Conductive Education

Conductive Education

Mária Hári and Károly Ákos

Translated from the Hungarian by
Neville Horton Smith and Joy Stevens

Photographs by Dénes Kökúti

R

TAVISTOCK/ROUTLEDGE
London and New York

First published as *Konductív pedagógia* by
Tankönyvkiadó, Budapest
© 1971 Mária Hári and Károly Ákos; Photographs by Dénes Kökúti

English translation
First published in 1988 by
Routledge
11 New Fetter Lane, London EC4P 4EE
29 West 35th Street, New York NY 10001
Reprinted in paperback in 1990

© 1988 Neville Horton Smith and Joy Stevens

Typeset in 11/13pt Caledonia Compugraphic by Colset Private Ltd, Singapore
Printed in Great Britain by T.J. Press (Padstow) Ltd, Padstow, Cornwall

British Library Cataloguing in Publication Data

Hári, Mária 1938–
    Conductive education.
    1. Conductive education
    I. Title   II. Konductiv pedagogia English III.
    Ákos, Károly
    616.7'06

Library of Congress Cataloging in Publication Data also available

ISBN 0-415-04745-5

Contents

Foreword

Dr András Petö's system of Conductive Education for the motor disabled has acquired international renown for the results it has achieved and this has led to a general demand to publish the details of this educational system, as being of interest not only to practising and prospective Conductors but for all those who work in related specialised fields of activity. Up to now, all that has been available consisted of some 30 volumes of privately circulated lecture notes and duplicated instructional material which was accessible only to practitioners highly skilled in Conductive Education.

Devising and developing this system was András Petö's life's work, continued now at the College he founded. The Petö Institute for the Motor Disordered in Budapest assesses dysfunctional children throughout Hungary, collecting data, in a nationwide network, responsible both for their education and for training Conductors.

This book gives detailed information on the general principles and practice of Conductive Education – no adamant routine but developed and shaped for each individual by skilled continual monitoring and adjusted at need.

Statistical data on the efficacy of this system is followed by a survey of the facts, inferences and opinions we have gathered from the findings of the most relevant disciplines. Factors taken from work in neurophysiology, neuropathology, psychology, psychopathology, clinical theory and practice are considered relevant to the satisfaction of human social, biological and educational needs. The discussion of the underlying concepts of Conductive Education which follows, with a general exposition of its theory and practice, shows that this is no closed method but a flexible system capable of integrating into a coherent whole any method, technique, or procedure reconcilable with its general principles or serving its educational purposes. Finally, photographs taken during activities within the Institute illustrate our specialist practices and show how individual (nero-motor dysfunctional) children have progressed orthofunctionally.

We would like to express our thanks to film director Laśzló Bánki for his advice on the visual presentation of our material.

Budapest, 1970

1 The field of application and results achieved by Conductive Education

The Petö system is applied in the Institute for Conductive Education of the Motor Disabled and College for Conductors in Budapest, under the authority of the Ministry of Culture of the Hungarian People's Republic.

The information which follows represents the work of the Institute as it looked on 31 December 1968, the day for the annual submission of statistics. At that time the Institute was treating 593 cases, 209 of them in-patients and 384 out-patients, classified as in Table 1.

Table 1

	In-patients		Out-patients	
	Children	*Adults*	*Children*	*Adults*
Cerebromotor dysfunctionals	182	7	257	96
Spinomotor dysfunctionals	18	1	2	9
Peripheral motor dysfunctionals	1	—	2	18

The following data may also serve to give an introductory picture of the results achieved. In 1968 the Institute discharged a total of 364 in-patients. This figure is larger than the number of in-patients present at any one time because they do not all stay in the Institute for a whole year. Of the 364 persons discharged, 48 (13.19 per cent) left the Institute with nothing achieved. Of the others

176 (48.35 per cent) were restored to health and
140 (38.46 per cent) were improved.

These figures immediately raise the question of what kinds of cases come to the Institute and what we mean by the terms 'restored' and 'improved'.

1

The simplest term to clarify is 'restoration to health'. A dysfunctional patient who is regarded as restored to health is one who has adapted himself to the orthofunctional conditions appropriate for his age, goes to a normal day-nursery, primary or secondary school, college or university, or has a job.

The data given in the following tables clarify 'improvement' and explain the details more thoroughly. Without any process of selection we recalled for assessment everyone discharged from the Institute between 1950 and 1965. Of the 1,002 people recalled 866 presented themselves between 1 January and 1 August 1968. Assessment results were processed by the University Computing Centre under the scientific direction of Miklós Hámori, senior research scientist. (We did not recall any Heine–Medin cases, since the Institute no longer deals with these, or any patients who had spent less than one month in the Institute.)

Table 2   Composition of the group recalled for assessment

Cerebromotor dysfunctionals	707
Spinomotor dysfunctionals	119
Peripheral motor dysfunctionals	33
Others	7

Table 3   Composition of the group in greater detail

Ataxia	28		
Diplegia	219		
Infantile hemiplegia	137	Cerebral Palsy	626
Double hemiplegia	29		
Athetosis	213	Cerebromotor dysfunction	707
Adult hemiplegia	79		
Parkinson's disease	1		
Multiple sclerosis	1		
Spastic paraplegia	42		
Flaccid paraplegia	36		
Quadriplegia	11	Spinomotor dysfunction	119
Spina bifida (myelomeningocele)	30		
Peripheral paralysis	33		
Others	7		
Total	866		

But diagnoses and figures given in this form are not really

enough to give a detailed picture of the condition of patients admitted to the Institute. Facts about their actual condition with degrees of dysfunction and orthofunction may make it clearer and we will discuss these in detail.

For our assessment we used a points system with a data-recording sheet which was not based on special tests or neurological or myological schemata but on a comprehensive review of the requirements for everyday living.

The most significant data derived from this assessment were, first, five criteria grouped under the heading of:

Degree of Self-sufficiency
   1 needs constant help (0)
   2 partly self-sufficient but needs guidance (1)
   3 self-sufficient but incapable of work or normal education (2)
   4 self-sufficient and able to work or study at home (3)
   5 self-sufficient and fit for work or going to school (4)

The number of points for each criterion is shown in parentheses. It can be seen that the five criteria correspond to gradations extending from the most severe dysfunction through to complete orthofunction.

Capability on admission and discharge can be compared most easily by calculating the index of averages. For this, the individual patient's scores on admission and discharge are multiplied by the number of people in each grade, the products added together and their sum divided by the total number of individuals. The result achieved is expressed as a percentage of the maximum possible number of points.

On this basis we can look at the development of self-sufficiency among the 866 cases assessed, as shown in Table 4.

Since the criteria for self-sufficiency are still largely unspecific we will review them again in more detail.

'Degree of skill in handling objects and eating utensils' is based on nine tasks. The performance of each task with one hand scores half a point. (A half in the total is rounded up.)

These are the skills assessed:

- buttoning
- tying shoe-laces
- use of eating utensils (spoon, knife, and fork)
- use of drinking vessels (one- or two-handled mug and glass)

Table 4   Degree of self-sufficiency

Criterion Number	Number of Points	Number of patients		
		At the time of admission	At the time of discharge	On recall
1	0	36	5	5
2	1	209	15	26
3	2	510	100	108
4	3	56	224	191
5	4	55	522	536
Totals		866	866	866
Index of averages		46.7%	85.9%	85.4%

- use of comb
- use of toothbrush
- clock or watch winding
- door and window opening and shutting
- use of key and purse, handling of money

The lowest possible score is 0, the maximum 9.

In choosing various tasks as criteria, as far as possible preference was always given to the achievement of goals which were both of the greatest practical importance and the easiest to assess. Naturally the tasks as noted here do not exhaust all the possibilities for 'handling skills': the aim in any case was to make the widest possible choice from among the relevant tasks.

Table 5 gives the results achieved by individual patients. Similarly points for skill in eating, dressing, undressing, writing, and drawing and for changing position and getting about are based on completely practical criteria.

Criteria for eating and drinking skills are:

1 difficulty in chewing and swallowing (0)
2 needs to be fed and given drink (1)
3 eats and drinks independently but only with great difficulty (able to raise the spoon or glass to the mouth three or four times) (2)
4 eats and drinks independently with a little help (meat has to be cut up) (3)
5 eats independently (with knife and fork) (4)

Table 5   Degree of skill in handling objects and eating utensils

Number of Points	*Number of patients at the time of*		
	Admission	*Discharge*	*Recall*
0	31	3	7
1	17	3	4
2	32	7	6
3	32	3	6
4	67	12	11
5	141	12	18
6	172	28	22
7	193	77	72
8	66	145	124
9	115	576	596
Totals	866	866	866
Index of averages	65.4%	92.2%	91.9%

Table 6   Degree of skill in eating and drinking

Criterion	*Number of Points*	*Number of patients at the time of*		
		Admission	*Discharge*	*Recall*
1	0	4	0	0
2	1	56	7	9
3	2	67	16	20
4	3	219	26	30
5	4	520	817	807
Totals		866	866	866
Index of averages		84.5%	97.7%	97.2%

The criteria for the degree of skill in dressing and undressing are:–

1 completely passive (0)
2 takes part in dressing (1)
3 dresses and undresses but with much help (2)
4 dresses and undresses (with some help in buttoning and shoe-lace tying) (3)
5 dresses and undresses independently (4)

Table 7   Degree of skill in dressing and undressing

| Criterion | Number of Points | Number of individuals at time of | | |
		Admission	Discharge	Recall
1	0	47	6	7
2	1	92	6	4
3	2	157	16	26
4	3	460	118	122
5	4	110	720	707
Totals		866	866	866
Index of averages		64.3%	94.5%	93.8%

The levels of skills in writing and drawing are:

1 cannot write or draw at all or even hold a pencil (0)
2 can hold a pencil but cannot make continuous lines or a dot (1)
3 can join two dots with a line (2)
4 can draw certain curved and straight components of letters (3)
5 draws letters in an exercise book with wide-spaced lines (4)
6 writes legibly though not neatly in an exercise book with standard lines (5)
7 writes and draws normally (6)

Table 8   Degree of skill in writing and drawing

| Criterion | Number of Points | Number of individuals at the time of | | |
		Admission	Discharge	Recall
1	0	183	32	33
2	1	81	7	8
3	2	42	21	13
4	3	230	289	121
5	4	3	26	16
6	5	139	243	371
7	6	188	248	304
Totals		866	866	866
Index of averages		51.8%	71.7%	79.7%

For describing changes in posture and getting about there are eighteen criteria:

1 cannot walk but only crawls and turns over on back and stomach (0)
2 can be seated with support (1)
3 can be seated upright but cannot stand (2)
4 sits up but cannot stand (3)
5 can move from one seat to another but cannot stand up (4)
6 stands up from a chair with support and stands with support (5)
7 stands for a moment without support (6)
8 can stand up from the floor (7)
9 can stand up and take one or two steps (8)
10 can walk from one room to another but cannot use stairs (9)
11 can walk, but unsteadily, and can climb stairs with support (10)
12 walks steadily indoors but is quickly tired (11)
13 walks steadily indoors and in the garden but not the street (12)
14 can walk in the street with an escort only for short distances (13)
15 goes out independently but needs help in boarding vehicles (14)
16 walks well in the street and uses all kinds of vehicles (15)
17 walks untiringly but with a trace of dysfunction (16)
18 as normal (17)

The following criteria are used in assessing receptive language:

1 does not understand speech at all (0)
2 occasionally understands something (1)
3 understands connected phrases (2)
4 understands connected sentences but with difficulty (3)
5 understands everything normally (4)

Table 9   Degree of changes in posture and getting about

Criterion	Number of Points	Number of individuals at the time of Admission	Discharge	Recall
1	0	51	1	6
2	1	45	1	5
3	2	24	4	9
4	3	57	1	11
5	4	16	3	3
6	5	203	135	155
7	6	20	12	9
8	7	1	1	1
9	8	36	54	42
10	9	29	11	7
11	10	220	7	12
12	11	41	22	8
13	12	31	29	15
14	13	39	56	46
15	14	13	93	74
16	15	3	58	39
17	16	14	329	356
18	17	23	49	68
Totals		866	866	866
Index of averages		43.4%	74.5%	73.1%

Table 10   Degree of receptive language

Criterion	Number of Points	Number of individuals at the time of Admission	Discharge	Recall
1	0	2	0	0
2	1	21	13	13
3	2	18	11	11
4	3	160	131	123
5	4	665	711	719
Totals		866	866	866
Index of averages		92.3%	94.5%	94.7%

Criteria of motor ability to speak are:

1 does not speak (0)
2 speaks unintelligibly (1)
3 can be understood with difficulty (2)
4 speaks intelligibly but occasionally with incorrect sounds and distortions (3)
5 speaks hesitantly, occasional confusions of stress and rhythm (4)
6 speaks normally (5)

Table 11　Degree of motor ability to speak

Criterion	Number of Points	Number of individuals at the time of Admission	Discharge	Recall
1	0	31	14	13
2	1	9	3	3
3	2	79	19	20
4	3	59	59	52
5	4	153	188	182
6	5	535	583	596
Totals		866	866	866
Index of averages		83.9%	89.7%	90.2%

Any improvement in the index of averages also traces development from admission to discharge for each condition diagnosed within this group.

Table 12 Degree of self-sufficiency for different types of dysfunction

Diagnosis	Index of averages at the time of	
	Admission %	Discharge %
Ataxia	48.2	82.1
Parkinson's disease	25.0	50.0
Hemiplegia	48.3	86.9
Double hemiplegia	26.7	62.1
Spastic paraplegia	42.3	94.0
Flaccid paraplegia	35.4	91.7
Quadriplegia	34.1	95.5
Diplegia	48.3	86.8
Athetosis	47.1	83.7
Spina bifida	51.7	85.8
Multiple sclerosis	50.0	75.0
Peripheral paralysis	56.8	94.7

Table 13   Degree of skill in eating and drinking for different types of dysfunction

Diagnosis	Index of averages at the time of	
	Admission %	Discharge %
Ataxia	89.3	100.0
Parkinson's disease	100.0	100.0
Hemiplegia	83.2	97.8
Double hemiplegia	61.2	87.9
Spastic paraplegia	97.6	100.0
Flaccid paraplegia	97.2	100.0
Quadriplegia	72.7	100.0
Diplegia	87.9	98.6
Athetosis	77.6	96.0
Spina bifida	100.0	100.0
Multiple sclerosis	75.0	100.0
Peripheral paralysis	87.9	100.0

Table 14   Degree of skill in handling objects and eating utensils for different types of dysfunction

Diagnosis	Index of averages at the time of	
	Admission %	Discharge %
Ataxia	69.0	93.7
Parkinson's disease	66.7	88.9
Hemiplegia	59.3	91.7
Double hemiplegia	36.0	69.3
Spastic paraplegia	86.2	97.4
Flaccid paraplegia	79.3	93.8
Quadriplegia	44.4	98.0
Diplegia	71.4	94.4
Athetosis	58.4	89.9
Spina bifida	88.9	98.9
Multiple sclerosis	77.8	100.0
Peripheral paralysis	74.1	97.3

Table 15   Degree of skill in dressing and undressing for different types of dysfunction

Diagnosis	Index of averages at the time of	
	Admission %	Discharge %
Ataxia	63.4	92.9
Parkinson's disease	25.0	75.0
Hemiplegia	63.0	94.7
Double hemiplegia	31.0	71.6
Spastic paraplegia	75.6	100.0
Flaccid paraplegia	75.7	99.3
Quadriplegia	52.3	100.0
Diplegia	66.8	96.3
Athetosis	61.6	92.5
Spina bifida	70.0	98.3
Multiple sclerosis	50.0	75.0
Peripheral paralysis	75.0	98.5

Table 16 Degree of skill in writing and drawing for different types of dysfunction

Diagnosis	Index of averages at the time of	
	Admission %	Discharge %
Ataxia	39.9	57.7
Parkinson's disease	83.3	83.3
Hemiplegia	55.6	74.2
Double hemiplegia	15.5	45.4
Spastic paraplegia	96.0	98.0
Flaccid paraplegia	98.6	98.6
Quadriplegia	42.2	83.3
Diplegia	46.6	67.8
Athetosis	37.6	63.5
Spina bifida	62.2	79.4
Multiple sclerosis	50.0	50.0
Peripheral paralysis	74.7	91.9

Table 17 Degree of receptive language for different types of dysfunction

Diagnosis	Index of averages at the time of	
	Admission %	Discharge %
Ataxia	81.2	83.9
Parkinson's disease	100.0	100.0
Hemiplegia	92.0	95.7
Double hemiplegia	76.7	81.0
Spastic paraplegia	99.4	99.4
Flaccid paraplegia	100.0	100.0
Quadriplegia	100.0	100.0
Diplegia	91.9	94.2
Athetosis	91.7	93.1
Spina bifida	96.7	99.2
Multiple sclerosis	100.0	100.0
Peripheral paralysis	100.0	100.0

Table 18   Degree of motor ability to speak for different types of dysfunction

Diagnosis	Index of averages at the time of	
	Admission %	Discharge %
Ataxia	65.7	73.6
Parkinson's disease	100.0	100.0
Hemiplegia	86.1	92.1
Double hemiplegia	62.1	75.2
Spastic paraplegia	100.0	100.0
Flaccid paraplegia	100.0	100.0
Quadriplegia	94.5	96.4
Diplegia	90.7	94.3
Athetosis	68.8	79.4
Spina bifida	98.0	100.0
Multiple sclerosis	80.0	100.0
Peripheral paralysis	100.0	100.0

The data just given illustrate what we mean by 'improvement' and what we regard as 'restored to health'. Conductive Education employs these terms in a very concrete sense, with orthofunction as its yardstick.

The tables given so far also show that the Petö system can be used without distinction for a very wide range of dysfunctions. We do not take the severity of the case into consideration at the time of admission.

In the literature on this subject, referring to a development in the condition of dysfunctional patients always raises the question as to the extent to which a result achieved in any particular case can be attributed to the method used or merely regarded as a spontaneous change. In some cases it is impossible to give a definite answer to a question like this, but statistics can settle the matter by the law of large numbers. These tables show that Conductive Education is very effective in influencing dysfunctional individuals towards orthofunction.

For example, it is widely known that the treatment of athetosis is usually seen as fundamentally hopeless. To show what can be achieved by the Petö system Table 19 lists separately the improvements shown in the skills of athetoid patients in various practical activities in terms of the difference between the index of averages on admission and on discharge.

Table 19 Differences in the index of averages for athetoid patients (discharge–admission)

Degree of self-sufficiency	36.6
Degree of skill in eating and drinking	18.4
Degree of skill in handling objects and eating utensils	31.6
Degree of skill in dressing and undressing	30.9
Degree of skill in writing and drawing	25.9

To complete the picture Table 20 relates to after-care.

Table 20 After-care of patients discharged in 1967, 1968, and 1969

Attending nursery school or school	170	
Under private tuition	51	
At work	44	
Working at home or doing house work	19	
Pensioned	66	
Total	350	73.38%
Readmitted	33	
Out-patients or attending 'parents' school	24	
Attending for regular check-ups	18	
Total	75	15.72%
In children's nursing or residential (social) homes	32	
Address unknown	16	
Dead	4	
Total	52	10.9%
Total	477	100.0%

2 The concept of motor disabilities (dysfunction)

Let us begin with an opinion which may be regarded as typical. Bernstein,[1] who spent decades in research on human movements, emphasized the point that although motor functions are of great biological significance, physiologists really pay very little attention to the problems of movement. Even those who do, adopt an extremely narrow approach for the most part.

What are 'movements', generally speaking?

The term 'movement' is generally understood to mean 'a change of posture or position'. Changing the position of the human body depends on a change of posture, in altering the position of the limbs. Postural changes are effected by the articulation of bones at the joints. Movements at the joint are caused by the contraction and relaxation of the parts of muscles attached to the skeleton; hence the skeleton and the skeletal muscular system are called organs of movement. Healthy body movements depend on the integrity of the motor organs.

Muscle function is regulated by the nervous system. Even in sound motor organs, serious disturbances of movement can follow injuries to the nervous system. These are referred to as motor 'disabilities' and we distinguish between cerebromotor, spinomotor, and peripheral motor dysfunction according to the site of the injury.

The commonest form of functional-anatomical description of motor disabilities is to present movements as taking place in a kind of abstract space. In fact the movements of an individual are not abstractions but take place in a real environment under complex biological and social conditions and serve the purposes of biological adaptation. The nervous system co-ordinates movements with complex environmental conditions in such a way that they assume that biological and social significance or, in other words,

1 Bernstein, A. (1967) *The Co-ordination and Regulation of Movements*, Pergamon: Oxford.

become actions. Motor disabilities are not merely impairments of the functioning of motor organs but dysfunctions, affecting the adaptive activity of the entire personality, disturbances of adjustment. So to understand dysfunctions and particularly to be able to transform them into orthofunctions, we must regard motor disabilities as disturbances in adaptability affecting the whole personality.

However, the origin of dysfunctions in any event is to be found in the functioning of the nervous system. It seems evident that to understand clearly problems connected with dysfunctions, we have to rely for a scientific basis on the principles which govern the structure and function of the nervous system, so we will survey these now – very briefly.

3 The nerve cell

The nerve cell (neurone) is only one type of cell in a many-celled organism and so it is understandable that many of its properties coincide with the organism's other cells'. We shall not discuss the details of the common properties of cells here, but we must say something about the special peculiarities of the nerve cell.

The most striking anatomical characteristic of a nerve cell is its extensions. Many widely varying extensions grow out from the cell body. One extension of this kind, the axon, is very long and in a human adult can even reach a length of 1 metre. The dimensions of a nerve cell's body may be exceedingly varied, with a diameter from 4 to 135 microns. The larger the cell, the longer the axon. An axon has a different structure from other cell extensions, the dendrites, of which there may be several hundreds.

Biologically, the nerve cell constitutes the basic unit of the nervous system but from a functional point of view, the axon must be discussed separately.

The axon

The function of an axon is to transmit signals. These signals travel along the axon in the form of specific excitatory processes.

Neurophysiologists have carried out some extremely important research into the way an axon functions.

An axon is a kind of tube contained by its membrane, which is polarized when in a state of rest, negative inside and positive outside, with a 'resting potential' amounting to about 70 millivolts.

Polarization of a membrane is caused by a difference in the distribution of ions in fluids within and around the axon. For example, there are about thirty times as many potassium ions inside as there are outside an axon, while the quantity of sodium ions is about ten times greater outside than inside. This difference in the distribution of ions between intracellular and extracellular fluids depends on the active functioning of the membrane.

From a variety of influences a point on the membrane can become momentarily permeable to the separate ions. A complex process of equalization of ions begins, as a result of which the polarization of the membrane not only ceases at that point but also is reversed so that the inner side becomes positive in relation to the outer. In the course of this process a discharge, or impulse, of about 110 mV is produced. This is the action potential.

An action potential lasts approximately between 0.5 and 2.0 thousandths of a second on a section of the axon ranging from a few millimetres to a few centimetres. Between the site of the discharge and distal parts of the axon a difference of potential arises and a flow of current results. This current is enough to bring about a discharge in the adjacent membrane which has so far been at rest and the impulse moves on like a flame on a fuse.

After discharging, the membrane ceases for a time to react to any influence and so the action potential spreads unidirectionally along the axon. Once an action potential has arisen it travels to the end of the nerve fibre. This is what gives the axon its capacity to transmit signals.

One of the most splendid chapters in the story of modern neuro-physiological research has been the discovery of many of the important points of detail playing a part in this signalling function of the axon. Yet there still has been no complete clarification even of such crucially important details as the functioning of the membrane which brings about that polarization.

Although this means that there are still considerable gaps in our knowledge, we do have a clear view of the function of the axon in conveying signals. The action potential transmits information and is therefore a signal. The speed of signal transmission may vary on different axons and from this point of view the axons have been divided into three groups according to whether they are connected with the muscles ('efferent' or 'motor' fibres) or with the intestines ('viscerals') or with the receptors ('afferents'). The speed of propagation of the action potentials is on

- A-type fibres 5–100 m/s,
- B-type fibres 3–14 m/s,
- C-type fibres less than 2 m/s.

A faster rate of conductivity is characteristic of thicker axons and a slower rate of thinner ones. According to Hursch's empirical rule the axon's speed of conductivity expressed in m/s is in general six times its thickness expressed in microns.

Production and propagation of impulses along an axon are quite independent of the body of the nerve cell and continue for a time even if they are separated. However, an axon cut off from its neural cell soon dies and the cell grows a new axon in its place.

Sensory cells of the spinal ganglia have a two-branched T-shaped axon. Through the 'stem' of the T the axon is linked with the body of the cell. One branch of the T carries the impulse from the periphery which is propagated along the other branch into the spinal cord and establishes contact with other nerve cells there.

Axons are enclosed in a myelin sheath (layer) the thickness of which is proportional to the axon's. This myelin sheath insulates the axon from its environment and on it at varying distances apart can be found the most readily excited points on the axon, the nodes of Ranvier. Action potentials 'jump' from one node to another in the course of propagation. On the A-type fibre the section under-going discharge at any one time averages 5 cm.

The different speeds at which impulses travel are of biological significance. Signals are transmitted most rapidly by those axons which form direct routes extending over relatively long distances. For instance, impulses travelling along the giant axons of a squid, now so very famous through neurophysiological research, effect the contraction of muscles of decisive importance in its escape movements.

Once generated, impulses are relatively simple processes of almost constant size and speed. But the way in which successive impulses are produced is much more complicated.

An action potential on an A-type fibre lasts for 0.5 of a thousandth of a second followed by an equal period of complete inactivity (refractory phase). Then for between 12 and 20 thousandths of a second there is a period of increased excitability and this is followed by a phase of diminished excitability lasting between 40 and 60 thousandths of a second. All this undoubtedly influences the rate of signal transmission but at present we do not know how. All we know is that between 10 and 100 impulses per second can travel on an A-type fibre. It seems likely that the actual number of signals and the length of interval between them are more important for the informational function of the nervous system than simply their rate in numbers per second.

Now we will consider how signals are generated on axons running from the environment towards the centre.

The receptor–axon link

Axons of nerve cells are signal-carrying 'cables'. Signal transmission can run from special stimulus-receiving mechanisms (receptors) to the nerve cells, or from cell to cell or, finally, from nerve cells to muscles or other 'effector' organs. We will begin with the receptors.

One of the simplest forms of receptor is the Vater–Paccini corpuscle, occurring in large numbers in the skin and elsewhere. It consists of lamellae which fit closely over one another like the layers of an onion and enclose the bare end of an axon. When a Vater–Paccini corpuscle comes under pressure, action potentials appear on the axon extension and these are the signals communicating the fact of the pressure. Loewenstein[1] in referring to the Vater–Paccinian corpuscle mentions patiently unpeeling the lamellae of a corpuscle under a microscope until nothing was left but the bare axon itself. It turned out that epithelial cells are not essential for stimulating the little receptor, for under pressure the bare axon responded by generating impulses just like an intact mechanism. It works like this: stimulation of an axon affects its membrane and the electrical potential across that membrane is reduced at the point of stimulation. If the reduction in potential is large enough the permeability of the membrane changes and ions begin to stream through (depolarization). Small electrical circuits are produced between the point of stimulation and its surroundings. If the pressure becomes so great that these electrical circuits extend as far as the first Ranvier node, they cause a complete discharge there and the nerve impulse at once travels right along the axon.

Generally every stimulation affecting receptors produces an electrical potential. If this is strong enough it sets off an impulse along the axons coming from those receptors. The simplest form of receptor is the end of an axon but a receptor may also be a more or

1 Loewenstein, W.R. (1960) *Scientific American*, 203 (2).

less complex 'end organ'. The potential produced in a receptor varies under the influence of every stimulus and is proportional to the strength of the stimulus' impingement. The number of impulses passing through an axon is also proportional to the size of the potential produced in a receptor, so this is called the 'generator potential', because of its capacity for generating axial impulses.

The generator potential of a receptor and the size of stimulus impinging on it are proportional to each other, this proportion varying with the excitability of the receptor. This in turn varies both with the influence of every stimulus and also, as often stated, with the degree of adjustment coming to that receptor from the central nervous system.

The generator potential produced is stronger than the size of the stimulus because the stimulus mobilizes the receptor's own energies. It is therefore not true – although often stated – that the energy of a stimulus is converted directly into the functional energy of the receptor. Similarly the impulse on an axon is all triggered and not converted energy (generated anew at each stage along the axon and constant in size). The organism adds its own energies to the reception and processing of information.

To turn to the opposite side of the system connections run between receptor and nerve cell, between nerve cells, and between nerve cell and effector organ. Let us see what happens when impulses along an efferent axon arrive at the muscle fibre.

The myoneural junction

The membrane of a motor-neural axon and the membrane of a muscle fibre produce a small mechanism at the point where they meet. This is a roughly circular plate, from 25 to 70 microns in diameter, formed by the two cell membranes with a gap between them 1 micron wide. Dale and his colleagues established in 1936 that when impulses on an axon reach this mechanism, the myoneural junction, acetylecholine is released into the gap. Acetylecholine changes the permeability of the membrane of the muscle fibre and depolarizes it. Consequently an 'end-plate potential' several millimetres across is generated between this point and the area around it. Acetylecholine is broken down very quickly by the always present enzyme acetylecholine-esterase and so the end-plate potential disappears. However, if impulses follow one another along the axon rapidly enough, the magnitude of the end-plate potential increases. If the potential reaches about 30 mV, the cell fires and the discharge runs through to the end of the entire muscle fibre. As a result the protein molecules of the muscle fibre rearrange themselves or, in other words, the muscle fibre contracts.

This means that muscle fibres behave in a similar way to axons. If the size of an end-plate potential exceeds its threshold it produces an action potential similar to the generator potential but the comparison ends there since the function of an axon is to transmit the impulse which serves as a signal, while the function of a muscle fibre on the other hand is the contraction which follows the firing of the action potential.

And with this we turn to connections between nerve cells.

The synapse

When two or more nerve cells are joined together, the axon of one of them ends in a small mechanism either on the body or on an extension of the other cell. This small mechanism, the synapse, is formed by the membranes of both cells. Between them, in the centre of the tiny mechanism, there is a gap as small as 150 to 300 A across. (The angstrom – A – is a ten-millionth of a millimetre, the diameter of a hydrogen atom.) Structurally, a synapse corresponds with the myoneural junction except that it is smaller. There are tens of thousands of synapses in each single nerve cell.

The functioning of synapse and myoneural junction is similar too. When the impulses on an axon reach a presynaptic membrane, chemical substances are released into the synaptic gap. The polarization of the postsynaptic membrane changes under the influence of this 'mediator' and two kinds of change are possible: either the membrane around the synapse is depolarized for some thousandths or ten-thousandths of a second, or it is hyperpolarized. If a sufficient number of synapses lying near to one another and depolarizing in nature are all activated within a few thousandths of a second, their effect can be combined to produce an action potential on the axon of the cell. In the case of motor neurones of the spinal cord a postsynaptic potential of about 10 mV is necessary to produce an action potential of 110 mV.

Operation of synapses with a depolarizing effect is inhibited by those with a hyperpolarizing effect. This reduces the possibility of an action potential's arising. Their functioning lasts for a very short time too. The effect of many depolarizing synapses must coincide in time and space for signals to be passed on from one nerve cell to others.

To add to the complexities of this situation, the excitability of nerve cells is variable, similar to that of axons and receptors.

Our knowledge of all these questions is incomplete, for instance there are some who assume that dendrites transmit rhythmically repeated impulses to axons and that the role of excitatory synapses is to modulate this rhythm. On the other hand, synapses which have an inhibitory effect impede rhythmic discharges along a neuron. It is assumed that between co-operating nerve cells the way for further contact is shaped or prepared, as it were (in German; Bahnung), and that it is precisely this which constitutes the neurophysiological foundation of learning. However, there is still a great deal of uncertainty and inadequately supported hypotheses on all these matters.

Our knowledge of mediator substances is also very uncertain. These neural transmitters are probably produced in the body of a nerve cell discharging through the synaptic vesicles and perhaps this explains the surprising fact that chemical processes occur in nerve cells on a scale comparable only with that in liver cells. Neural plasma is renewed several times a day and there is a constant flow moving through the axons towards the periphery at a speed of 2.5 mm a day, according to Gerard.

However, apart from acetylecholine we do not know for certain what other kinds of neural transmission substances the synapses possess. 'The excitatory transmitters at neuro-neural synapses include acetylecholine, an adrenaline-noradrenaline complex and probably others not yet identified.' (Brazier[2])

Krnjevič[3] succeeded in demonstrating that glutamic acid has a depolarizing effect on some of the neurones in the brain but that the gamma-amino-butyric acid (GABA) forming with the alpha-decarboxylation of the molecule of glutamic acid hyperpolarizes the membranes. Both molecules are present in the brain and it is

2 Brazier, M.A.B. (1966) *The Electrical Activity of the Nervous System*, New York: Macmillan.
3 Krnjevič, K. (1966) *Endeavour*, XXV (94).

conceivable that they constitute the excitatory and inhibitory mediators in the synapses of cerebral neurons.

All this is still rather uncertain. For the time being we cannot even explain the cause of the various nerve cells being unequally sensitive to certain damaging agents. For instance the Heine–Medin virus attacks motor neurones in the spinal cord, streptomycin injures neurones of the nucleus of the eighth cranial nerve, alcohol damages myelin sheaths on the axons of cells of the corpus mamillare, and so on. These variations indicate subtle differences between the nerve cells, but at present we know practically nothing about them.

As far as details are concerned, then, there are still many unsolved problems but the overall picture in relation to signal transmission is already clear, at least in principle. Axial functioning ensures that a signal is not lost in transit. Once an impulse has been produced it continues to the end of the axon. On the other hand synapses screen conditions for signal transmission very carefully and so a signal is passed on only when very rare and favourable circumstances are present and then by extraordinarily complicated routes. It seems that the course of these routes is determined partly by heredity and partly by experience (learning). At present we do not know how.

4 Stimulus, excitability, excitation, and inhibition

As we have seen, our knowledge of the activity of nerve cells continues to grow even if very many details have still to be clarified. The main functions of the nerve cells are grouped around biological processes, the capability for which is provided by neurophysiological processes yet, at the same time, it is the biological processes which set the course for the entire functioning of the nervous system. What are they?

Neural activity combines two fundamental roles: reception, in the form of signals, of influences from the environment and the transmission of those signals. Physiologically impulses are discharged as axial or synaptic potentials. If we consider the biological significance of the nervous system, impulses convey information important for the organism about either its internal state or its environment. Through the reception and processing of this information and by transmitting it to the various organs, the nervous system enables an organism to adjust to its environment. Biologically the nervous system processes information and initiates action. Neural signals serve these purposes.

We are talking about the same phenomena from both a biological and a physiological point of view but important distinctions have to be drawn between the two. In healthy physiological states impulses transmitted along an axon have an informational significance which is valuable biologically but which can be interpreted incorrectly in impaired conditions. Consequently not physiological but biological functional considerations are able to give valid practical information on whether neural function in receiving and transmitting signals is normal or impaired. This can be judged only from the adjustment an organism makes to its environment and it is only subsequently, after making a decision based on that biological condition, that we can attempt to trace a physiological–pathological explanation.

Any stimulus which evokes an axial action potential has

important biological connotations yet from a physiological point of view the same potential can be produced by environmental influences which vary very widely, and once produced it will have an identical effect.

Now we will look at the concepts of causal impingement (stimulus) and excitatory effect (response) in more detail. The response is a result of the stimulus. An environmental influence stimulates a receptor's response, its excitation producing a generator potential. The generator potential is the stimulus which affects an axon. If this stimulus is large enough it arouses excitation on that axon and this axial action potential discharges and affects a synapse. Synaptic activity in turn is the stimulus affecting the axon of the post-synaptic nerve cell, but only if a sufficient number of synapses deploy a large enough depolarizing influence at the same time. Impulses travelling along the motor neurone's axon stimulate a myoneural junction and this excitation evokes an end-plate potential which, if it is large enough, becomes the stimulus for the action potential on a muscle fibre, and so on. Stimulus and excitation thus represent a directional link. In appropriate conditions the excitation of every link in this chain can become the stimulus which affects the next.

In this pattern of links between stimulus and excitation the stimulus always mobilizes greater energies than its own. For example the discharge on the axon of a motor nerve cell of the spinal cord is about eleven times as great as the potential of the stimulus which triggered it. The energy of impulses on the motor axon and the end-plate potential of the myoneural junction seem negligible beside the energy released when muscle fibres contract. Between stimulus and excitation this progression is general with a tendency for it to increase from receptors to effectors. This is one factor contributing to the relative independence of the living organism, at least in terms of energy.

Yet the energy gradient of the neural links from receptors to effectors does not mean that the chain of stimulus and excitation follows a rigidly set path: in fact, the range of possible routes is very wide and extremely varied. Any particular link that may be established is determined in the first place by the actual excitability of individual nerve cells. The same stimulus can affect or fail to affect the same cell in varying circumstances, that is to say it can produce excitation or may remain ineffective. We can express this by saying that excitability has a threshold and stimulation below that threshold has no effect. The level of the threshold stimulus varies and its variation is influenced by very many factors such as the length of time elapsed since the preceding excitation or even by the stimulation itself.

Variations in the excitability of nerve cells are extremely important for biological function. As excitability decreases, previously effective stimuli fall below the threshold, do not produce excitation, and therefore lose their excitatory character. At the same time stimuli below the threshold (subliminal) can influence excitability: they still have an effect but only in a concealed form.

If a stimulus which happens to be just above the threshold reaches an axon, its effect is shown by the production of an action potential. For a short time afterwards the same stimulus remains ineffective indicating that the threshold has risen. The raising of a threshold in relation to the size of the stimulus has been called 'accommodation' and conversely the lowering of the threshold, or the effect on excitation when two stimuli below the threshold are applied at the same time, is 'facilitation'.

Strictly speaking, every stimulus has an effect on excitability. In the course of successive repetitions of the same stimulus axial action potentials steadily decrease until in the end the stimulus has no effect at all. This process is called 'adaptation'. In this way a stimulus which is physically identical does not remain biologically uniform in effect. In the course of adaptation the number of discharges diminishes steadily and this leads to a negative exponential correlation between the stimuli and the number of discharges.

The apparent effect of a stimulus can be seen comparatively easily through excitation, but it is much more difficult to trace a latent influence only revealed by variations in threshold level. Makarov[1] demonstrated that this latent effect, which he called 'functional shift', spreads steadily along the axon.

In an axon the development of excitability is relatively simple but at the synapses it becomes a very complex combination of influences. On the axon the picture is complicated already by the

1 Makarov, P.O. (1956) *The Neurodynamics of Man, Excitability, Lability, and Adequacy*, Leningrad.

appearance of inhibitory processes which reflect all the phenomena characterizing excitational processes but which are much more difficult to trace. Latent phenomena connected with inhibitory processes can be demonstrated only in particular circumstances. So it can be shown that the inhibitory effect is also of an adaptational nature. This is very noticeable when the inhibitory effect ceases and impulses appear, their number decreasing in a negative exponential curve. This phenomenon corresponds to the adaptation to be seen when stimuli are repeated monotonously. Yet although no kind of actual stimulus is present or repeated, inhibition has ceased. In this way, as Florey[2] emphasized, the same environmental factor which produces excitation by its presence inhibits by its withdrawal and conversely the withdrawal of an inhibitory factor generates excitation.

Biologically the processes just described can be summed up by saying that every change has important informational value but that constancy has no such value. (Constancy is merely a basis for comparison with any change, the starting-point and standard for determining the extent of that change.) The system constantly adjusts itself according to the significance of incoming information by means of complex physiological processes. Although the picture is very intricate and details to a large extent are not clear, we are beginning to get a picture of the biological role of this functional system. This involves weighing up one item of information against another and laying stress on the significance of that information and its importance biologically.

2   Florey, E. (1961) *Nervous Inhibition*, Oxford: Pergamon.

5 Motorium

The motor unit

We have outlined the activity of the nerve cells and their connections and now we will go on to review briefly the structure and functional principles of the nervous system. Since motor disabilities are the most conspicuous dysfunctional signs of damage to the nervous system we will discuss the organization of movement first of all.

The most generally held view at present accepts a hierarchically integrated structure of the nervous system and sees the basis for the organization of movement as formed by 'motor units'. This name was chosen by Liddell and Sherrington in 1925 in order to emphasize the extraordinarily close link between a nerve cell and muscle fibres meeting at a myoneural junction. A motor unit is therefore formed by a nerve cell and muscle fibres with common myoneural junctions.

Nerve cells forming motor units of the skeletal musculature are motor neurones and there are about half a million of them (Clara[1]). They are very large cells with bodies chiefly situated in the ventral, or anterior, horn of the spinal cord and axons branching to connect with varying numbers of muscle fibres, apparently according to their functional patterns. In the gastrocnemius muscle for instance there are about 1,500 muscle fibres for each motor neurone and there are about thirty in the muscles moving the eye (Adams[2]).

If a motor neurone is destroyed for some reason, the muscle fibres associated with it are destroyed too, although in a biological sense as cells they are independent units. If the motor

1 Clara, M. (1959) *The Human Nervous System*, Leipzig: Johann Ambrosius Berth Verlag.
2 Adams, J.C. (1964) *Disorders of Voluntary Muscle*, Boston, Mass.

neurones gradually deteriorate for an unknown reason, for example in the course of a disease like progressive muscular atrophy (Aran-Duchenne), then corresponding with their decay, the muscles of distal parts of the arms begin to weaken first: the musculature of the hand begins to waste away. If medullary motor neurones decay too, the results will be difficulty in swallowing, slurring of speech, and so on. Muscle fibres forming the motor unit with a motor neurone attacked like this will show feeble rapid twitchings (fasciculation) and are slowly destroyed completely, the process taking a few months or occasionally years.

The fact that the decay of a nerve cell or the permanent breaking of a link between a muscle and a nerve (axon) is followed by the deterioration of the muscle fibre is very important. The nerve cell has a vital, trophic effect on the muscle fibres of a motor unit. (Skin and even bone waste away if they lose their neural links.)

Now we ought to deal in detail with the physiological explanation of the trophic effect. But for the time being there is no possibility of doing so since this problem is one of the least clarified of neurophysiology and neuropathology, despite the fact that medical experience has repeatedly called attention to its importance. For instance the often very severe deterioration of tissues deprived of their neural connections is the cause of deformations from leprosy and persistent ulcers in patients suffering from tabes and syringomyelia.

More than one researcher has been concerned with neural trophic effects. For instance, Pavlov demonstrated that the heart has special trophic nerves and one of his pupils, Orbeli, primarily investigated vegetative neural trophic effects while another of his pupils, Speranskij, demonstrated the role of trophic nerve-effects in a number of diseases affecting organs over a wide range. More recently a great deal of interest has been caused by observations on substances produced by nerve cells, which seem to indicate that neural cells can be compared with glandular cells here. It may be assumed that the substances which flow in an axon supply innervated tissues with enzymes. But this assumption is contradicted by the fact that relatively large molecules have no gates on the membrane of a nerve cell, or on the membrane of a muscle fibre or of other cells. At the same time 'it is widely accepted that proteins made in the cell body move down the axons to their endings where they may be released to carry out metabolic functions' (Lebovitz and Singer[3]).

It is not only destruction of a nerve cell that may impair motor unit function. Sometimes impulses passing along the axon of a motor neurone do not excite a muscle fibre because of a functional disorder of the myoneural junction. The muscles most frequently affected by this are those of the eye movements, the mimetic, masticatory, and the tongue, those used in swallowing and making sounds. The affected muscles after a few contractions of normal strength become progressively less and less capable of functioning. The patient's eyelids sag, his face looks exhausted, and his voice becomes inaudible. This illness is myasthenia gravis. Its symptoms are ascribed to an insufficient production of acetylecholine (Desmedt 1958), so that the membrane of a muscle fibre does not depolarize, or does not depolarize enough, even though the motor neurone sends appropriate signals.

There is another case in which the functioning of a myoneural junction is pathologically prolonged. Contraction of a patient's muscles is followed only slowly by relaxation; if he shakes hands he cannot relax his clasp. If one of his muscles is tapped with a reflex hammer a lump comes up after the contraction which is slow to subside. This illness is myotonia. It is assumed (Jenerick and Gerard 1953) but disputed (by Van der Meulen, Gilbert, and Kane 1961) that here the functioning of a myoneural junction would be of a progressively depolarizing nature.

Even when myoneural junction and motor neurone are in fully functional order a motor unit may be injured by a lesion in a muscle but then it is not a case of dysfunction in a motor unit, but of a disease of the organs of movement.

We have gained more detailed knowledge of the functioning of the motor unit in many respects through modern electrophysiological investigations, in which it has become possible to register changes in the electrical potential of muscle fibres. This method, electromyography, was brought into clinical use by Adrian and Bronk (1929) to study muscle function. By inserting a needle-like electrode it became possible to register electrical events in approximately 10 to 20 muscle fibres associated with

3   Lebovitz, P. and Singer, M. (1970) *Nature*, 225 (6235), 28 February, p. 827.

one motor unit and occupying an area of a few millimetres in diameter.

In a completely relaxed muscle there is electrical silence. Contraction of muscle fibres in one motor unit is initiated by a synchronous action potential travelling at a speed of 4 to 5 m/s and lasting for between 2 and 10 thousandths of a second at a given point. Its duration is not uniform in the fibres of different muscles and generally it increases with increasing age. The amplitude of action potentials, that is, the difference between maximum potential change and zero, is between 100 and 10,000 microvolts, depending on the method of registration. In the case of fatigue it is generally less. The frequency of successive impulses in the case of voluntary movement of minimum strength is 1/s and maximum 150/s. (These are not defined established values but only the most typical measurements taken over a number of investigations.)

When a motor neurone is destroyed, the motor unit disintegrates electrophysiologically. Some muscle fibres independently display spontaneous action potentials with a comparatively low amplitude. This is the electromyographic picture of fasciculation, which we met earlier. With electromyography it is possible to demonstrate 'fasciculations' which do not even cause quick feeble twitches. Contractions like these, only to be detected electromyographically, are called 'fibrillations', to distinguish them from visible fasciculations.

The general structure of the nervous system

In order to be able to talk about the higher levels of the organization of the nervous system we must look briefly at its structure.

The formation of the nervous system commences in the third week of the development of the human embryo. From the ectoderm of the embryonic shield grows the medullary swelling which becomes a neural plate and then a groove. The medullary groove closes to form the medullary tube and sinks into the mesoderm. The ectoderm closes over it by the end of the fourth week. Even before the medullary tube closes, some groove cells travel into the surrounding mesoderm. These mainly develop into the ganglia of the cranial nerves, the spinal cord, and the vegetative nervous system.

At the cranial end of the medullary tube three vesicles appear, and with them the development of the brain begins. The spinal cord develops from the rest of the medullary tube and the three vesicles are the forebrain (prosencephalon), the midbrain (mesencephalon), and the hindbrain (rhombencephalon).

The greatest development takes place in the forebrain, which is transformed into the telencephalon consisting of two hemispheres, and the diencephalon.

Retinas for the eyes and two optic nerves grow from the initial diencephalon.

The midbrain retains its unified structure even in its fully developed form.

The hindbrain is developing into two parts, the metencephalon and the myelencephalon. The metencephalon becomes the pons and the cerebellum.

The initial cavity of the medullary tube develops into the two lateral ventricles of the hemispheres as well as a third linking these two, and a fourth ventricle, which is connected with the third by the aqueduct. The remainder of the medullary tube in the spinal cord is the rudimentary canalis centralis.

Apart from this evolutionary division there is another simpler practical way of dividing the brain. On this basis the anterior portion of the brain is the cerebrum, corresponding to the telencephalon and the diencephalon in the evolutionary division. The posterior part of the brain is the cerebellum. Between these two comes the brainstem which therefore consists of, and is the common name for, midbrain, pons, and myelencephalon.

For the time being this brief survey is sufficient for our purposes. At most it needs only to be amplified by stating that bodies of nerve cells clustering around the cavity of the medullary tube produce the grey matter and axons produce the white matter surrounding the grey. The grey matter can be divided into dorsal (alar) and ventral (basal) parts. Cells of the dorsal part receive information from receptors and cells of the ventral part send signals to effector organs. This layout corresponds to the shapes of the ancestors of present-day vertebrates, which lived in the depths of the oceans, crawling on their bellies on the sea-bottom and exposed to danger from the living world in the water above them. Cerebral development also points to ancestral conditions of existence: the most important receptors took shape around the mouth and the brain took shape in connection with these.

The cells organizing contacts with the environment are placed to the side in both dorsal and ventral parts of the grey matter and cells collecting information on the interior of the body or regulating internal body functions are located in the centre.

The inner part of the grey matter of brainstem and spinal cord is the 'nucleus', around which accessory cells are sited. According to Szentágothai the nucleus plays a dominant role in organizing complex forms of movements.

As a result of the vast development of the brain the original principle of the layout of cells is no longer traceable. The majority of cells of cerebrum and cerebellum have migrated to the surface and help to form the cortex or very large nuclei in the white matter.

The bodies of neurones directly connected with receptors are situated outside the central nervous system, for example, in spinal ganglia, eye, ear, and so on.

Neural cells in the brain and the spinal cord are surrounded by a peculiar and still fairly mysterious type of cell, glia. There are many more glia than nerve cells. These glial cells not only play a very important part in feeding nerve cells but they also – it appears – play some part in their functioning as regards processing information.

After this short survey we will go back to the lowest level of spinal cord organization including the motor units, the gamma system.

The gamma system

Around the turn of the century Sherrington[4] made an extremely significant discovery. If the forebrain of a cat or monkey is cut off from the functioning of the nervous system by severing the mesencephalon and the animal is suspended standing on all four feet, it adopts a peculiar stance. Its limbs extend at the elbow and the knee. Its tail is held horizontally or erect. Its back is excessively hollowed in the lumbar-sacral region (opisthotonus), its head held up with the mouth closed. The cat stiffens in this

4 Sherrington, C. (1961) *The Integrative Action of the Nervous System* (ed. O. Zangwill), New Haven: Oxford University Press.

position like a statue. If it is given a gentle push it holds its position but becomes a little more rigid than it was before.

This posture is induced by the continuous spasm of the 'voluntary muscles'. The muscles taking control are those which extend the neck, raise the chin and tail and tense shoulders and haunches. This 'decerebrate rigidity', as Sherrington called it, lasts for about four days and if not any passive movement will bring it on again.

Since decerebrate rigidity is produced by disconnection from the forebrain we can assume that the forebrain exercises an inhibitory effect on the lower centres of the brainstem influencing the spinal cord motor neurones. When this inhibition ends the stimulatory effect of those centres is reasserted and decerebrate rigidity appears.

Sherrington checked this hypothesis by severing the medulla of an animal with decerebrate rigidity (and so eliminated the influence of brainstem centres too). The animal became flaccid. However, when he cut through the anterior and lateral funiculi of the white matter on one side of the spinal cord of the animal with decerebrate rigidity – it is in these front and side funiculi that the efferent or 'descending' fibres run from the brain to the spinal cord – the rigidity on that side disappeared.

Sherrington proposed that cerebral efferent influence can be ascribed to afferent excitations travelling to the brain from the periphery. A brainstem, deprived of the inhibitory influence of the forebrain, responds to that excitation by inducing decerebrate rigidity. If that is the case, decerebrate rigidity must cease with the severing of the afferent or 'ascending' tracks running through the dorsal funiculus of the spinal cord. But severing the dorsal funiculus did not affect the decerebrate rigidity.

However, the decerebrate rigidity of a given limb can be terminated by cutting the axons which bring information from the receptors of the limb to the spinal centre, the 'posterior roots' of the spinal cord. From this it seems decerebrate rigidity really is subject to an afferentative conditioning factor, too, not from the brain but from the spinal cord. That is why there was no effect from severing the ascending afferentational tracks of the dorsal funiculus running towards the brain.

From these experiments Sherrington inferred that muscle function is subject to a form of regulation by the spinal cord in which the 'proprioceptive' information arriving from those muscles plays a decisive role. In this process stimuli from the force of gravity are the most important. This control is subject to a twofold influence at a higher level. Corresponding with this the 'voluntary' muscles have a permanently operative 'tone' maintained by the organization of the brainstem, of which decerebrate rigidity is an intensified form. In normal conditions brainstem tone is subject to a secondary inhibitory influence from higher brain centres, accounting for the prevalence of rapidly passing 'phasal' contractions originating from the higher organization.

Terminating decerebrate rigidity involved eliminating proprioceptive information and could be done by means of a physiological mechanism of deafferentation not explained until around the middle of the twentieth century. In 1945, in the Institute directed by Sherrington's Swedish pupil Granit, Leksell demonstrated that efferent fibres coming from the spinal cord belong to two different systems. Amongst them are thick A alpha fibres along which impulses travel at a rate of 60–115 m/s. (Greek letters are used for subtypes of types already known.) These fibres are axons of the motor neurones known earlier, alpha motor neurones forming the motor unit. The other type consists of fibres of the A gamma category. They are thinner and their conductive velocity is also lower: 20–44 m/s. Similarly, they are axons of cells with bodies in the anterior horn of the spinal cord, the 'gamma' motor neurones. The difference between the two types is that, while the alpha motor neurones stimulate contraction in common muscle fibres, gamma motor neurones stimulate the tiny muscle fibres of muscle spindles.

Human muscle spindles are 2–20 mm long and 0.15–0.4 mm thick, enclosed in a layer of connective tissue and consisting of small striated muscle fibres. Because they are enclosed, muscle spindle fibres are called 'intrafusal' fibres as distinct from the other 'extrafusal' fibres. Intrafusal muscle fibres are found among extrafusal fibres and parallel with them, chiefly in places where the muscle is capable of the greatest stretch. As on extrafusal fibres, myoneural junctions can be found on them but are extremely small and formed on the intrafusal fibres of the muscle spindle by the axon of the gamma motor neurone. However, both efferent and afferent axons end in muscle spindles and again there are two kinds of afferent end-organ. There is generally one primary (annulospiral) end-organ in a muscle spindle. This is connected with a thick 'Ia' fibre with a conduction rate of 70–110 m/s. As many as five secondary ('bunch of flowers') receptors may also be present and these are connected with a thinner II fibre with a conduction rate of 40–80 m/s (Boyd[5]).

The shape of muscle spindles at any given time is determined by impulses arriving on the gamma efferent fibres and the contraction of intrafusal fibres. If extrafusal fibres around a muscle spindle stretch, if for example leg muscles are stretched by the weight of the leg lifted in walking, intrafusal fibres come under pressure in the muscle spindle and primary end-organs with lower stimulus thresholds are excited as a result. This leads to action potentials arising which can be registered on the Ia afferent axon. These fibres enter the spinal cord by way of the dorsal roots and form synapses with the alpha motor neurones. Their impulses excite the alpha motor neurones and so impulses pass along their axons to the extrafusal fibres surrounding the muscle spindles concerned. They respond by contracting, stopping the stretching of that muscle area and with it the pressure on the muscle spindle. With this excitation of the primary end-organs also finishes, so discharges no longer pass along Ia fibres to the alpha motor neurones and these in turn cease to supply the impulses causing the contractions in extrafusal fibres.

This whole process is called 'autogenous facilitation' since the alpha motor neurone function is set off by signals originating from the muscles which also control their contraction. This process, muscle contraction as a result of its own expansion, is called the 'stretch' or 'myotatic' reflex.

We call this a reflex because an external influence produces a defined response, but it is in fact part of a feed-back regulatory circuit. First of all the excitability of the muscle spindle is adjusted, determining the degree of autogenous facilitation and the threshold of the myotatic reflex. It is assumed that if this facilitation is too intense, muscles affected become excessively tense: this is called 'gamma rigidity'.

So the discovery of the gamma system has reduced the factors

5   Boyd, J. (1964) *The Role of the Gamma System in Movement and Posture*, New York: Interscience Publishers.

which influence decerebrate rigidity to a common denominator. The regulatory function of gamma efferents is carried on by means of spinal cord efferent pathways. Autogenous facilitation is effected through the dorsal roots and thus deafferentation of the limb ends the decerebrate rigidity.

This physiological mechanism has given clinicians an explanation for a spastic condition characterized mainly by the pathological heightened tone of particular limbs. The stretch reflexes of a spastic patient are much brisker than usual and the reflexogenous zone producing them extended. A neurophysiological explanation for these clinical symptoms would be to assume that the threshold of excitability has fallen in the muscle spindles due to intensified stimulation on gamma efferent fibres.

But this explanation lights up only part of the picture characteristic of spastic patients, for if passive external pressure is applied to the patients' stiffened joints, forcing them to flex or extend, resistance suddenly ends. At first the joint resists flexion or extension and then the resistance ceases altogether, in the same way in which the blade of a penknife can be opened or closed (a phenomenon of stretching).

To have found an explanation for this phenomenon was another great achievement in neurophysiology. However it is the regulatory cycle of the 'tendon' spindles and not the muscle spindles which participate in this function. These Golgi tendon spindles are also receptors. They are found at the boundary of muscle and tendon, connected 'in series' with muscle fibres as continuations branching off on the fascicles of the tendon. Tendon spindles are connected with Ib afferent fibres. The terms 'Ia' and 'Ib' fibres serve to clarify them linguistically although physiologically they do not differ at all.

The stimulus threshold of tendon spindles is relatively high. These receptors become excited only when tendon muscle stretch is already extremely great and then discharges pass rapidly along Ib axons forming synapses with alpha motor neurones. These synapses, however, do not produce an exciting (depolarizing), but an inhibiting (hyperpolarizing) effect. When they function the efferent influence of alpha motor neurones diminishes and consequently the muscle fibres in the corresponding motor unit relax – an autogenous inhibitory process, an inhibition originating from the muscle itself. Its result is also a reflex, the 'inverse stretch reflex'. The muscle responds to strong stretching by relaxing and this protects overstretched muscles from injury.

It is assumed, for example in walking, that the weight of a raised leg is a peripheral stimulus causing a contraction in leg muscles so that when that leg is put down again, it stiffens into a pillar which holds the body's weight firmly. However, this is only one factor in the activity of walking. In fact the process we have described is, as Bernstein insisted, very much more subtle than that because when walking a leg continually adjusts to every irregularity in the ground surface or, as Bernstein put it, the final form of walking is ultimately determined by information arriving from the peripheral receptors.

We do not know what types of receptors play a part in this. Afferent fibres connecting with secondary receptors of muscle spindles may perhaps assist in co-ordinating the muscles involved. It is also thought that Ib fibres connected with tendon spindles form synapses not only with alpha motor neurones but also with 'intercalated' nerve cells and that through these their influence extends simultaneously to a larger number of motor units.

We have already referred to the fact that when a clinician diagnoses musculature as spastic, a physiologist explains it in terms of gamma rigidity. Physiologists consider that there is an alpha rigidity, too, which may be interpreted as follows.

Sherrington has demonstrated that decerebrate rigidity can be ended by stimulating the anterior section of the cerebellum and this was why he explained spasm occurring in cases of damage to the cerebellum as being due to a loss of cerebellar influence. Pollock and Davis (1930) also showed that there is a form of decerebrate rigidity which may be ascribed to loss of function of the anterior part of the cerebellum. This cannot be terminated by severing the corresponding dorsal roots or, in other words, the rigidity is not relieved by deafferentation of the limb. It is assumed that in these circumstances alpha motor neurones are in a state of maximum activity and that is why the term 'alpha rigidity' is used. Many details of the whole complex system are still not clear.

Spinal cord regulation

Neurologists divide the spinal cord into segments corresponding to points where spinal cord nerves enter and emerge between vertebrae, classifying them to correspond with vertebrae (cervical, dorsal, lumbar, and sacral).

For several reasons this classification by segments is very difficult to apply. One is that nerves passing between vertebrae run for a shorter or greater distance in the spinal canal before entering or leaving it. There is a great difference in the proportion of spinal cord and spinal canal in child or adult. A child's spinal cord is relatively longer than an adult's and so the segments are positioned differently.

Cipault's rule helps in remembering how adults' segments relate to vertebrae. There are seven cervical vertebrae but eight segments, because spinal-cord nerves emerge both above and below the first cervical vertebra. We can locate the particular cervical segment by adding one to the number of the cervical vertebra level with it. For example, the third cervical vertebra is level with the fourth cervical segment. To the serial numbers of the six upper thoracic vertebrae two must be added for the number for the corresponding segment on the same level. For the sixth to eleventh vertebra three must be added. The first lumbar segment is on the same level as the upper half of the eleventh dorsal vertebra and the remaining four lumbar segments are level with the lower half of it and the twelfth vertebra.

The five sacral segments are level with the first lumbar vertebra and the end of the spinal cord comes between first and second lumbar vertebrae.

This clumsy segmental classification only identifies neurological position and does not correspond with the anatomy of the spinal cord or its embryonic development. It is true that in a very early stage of the development of the human embryo, segmentation does in fact appear as a vestige of an extremely remote phylogenetic past. But this ancestral segmentation relates only to part of the skeleton, to the musculature of the trunk, and to the vascular system, in other words to the small parts with mesodermal development. The spinal cord is not segmented in any stage of its development and nor is there a segmented arrangement in cells serving originally segmented muscles.

The spinal cord is capable of performing important organizational tasks independently. We can see this, for example, in the co-ordination of spinal-cord reflexes. If a cat's head is cut off so that it is deprived of its brain and the preparation is kept alive by artificial respiration and circulation, movements can be induced in it. If one of its legs is stimulated with a weak electric current the leg extends. If the strength of the current is increased the leg flexes suddenly. These are simple reflexes which are combined into larger organizational units, such as when a leg on one side of a cat bends the opposite leg straightens. So there is an inverse co-ordination between the movements of limbs on the two sides.

What would happen if one wished to induce two reflexes with opposite effects simultaneously by compelling the reflexes to compete against each other? Both hind legs are stimulated at the same time with electrical currents of the same strength. When the current is weak both legs extend. These are two one-side reflexes. If the stimulus is increased both legs flex. It follows that the flexion reflex on one side suppresses the extension reflex set off on the other side. In the rivalry between the two influences their effects are not added together but one reflex becomes dominant over the other.

Sherrington carried out these experiments. He increased the strength of the electric current, simultaneously affecting the two hind legs. Suddenly one of the cat's legs flexed whilst the other remained extended, then the leg which had been extended, flexed and the leg which had been flexed, straightened out. This alternation continued. Alternate bending and straightening of the legs is reminiscent of stepping and presumably Sherrington triggered the elementary regulation of that activity. A pupil of his, Graham Brown, also demonstrated that the rhythm of the stepping reflex is not dependent on the strength of stimulus applied but is a datum in spinal-cord organization itself. Within the rhythm of the stepping reflex there appears the inherent rhythm of the alternating dominance of rival reflexes and this rhythm too has a part in the organization of the spinal cord.

Transitorily alternating regulatory systems like this are very important for the whole functioning of the nervous system. They are usually called 'stereotypes', 'patterns', or 'models'. The stepping reflex just described is a very simple spinal-cord pattern.

Spinal-cord functions resulting from cerebral disconnection in animal experiments can be investigated in humans in pathologies where the link between brain and spinal cord has been severed. The first effect of this kind of transverse lesion is that every spinal-cord function ends for a time. After an interval, however, there is a progressive restoration of spinal-cord function below the site of the lesion, where it is isolated from its higher connections. Then, though only vestigially, reflexes appear which form the elements in walking. For example if the sole of the foot is stimulated the big toe extends and if this reflex is induced on both sides at once, there is a co-ordination which corresponds with alternating dominance. On one side the flexed big toe extends and on the other the extended big toe flexes into its normal position, alternately. According to Fortuyn this is a vestigial stepping reflex.

The alternate working of the muscles can be traced electro-myographically, too, for there is a form of electromyography where electrodes are not inserted but activity registered from the surface of the skin, so that the complete picture of activity in several muscles can be traced at the same time.

In flexion, for example, the extensor quadriceps muscle also contracts. This corresponds to the phase in walking when the leg flexes for the foot to push up from the ground.

Using a multiple method of electromyographic recording Fortuyn[6] distinguished two different forms of spasticity in spinal cord organization and according to him, one is connected with swinging the leg and the other with weight-bearing. Both are achieved by spinal cord organization.

Fortuyn also called attention to the fact that discrete delicate movements of the toes can be detected from plantar reflexes – responses produced by stimulating the soles of the feet of patients with transverse lesions of the spinal cord. According to him this indicates that differentiated toe movements usually associated with the cerebral cortex are also regulated by the spinal cord control system.

Taking all these facts into account, Fortuyn made a very important suggestion which deserves to be taken to heart in discussions on encephalization. The basis of the current concept of encephalization is that directive cerebral activity increased steadily with evolutionary progress. Evolution from the lower vertebrates to man brought with it not only a vast cerebral

6 Fortuyn, A. (1960) *Proceedings of the International Study Group on Child Neurology and Cerebral Palsy*, Oxford: Oxford University Press.

development, but also a subordination to cerebral control of more and more functions originally operating at the lower levels of the nervous system. But it would be a mistake to think that encephalization has definitively transferred the organizational 'centres' from lower 'storeys' of the nervous system to higher ones. In the course of the immense development of the upper, cranial end of the nervous system lower structures still remain and function that characterized ancient vertebrates, but have become subordinate to human structures at a higher level and are, so to speak, 'built into' integrative activity. Consequently lower centres even when cut off from higher ones are often capable of organizing surprisingly complex movements. In certain cases the brain can learn to control reafferentatively these isolated functions and even apply them indirectly.

The reflexes

We have referred to the reflexes several times already so let us concentrate our attention on them now. The term 'reflex' was originally understood to mean that living beings respond mechanically in a manner defined in their own structure to influences affecting them, that is, to stimuli. Later this biological concept of the reflex was linked with the nervous system and attributed to its functioning. Nowadays, especially in neurology, only a simple stimulus–response relation is called a reflex and investigated for diagnostic purposes. Doubt is often thrown on the reflex nature of more complicated functions.

Let us begin with a simple reflex like the extension of a flexed knee after tapping the quadriceps tendon. It is supposed that the ability to produce this reflex depends solely on stimulated receptors, on afferent and efferent routes and on the healthy state of the effector organ. The reflex arc runs from receptor to effector and determines the functioning of the reflex link.

In the simplest reflexes a reflex arc is formed by a single afferent and efferent nerve cell. This is the 'monosynaptic' reflex. In a myotatic reflex the efferent cell is the alpha motor neurone and the afferent is the neurone which supplies the Ia axon. We already know from the description of the motor unit that a single alpha motor neurone can activate a number of muscle fibres.

The position of every joint is determined during actual

movements by the complicated collaboration of a significant number of muscles. In this collaboration there are muscles which assist each other, the synergists, and muscles which exert a contrary influence on each other, the antagonists.

In discussing the gamma system we saw what finely regulated connections come into play in even the simplest reflexes. To execute every movement depends not only on the reflex arc, but also on the preparatory adjustment of receptors and other reflexes operating at the same time, and so on.

Excitational processes may result not only in signals travelling along but also in the appearance of inhibitory processes. The 'Renshaw-cells' in the ventral horn of the spinal cord among the motor neurones have an inhibitory effect and some of the afferent fibres entering the dorsal roots of the spinal cord form synapses with them. Under their impact axons of the Renshaw-cells have an inhibitory influence on the motor neurones near them.

Postsynaptic inhibition is where the membrane of a nerve cell is hyperpolarized by inhibition. Presynaptic inhibition is where excitation can be prevented in axons ending in synapses with a stimulatory effect.

Various axons form synapses with a number of nerve cells and it is usually a case of polysynaptic reflexes which correspond to whole collections of nerve cells. Because circumstances are so complicated stimuli have varying effect in space and time in different reflex processes and there are still many riddles for neurophysiological research.

From the neurophysiological implications of this complexity the concept of the reflex is not rated at all highly in some quarters. 'In neurophysiology the old concept of the reflex is no longer of central significance', writes R. Jung.[7] In fact one needs only to return from an anatomical-physiological to the original biological principle of the reflex, the substance of which is that every function of the organism is determined, to see that this determination is not affected by the obvious complications of functional-anatomical relations. Let us take as an example the movement of a leg in walking, starting from the moment in which gravity pulls the muscles of the lifted leg to extend and the excitation of muscle spindles stimulates the corresponding alpha

7 Jung, R. (1967) *Psychiatrie der Gegenwart*, I/1A, Berlin.

motor neurones through signals along the Ia fibres. As a result of the increased discharges of these motor neurones muscle fibres of the motor units contract. This describes a simple reflex. However, the myotatic reflex just described occurs in this isolated form only rarely and only in the context of other more extensive movements. The movement is not just of the leg but the whole individual and forms not just a simple movement but a phase of an activity. The process we have outlined is part of the functioning of a system which consists of increasingly comprehensive regulatory circuits. Yet the functioning of regulatory cycles corresponds to the biological principle of the reflex and is therefore determined. This can be clearly seen even though the functional anatomical details escape us.

Feedback circuits

The simplest robot consists of a single feedback circuit. Every robot is a structure with a defined functional purpose in which the result of the function is 'sensed' by an apparatus and this in turn influences its function.

To take a refrigerator as an example: its motor keeps a cooling liquid in circulation and this coolant draws off heat from its interior. A built-in thermometer registers how much heat has been extracted from how much the mercury contracts. If the mercury column falls below a predetermined level it breaks the electrical circuit operating the refrigerator motor and so the motor stops running. Coolant ceases to circulate and influenced by the external temperature the space inside the refrigerator slowly begins to warm up, causing the mercury in the thermometer to rise. Eventually the electrical circuit is closed once again, the motor begins to function, and refrigeration recommences.

This kind of robot function is called a 'servomechanism'. Relatively large amounts of energy are needed to work the robot but very small amounts are enough to control it. Control is exercised by the sensor registering the result of the robots' working. If change registered by the sensor moves in the direction of a preselected value, the difference between the selected value and the value representing the current situation will produce a discrepancy signal. When the discrepancy is cleared, the control system connected with the sensor stops the robot working. Thus the working of the robot itself affects the control system and that is why this kind of regulation is called a 'feedback regulatory circuit'.

In feedback circuits functioning can begin in two different ways, either a discrepancy signal registers any deviation from a zero value in response to an external influence or else the zero setting is changed, with the same result. It is easy to see that any alteration in the environment corresponds to a reflex stimulus and that there is no difference in principle between a stimulus from an external change where the stimulus threshold does not vary and the result of a change in stimulus threshold where environmental circumstances do not vary.

Functions of the nervous system which correspond with the reflex principle can also be described as functions of feedback circuits. Indeed a cybernetic description based on the principle of feedback circuits is better adapted to explain the complicated relations of reality than the kind of neurophysiological description which analyses particular details. As an example, we can refer to the alpha motor neurone.

Each alpha motor neurone is a huge cell with a large array of dendrite extensions. These dendrites branch out along the longitudinal axis of the spinal cord. Synapses are to be found on them by the thousand. It is enough to take a closer look at a single alpha motor neurone to see what a vast number of factors share in the regulation of its activity. Even in the simplest case exact and detailed investigation is impossible. In science this type of complicated regulatory structure is usually called a 'black box', that is, a structure of which we have no exact knowledge.

But ignorance of the internal details of a structure does not mean that its functioning cannot be studied. In view of its robot-like character the behaviour of the black box can be described by comparing relations between the input signal, corresponding to environmental changes, and output response, the change taking place in the functioning of the structure, in accordance with the reflex principle.

The consistent relationship of stimulus to response, that is the relationship of input to output, gives valuable data on how the black box functions.

A combined regulation of a number of motor units is achieved in both the myotatic, and the inverse myotatic reflex.

Co-ordination and combination of myotatic and inverse myotatic reflexes form an important part of postural controls which maintain body attitudes, and these postural regulations also form only a part of the organization of activity. Simpler regulations are parts of more complex control systems. It is a hierarchy of feedback circuits.

Describing the functional rules of feedback circuits avoids the difficulties attendant on investigating the structural details of the black box. But even so in practice we are very far from seeing the details clearly. Even the experimental results are very contradictory.

Szentágothai and Székely, for instance, demonstrated (in 1962) that normal limbs develop from limb buds implanted in the sides of chicken embryos. Nerves grow out from the spinal cord into these limbs. Supernumerary limbs equipped with nerves will move too but only if nerves grow into them from those segments of the spinal cord which would contribute in other circumstances to innervation of the extremities. If a supernumerary limb receives its innervation from the part of the spinal cord supplying nerves to a fore-limb, its movements will be like those of a fore-limb and if from segments supplying the hind-limb it will move in that way. This movement pattern is independent of whether the transplant was a fore- or hind-limb and even if as many as ten limbs have been transplanted.

These experiments indicate that particular segments of the spinal cord are not uniform from an organizational point of view and that specialized limb movements are decided in the nucleus of the spinal cord.

These results are definitely at odds with those from experiments performed by Weiss (1970). He interchanged the two fore-limbs of tailed amphibians. When the nerves had regenerated, movement was restored. Both retained their original movement in their new placement and so of course the animal became incapable of moving purposefully. Weiss concluded from these experiments that it is not the nucleus but the periphery which decides the character of movements. This conclusion is completely opposed to that arrived at by Szentágothai and Székely.

We might think that the contradictions between these experimental results and the conclusions derived from them are due to their having been carried out on birds in one case and on amphibians in the other. However, Szentágothai obtained results contrary to Weiss's with amphibians as well.

In fact the lesson taught by these contradictions is really the extreme complexity of studying relationships in the organization of the nervous system. Small and apparently insignificant differences in experiments can often lead to contradictions. The extraordinary intricacy of relationships is shown very clearly by Szentágothai's experiences in the following experiments.

One of the central problems in Szentágothai's work concerns the connections between oculomotor nerves and the vestibular organ. He demonstrated on a dog that when an oculomotor nerve has been severed its fibres do indeed regenerate, but their normal anatomical layout is not restored. This anatomical finding coincides neatly with a functional result, where the excitation of certain semicircular canals of a healthy vestibular organ is followed by regular eye movements. In normal circumstances these are very selective reflex correlations but they lose their selectivity after severance of the oculomotor nerve and fibre regeneration. The situation is still the same even eight months after the operation and corresponds completely with the anatomical picture.

However, apart from severing a dog's oculomotor nerve its fasciculus longitudinalis medialis can be cut. This is the pathway connecting the nuclei of the oculomotor nerves with those of the vestibular nerves and plays an important regulatory role in the positioning of head and neck. The result is very surprising. Instead of the reflex functions deteriorating still further as earlier they recover their lost selectivity. 'No explanation can be given for this odd result' wrote Szentágothai, 'but at the same time we obtain a clear picture of the plasticity to be observed at simpler levels of the nervous system.'[8]

It must not be concluded from all this that neurophysiological research projects, investigations into the reflex principle and the feedback circuits are inadequate in finding out how the nervous system functions. It is simply that the nervous system is extraordinarily complicated and any attempt to over-simplify the facts or to schematize reality is doomed to failure sooner or later.

8   Szentágothai, J. (1967) *Results in Neuroanatomy, Neurochemistry, Neuropharmacology, and Neurophysiology*, Budapest.

Tonus

The concept of tonus was first indicated in clinical work based on experience with patients.

Doctors had noticed that muscles deprived of their motor nerve connections become flaccid. They assumed therefore that in healthy condition muscles never relax completely, never become flaccid. So muscle fibres connected with a motor neurone have a basic tension, 'tone'. Tone is so to speak a muscle's state of readiness. They supposed that tone is maintained in the muscle by a few muscle fibres contracting in relays.

Understandably neurophysiologists carried out a number of experiments to check the clinicians' hypothesis and their results corroborated the clinicians' opinions. In animal experiments, too, if peripheral nerves were cut flaccid paralysis appeared in the corresponding muscles. In human beings a diminution in the basal metabolism could be established ('basal' – measurable metabolism in a state of complete rest) after injecting curare which has a paralysing effect on the myoneural junction. It was thought that this paralysed the contraction of muscle fibres maintaining tone, causing metabolic decline. Muscles in a state of flaccid paralysis were shown to have a temperature often as much as two tenths of a degree Celsius lower than that of healthy muscles. This was regarded as another proof for the hypothesis of tonus.

Sherrington, too, succeeded in demonstrating that the nervous system provides muscles with separate tonic and phasal functions. We have seen that the unveiling of the gamma system largely confirmed his conclusions.

However, the hypothesis of tonus in relation to the alternating contraction of individual muscle fibres was shaken to its foundations by electromyography. This extraordinarily sensitive method of investigation established absolutely that there is no kind of electrical activity in tonic (that is, not flaccid) muscles at rest. This meant that the neurophysiological theory on the part played by individual muscle fibres in maintaining tone had to be discarded.

In science it is not unusual that a number of initial arguments in favour of assumptions are proved to be misleading later. That is why valuable hypotheses are those formulated in such a way that crucial experimental procedures can prove them right or wrong (Popper[9]). In the case of tonus electromyography provided the crucial test which rejected the idea of alternating contraction in individual muscle fibres and so caused the collapse of the current tonus theory. Nowadays researchers look for a basis of tonus partly in the elastic property of muscles, and partly in the assumption that it is maintained by the contraction of muscle spindles (Nelson[10]).

As usual there was trouble with the clinical concept of tonus, too. In clinical practice the problem presents itself quite differently from the way it looked to physiologists, who were concerned with normal tone and looking for its origin. They supposed that knowledge of normal tone would make it possible to explain its clinical deviation. But in clinical practice it is not normal tone one sees, but an increased muscle tension (hypertonus) impairing movements and posture, or else its antithesis, 'hypotonus'.

Prechtl and Beintema[11] write:

in the entire book the use of the word tonus has been avoided. We think that so much confusion has already been caused by the use of this technical term that it is best to dispense with it altogether. At the same time the expressions hypertonia and hypotonia of a newborn infant are so useful in practice that their elimination seemed to be impossible. In short: if we speak of a hypertonic infant we mean by this that it is in general 'stiff' and that it displays definite resistance to passive movement, while the hypotonic baby is just the opposite of this.

For a clinician, then, both increased and reduced tonus are important but not tonus as such. The crux of the matter is the problem of both pathologically flaccid and pathologically overtense musculature often seen in the same patient and at the same time. If a clinician finds neither hypertonia nor hypotonia he calls their absence normal tone.

The physiopathological basis for these phenomena has not been clarified nor whether they may be homogeneous.

9 Popper, K. (1966) *Logik der Forschung*, Tübingen: Mohr Siebel.
10 Nelson, A.J. (1967) *Physical Therapy*, 47, 48.
11 Prechtl, H. and Beintema, D. (1964) *The Neurological Examination of the Full Term Newborn Infant*, London: Spastics Society.

A clinical distinction is made between the increased muscular tension in spasm and rigidity. Spasm is characterized by brisk tendon reflexes and by a sudden ending of resistance to passive bending. In rigidity resistance is always uniform or 'plastic' and tendon reflexes are not brisk ('lead pipe' phenomenon).

We have said that a neurophysiologist uses the concepts of gamma and alpha rigidity but not in a way altogether coinciding with the clinical description. The Nobel prize-winner and neurophysiologist, Granit[12] described the situation like this:

> In the problem of motor regulation one is confronted with a biological mechanism and this mechanism is obviously much more complicated than an ordinary clock. If a little piece is removed from a clock the clock stops or else it begins to go too fast or too slowly. The clockmaker tells us that the clock is wrong for this or that particular reason but he will not necessarily take the trouble to explain how many other reasons might cause a similar fault in the running of the clock. On the other hand the clockmaker can point out the important and less important parts of the mechanism and we can understand from this how the clock works. Similarly the physiologist can show the clinician which are the important parts of the biological mechanism effecting increased tonus. But this does not solve the clinician's problems. Here the comparison ends, for the clockmaker makes the clock himself but the neural structure is like a 'black box' whose unknown inner structure spurs us all on to efforts to understand how it works.

In other words the clinician has to wait for an answer to his questions from the neurophysiologist if he is curious about what is wrong with the biological 'clockwork'.

The centres and storeys of the nervous system

In any description of the functioning of the nervous system there is usually some mention of the concept of 'centre'. What is a centre?

The name 'centre' is given to that part of the nervous system on whose healthy condition the organization of reflexes and

12 Granit, A. (1964) 'Symposium on skeletal muscle hypertonia', *Clinical Pharmacology and Therapeutics*, 5:6/2.

feedback circuits depend. In the connective system of nerve cells a 'centre' is always a cell-to-cell connection.

When the palm of a monkey is tickled its thumb bends in and adducts, its wrist and fingers stretch out, its elbow flexes, and its shoulder retracts. These movements are the reflex response and occur even if the cervical segments of the animal's spinal cord supplying the fore-limb are completely isolated above and below the point at which the spinal cord is severed. (Initially the lesion brings a complete lack of response, but in time the reflex reappears.) So for these movements the cervical segments form the centre.

In a healthy animal this reflex seldom appears in isolation but is usually combined with other movements, contributing to preserving balance for instance, or defence. Accordingly any given movements always have their centre in the part of the nervous system where the organization of that composite movement takes place. In this sense we usually speak of 'centres' as arranged one above the other or of the 'storeys' of the nervous system. These are all metaphors and not especially happy ones. The concept of centre cannot be defined very exactly in relation to the reflex principle and even less so on the basis of the principle of feedback circuits, while in terms of buildings any comparison with storeys is not very apt either. An inverted pyramid would be much more to the point for the fact is that far more neurones take part in any relatively high-grade regulation than at the lower levels. There are about 10,000,000,000 nerve cells in the cerebral cortex at the highest level whereas the spinal cord has only a few million. So it is quite easy to see why the magnitude of energy brought into action varies directly with the complexity of connective systems and the number of nerve cells participating in it and it is also clear why the higher authority plays the leading role.

We shall be returning to this question but must emphasize now that the simplest regulations are the most vulnerable. Nowadays the opposite view is expressed constantly. It is thought that resistant functions are those organized in the lowest centres and the most vulnerable are those connected with the cerebral cortex. The actual situation is completely the opposite. For instance, the loss of comparatively few alpha motor neurones as a result of the Heine–Medin disease leads to very severe paralysis. In contrast, even removing the whole of one cerebral hemisphere quite early in a child's life does not prevent it from growing up to become a completely normal adult or even an outstandingly able person. This means that the most resistant functions are the ones in which a very large number of neurones take part.

We have already pointed out that relatively highly complicated organizational processes can take place even at spinal cord level, and that consequently it is a great mistake to underestimate the functions of the nervous system organized there. But it must be said, too, that after any kind of injury the cerebral capacity for compensation is much greater than the spinal cord's.

Anochin[13] reports an experiment on a cat. An extensor muscle (quadriceps femoris) in one of the cat's hind legs was divided into two lengthwise. One half of it with its tendon was transplanted so that when it contracted the cat's knee flexed but otherwise the muscle retained its original innervation, yet the contraction caused the cat severe difficulty in its movements. But it gradually learned to use its legs correctly until ultimately its movements were completely normal again after a few months. Evidently there had been a complicated restructuring of the nervous system in the way the corresponding centres functioned. Next a Sherrington decerebration was done on the cat and decerebrate rigidity set in, the transplanted muscle section acting as an extensor just like the other half. This means that the transplanted muscle functioned as a flexor in moving about but kept its extensor character otherwise. It follows that a functional change took place above the level of spinal cord organization at a point where the whole activity was integrated into a functional unit and co-ordinated there. Anochin called this a 'functional system'.

Any reference in what follows to the residual capacity of the nervous system refers principally to cerebral function.

The brainstem organization

Sometimes an unusually severe developmental disorder can result in a child's being born completely without a forebrain (prosencephalon). One case of an unfortunate little anencephalus baby is well known from the literature. Cared for carefully and given the correct nourishment the child lived for several months, even

13 Anochin, P.K. (1967) *Das funktionelle System als Grundlage der physiologischen Architektur des Verhaltensaktes*, Jena.

though it had neither cerebral cortex nor 'basal ganglia' and only traces of a diencephalon. The child's nervous system therefore began cranially (rostrally), with its midbrain (mesencephalon) as its highest level. What effect did this appalling defect in the baby's nervous system have on its behaviour? One might perhaps expect the most horrifying symptoms but actually it spent its days awake and asleep just like any other baby. In response to visual stimuli it turned its head and its eyes toward the stimulus. It cried at times like all babies do. When it yawned it stretched out its arms. In general it had every reflex characteristic of babies. For instance if its lip was touched it turned towards the finger touching it, watched the finger as it was withdrawn and reached after it with its mouth. From time to time it sucked its finger. When its feet were held down it sat up (Gamper 1926).

What is to be learned from this? At the level of the brainstem very complex regulations of movement and behaviour take place and obviously these play a leading role in the development of a healthy baby, too.

The principal difference between spinal cord organization and the brainstem control system stems mainly from the fact that their respective output instructions are formulated on the basis of information coming from different receptors.

Spinal organization of movements primarily utilizes proprioceptive information from muscles and tendons. These input signals are joined and complemented by information arriving from the joints and skin. It can be shown that these other receptors are less important than the receptors in muscles and tendons, for removing skin and thus the skin receptors, does not affect the decerebrate rigidity of an experimental animal at all. Yet receptors in the skin do have some significance and this can be seen not only from spinal cord preparations in animal experiments but also in humans with a transverse lesion of the spinal cord. In both cases stretching the skin is followed by the tensing of extensors lying under that area of skin. Equally it has been shown that signals from receptors of internal organs influence spinal cord organization.

However information from the vestibular organ becomes an important influence at brainstem level. This inner ear receptor consists of five composite receptors, two maculae and three cristae which are stimulated by straight-line and rotational accelerations and gravitational acceleration.

The vestibular organ is often incorrectly called the 'balance' receptor. In fact information on equilibrium obviously cannot be limited to the functioning of just one receptor but has to relate to a congruity from several different receptors or to any changes in that (disturbance of balance).

Afferent fibres of the eighth cranial nerve originating in the vestibular organ run into the medulla oblongata (myencephalon) where some of them form synapses with cells of the two sets of four vestibular nuclei and others continue to the cerebellum. The vestibular system of nuclei forms a single functional unit. Fibres from the two lateral (Deiters) nuclei reach the motor neurones of the spinal cord either directly or through the reticular formation.

Excitations of the vestibular organ primarily influence the poise of the head and every change in head position affects the whole skeleton through the neck reflex. A cat generally lands on its feet after a fall because first of all its head moves into an erect position and then the whole body comes into line with the head. We know from Magnus's fundamental investigations published in the 1920s and research that followed that any change in the position of the head affects the musculature of the entire body. If for example an animal's head is bent forward the tensors of the forelegs relax and if its head is raised those muscles tense.

It has been suspected that when decerebrate rigidity disappears on severing the myelencephalon it may not be from eliminating the vestibular organ but the formatio reticularis, a huge group of cells running the whole length of the brainstem and taking its name from its luxuriant mesh of cell fibres. Undoubtedly the formatio reticularis is the principal seat of brainstem organization and it is certain that its facilitatory and inhibitory influence extends not only to every detail of spinal cord organization but even to the cerebral cortex. It seems that a non-specific, generally stimulatory or inhibitory, influence is associated with every item of specific information that reaches the cerebral cortex. In investigations of cerebral function the role of the brainstem (and including the formatio reticularis) has made such a profound impression that some have located the centre of integration of the entire function in a 'centrencephalon'.

But again, with increasingly extensive research the formatio reticularis has lost its image as an homogeneously functioning system and presents an increasingly baffling tangle of complex rival feedback circuits. It certainly has a great influence on motor organization but its functioning is not by any means restricted to the motor system.

The pyramidal tract

Now we will turn from the organization of movement in the spinal cord and the brainstem to the forebrain and approach its role in motor organization rather by looking at the role of the pyramidal tract first. It begins in the cerebral cortex and is the only direct efferent connection between the forebrain and the spinal cord. This in itself aroused a great deal of interest among researchers and so the function of the pyramidal tract became highlighted anatomically and physiologically.

In 1870 Fritsch and Hitzig's pioneering experiments on animals showed that if certain areas of the cerebral cortex were stimulated by a galvanic current, movements occurred on the other side of the animal's body. Later the areas of the cerebral cortex concerned with producing those movements were defined exactly and in 1873 Ferrier also established that injury to an area caused paralysis in the opposite half of the body. This discovery was followed by Betz's anatomical observation that 'giant pyramidal cells' can be found in the cortex behind the sulcus centralis with axons running into the spinal cord. This is how the concept of the pyramidal tract made its appearance in science. Betz considered the gyrus praecentralis to be the origin of the pyramidal tract, calling it the 'motor' area and the gyrus postcentralis the 'sensory' area.

This seemed a great achievement. It had become possible to localize fundamental psychological facts in the nervous system.

Another fact learned about the pyramidal tract from these experiments was that it runs across into the spinal cord, explaining why when the area of origin was stimulated or destroyed a reaction occurred on the opposite side of the body. The fibres of the pyramidal tract certainly end on the motor neurones of the spinal cord, so there was good reason for thinking that these reactions were motor responses to cortical excitations.

After this research into the significance of the pyramidal tract became more and more comprehensive. For instance the comparative anatomists demonstrated that in the course of evolution in mammals the proportion of pyramidal tract fibres in the white matter of the spinal cord grew steadily as compared with other fibres. In a marsupial rat fibres of the pyramidal tract constitute only 3.6 per cent of the white matter, 4.8 per cent in elephants, 10 per cent in dogs, 20 per cent in Cebus monkeys, and finally around 30 per cent in man (Clara 1959).

From all this came the view, still fairly widespread, that the forebrain organizes the most complex and precise movements by means of the pyramidal tract. Following tradition these movements were called 'voluntary'. On the other hand those movements which take place unconsciously, spontaneously, and involuntarily were thought to be connected with structures outside the pyramidal tract and were called 'extrapyramidal'.

However this beautifully designed scheme fell to the ground later on. It turned out that movements can be produced not only by excitation of the 'motor area' but from other areas of the cerebral cortex as well. The number of fibres forming the pyramidal tract was calculated and it was shown that there were a million on each side. This figure was compared with the number of Betz's giant pyramidal cells and it was found that, of the million fibres, only 3–4 per cent were really pyramidal fibres. Furthermore only 60–70 per cent of the fibres of the tract originate from other cells of the motor area or from the premotor area in front of it, similarly thought to be motorial. The remainder – and this really seemed incredible – were axons of cells of the gyrus postcentralis although this area of the cortex was considered to be 'sensory' (Ruch[14]).

It is still very common for clinicians to explain the loss of voluntary movements as due to lesions of the pyramidal tract, even though, for example, Tower's exact investigations have shown that in cats, monkeys, and even chimpanzees severing the pyramidal tract causes hypotonic and not spastic symptoms. True, the movements of the experimental animals lose something of their precision but still remain purposive, or 'voluntary'. 'It is therefore erroneous', Ruch writes, 'to associate voluntary movement exclusively with the pyramidal system.'

14   Ruch, T.C. (1951) *Handbook of Experimental Psychology*, New York: Wiley, p. 182.

So a distinction between the pyramidal tract and the extra-pyramidal system that is based on anatomical and physiological definitions would not be tenable either morphologically or functionally. Nevertheless the sharp contrast between voluntary and involuntary movements and their respective association with pyramidal tract and extrapyramidal system obstinately persists in the literature and defies factual criticism. This odd state of affairs is a result of the inertia of concepts. A separation between voluntary and involuntary movements echoes our everyday experiences and a neurophysiological justification would be welcomed generally. Clinicians and neurophysiologists look to one another hopefully for a solution.

Paillard[15] described the situation in his chapter on movement pattern in *Neurophysiology*:

> If the neurophysiologist attempts to probe into questions concerning the elaboration and voluntary control of activity, he has to recognize very quickly the inadequate state of our present knowledge and the inappropriate nature of our research methods. . . . It is on the clinician and the researcher in pathological anatomy that the neurophysiologist now pins his hopes of finding new phenomena, accessible to the experimental method.

However, all we can do in this situation is to examine the facts without bias or conceptual prejudice.

The cerebellum

Sherrington (1961) still considered the cerebellum to be the principal organizer of movements. According to his opinion, still often quoted, 'the cerebellum is the head ganglion of the proprioceptive system which incorporates muscles, tendons and joints and the head ganglion here as elsewhere is the principal ganglion'. This was the neurophysiological view of the cerebellum at the beginning of this century. What is it now?

The motor organizational activity of the 'forebrain' has proved to be more complicated than was expected. It has not been possible to find the supposed difference between the pyramidal

15 Paillard (1959/60) in *Handbook of Physiology: Neurophysiology*, Washington, DC: American Physiological Society.

tract and extrapyramidal systems. Is what we know about 'hindbrain' function any more encouraging?

The cerebellum can be divided into several parts. Its oldest part in evolutionary terms, the lobulus flocculonodularis, is common to all vertebrates. The corpus cerebelli was present only in amphibians and developed to very large proportions in mammals. This indicates in itself that the cerebellum developed at the same rate as the cerebrum.

The corpus cerebelli is divided into three parts corresponding with its connections. The vestibulocerebellum is connected with the vestibular organ, the spinocerebellum with the spinal cord, and the pontocerebellum (across the pons) with the forebrain.

In 1943 when Adrian showed by electrophysiological methods that proprioceptive excitations are localized in the cerebellum according to regions of the body, 'somatotopically', it was a great triumph for the Sherrington view. There was some unease a year later when Snider and Stowell demonstrated that tactile skin stimulation also produces an electrical effect in the cerebellum in a pattern which coincides with proprioceptive somatotopy. Again, auditory and visual afferentation was found later to be localized in essentially the same area and a motor response could be obtained by stimulating these points. So the picture which had seemed so clear originally became completely confused.

For it follows from these experimental data that the cerebellum regularly receives not only the proprioceptive information connected with motor organization but all the other incoming information as well. It was a bitter blow to the researchers' expectations when they found the same area of the nervous system to be both motor and sensory, connecting both with 'conscious' visual and auditory information and with 'unconscious' proprioceptive information. All of this implied a blurring of any line between voluntary and involuntary movements.

We always come back to the same fact: there is a contradiction between the way we describe our everyday experiences and the results of scientific research. It seems to be self-evident that there is a difference between movement and sensation and so we expect the motorium and the sensorium to be sharply separated from each other in the nervous system.

But just as it was impossible to connect the organization of voluntary and involuntary movements with the pyramidal tract and extrapyramidal system respectively, so in cerebellar function boundaries between motor and sensory systems have not been clearly defined.

But what may seem to be self-evident is by no means always true! Input and output correspond with important practical differences in the relationship between an individual and his environment, but this distinction loses its point when we try to extend it to the functioning of the nervous system. Even in the simplest feedback circuit any distinction between effector organ and sensory receptor becomes self-contradictory. Just let us look at the functioning of a motor unit from this point of view.

A muscle is a motor organ. That is obvious. The alpha motor neurone is a 'motor' nerve cell. That is indisputable too. But is that really the whole truth? Its impulses are facilitated or inhibited by synapses formed with the axons reaching it and synaptic excitations stimulate the alpha motor neurone, which therefore responds to them as a 'sensory' cell. So even in the case of the alpha motor neurone, sensory and motor characteristics, input receptor and output transmitter, merge into one.

Then again the muscle is not purely a motor organ for it is also a receptor. Sherrington included proprioception in the motorium but his pupils showed that movement and sensation meet in the gamma system. The higher up we go in studying feedback circuits the more we find that increasing numbers of items of information play an active part in shaping the output measures that produce movement patterns. There is never a sharply defined boundary between motor and sensory systems.

And now let us look at the picture of cerebellar function given by Eccles, Ito, and Szentágothai.[16] The cerebellum is an organ with a surprisingly regular and homogeneous structure. Its cortex has the greatest density of cells in the entire nervous system. Two types of input axon lead in and only one type of output axon, the N cells, leads out of it. Five types of cell are represented in the structure of the cerebellum. Only the axons of Purkinje cells (P axons) come from its cortex and form synapses of an inhibitory nature on the N cells of the nuclei of the cerebellum. On the other hand N cells' output axons form synapses with a stimulatory influence on the cells of widely varying areas of the nervous

16   Eccles, J.C., Ito, M., and Szentágothai, J. (1967) *The Cerebellum as a Neuronal Machine*, Berlin: Springer Verlag.

system. N cells have their own impulse rhythm inhibited by P fibres and facilitated by fibres entering the cerebellum.

An inhibiting influence does not necessarily lead to an actual inhibition since there may be inhibition of another inhibition (disinhibition) and so facilitation. Conversely, if an inhibitory cell is affected by a facilitating influence inhibition is increased (disfacilitation).

Although details like this can give us profound insights into cerebellar function, it is still not possible to see the whole picture. Eccles and his associates assumed that it is involved like a computer in every afferent–efferent regulation.

True, injuries to the cerebellum usually cause the kind of symptoms which in technical terms would be called 'regulatory disturbances'. Movement may be associated with a form of trembling which increases before the movement reaches its goal (intention tremor), equilibrium may be upset by swaying, and so on.

Having said that the cerebellum takes part in every regulatory process, it must be admitted that if it does not function the effect will be paradoxical. In fact there is one congenital condition where the cerebellum is absent yet there are no particular consequences in life and it is only evident in an autopsy. Injuries to the cerebellum developing slowly and gradually may remain virtually without any clinical symptom, too. This paradoxical evidence points up the huge compensatory possibilities characterizing the higher storeys of the nervous system, that is, residual cerebral capacity.

But disordered cerebellar function can produce very varied symptoms and it was precisely from clinical indications like this that neurophysiologists hoped would provide clues to clarify motor organization. Actually they only increased the conceptual confusion. One significant factor in this has been the peculiarity that clinicians and physiologists often give different names to functional changes originating from the cerebellum (Brookhart[17]).

In summarizing them we will follow Brookhart who followed Holmes. Cerebellar functional disorders all share the name of

17 Brookhart (1959/60) in *Handbook of Physiology: Neurophysiology*, Washington, DC: American Physiological Society.

'cerebellar ataxia' and within this the collective name for disorders affecting voluntary movements is 'dysmetria'. ('Voluntary' refers to a series of purposive movements.) Hypermetria is a motor disorder in which movement overshoots the mark and in hypometria movement ceases before a goal is reached. We refer to decomposition of movement when individual links in an activity become confused or disproportionate in timing. A tremor is a movement which is independent of its purpose and oscillates rhythmically. It can be present in a state of rest (static tremor) or may occur only in the course of a movement (dynamic tremor). In cerebellar ataxia musculature may be either hypertonic or hypotonic.

The multiplicity of these symptoms indicates that the cerebellum takes part in many different kinds of regulation and that the symptoms are not so much characteristic of the cerebellum itself but rather of regulatory impairment. The complexity of the situation has been proved experimentally like this.

Fulton with Aring, and Fulton with Liddell and Rioch induced tremor in a cat by removing half of its cerebellum. They next extended the injury by destroying the motor area of the cerebral cortex, when the tremor ceased. The explanation is complicated. Tremor apparently arises in two different ways, either because there is *direct* damage to the part of the cerebral cortex which carries out the definitive formulation of 'voluntary movements' or else because this regulation is *indirectly* impaired by an injury to the cerebellum. Both cerebrum and cerebellum participate in this regulation. At whatever point this feedback circuit is damaged the result is the same: a tremor ensues. It is therefore a precondition of tremor that the function of one component in the cerebral-cerebellar feedback circuit remains intact while the other is not. But if the functioning of both components is impaired, tremor originating from injury to either component ceases.

To sum up, as the disorders of a damaged cerebellum show, the more comprehensive the functioning of the individual 'centres' of the nervous system, or the more numerous the feedback circuits with which the particular structure is connected, so much the more varied will be the symptoms of that injury, but so much the greater, too, will be the possibilities for compensation for its consequences.

The extrapyramidal system

As regards the pyramidal tract system, we mentioned earlier the efforts to connect voluntary movements with the pyramidal tract and involuntary activity with the extrapyramidal system but that they had failed. Nevertheless the extrapyramidal system will be discussed separately because as a result of the peculiar inertia of concepts this term is still frequently used, principally with reference to lesions and pathological symptoms. (All this tends to remind one of the well-known saying: 'We do not know whether Homer really lived but it is certain that he was blind.')

The functioning of the extrapyramidal system is most commonly said to be connected with movements which form the background for intended activity and ensure its preconditions. So, for example, in raising a glass, we also make movements to ensure our balance, manual grasp, and to lift the shoulder. The two different groups of movements form a single unit and the greater the skill with which the intended activity is done – precisely because of those movements forming its background – the smoother it will be and the less effort will be required. (An outstanding Hungarian pianist, Richard Wank, whose death prevented him from working out his theory, maintained that the secret in playing really well is to make the arms weightless.)

The extrapyramidal system has no clearly definable limits. In his monograph on basal ganglia and posture, J.P. Martin[18] writes: 'Since the cerebrospinal fibres which serve the mechanism of the basal ganglia are comprised within the pyramidal tract I have avoided the expression "extrapyramidal" and *a fortiori* I do not use the term "extrapyramidal system" either.' His book is about basal ganglia and its first sentence reads: 'There is no precise definition for the term basal ganglion.'

However, the extrapyramidal system mentioned in the literature means principally the basal ganglia, the subcortical nuclear system of the hemispheres. Martin included only the pallidum, nucleus caudatus, putamen, and corpus Luysii, but some writers include the thalamus and even some defined and diffuse parts of the grey matter of the brainstem as well, while

18   Martin, J.P. (1967) *The Basal Ganglia and Posture*, London: Pitman.

others even include the cerebellum and significant parts of the cerebral cortex.

Classifications of extrapyramidal motor disorders vary widely, too. Jung and Hassler (in *Neurophysiology*, 1959) classify the symptoms in two groups, the 'hyperkinetic-dystonic' referring to pathologically exaggerated movements and posture disorders and the 'hypokinetic-rigid' group distinguished by rigidity associated with static tremor.

According to Jung and Hassler these are the subgroups within the hyperkinetic-dystonic group.

The Chorea group of symptoms: These are characterized by involuntary rapid fragmentary movements in the proximal parts of the limbs rather like gesticulation, and in the trunk and head muscles exaggerated and distorted with facial movements rather like grimaces. These movements are of short duration and do not run together. They increase with excitement or in the course of intentional movements and cease with sleep. They impede intended movements. The musculature is hypotonic. These symptoms are attributed to damage to the small cells of the putamen and to the nucleus caudatus.

Ballistic motor disorder: This is characterized by agitated beating movements beginning in the proximal part of the limbs and extending along their whole length. They are accompanied by relatively slow bending and stretching movements in the peripheral joints. Agitated movements extend from the limbs to the face. The entire process of exaggerated movement begins suddenly and presents itself with such force that patients fall down and roll about helplessly. Attacks can be brought on by an intentional activity, an unexpected stimulus, or strong emotions. They are ascribed to damage to the nucleus subthalamicus (corpus Luysii) on one side and appearing in the opposite side of the body.

Athetoid syndrome: In face and limbs, principally in the distal parts, the fingers and toes, slow irregular writhing movements are accompanied by excessive extension of the joints from the simultaneous contraction of agonists and antagonists. These movements increase on stimulation and often frustrate any voluntary activity. Musculature is hypotonic. A characteristic feature is the very bizarre positions in which joints become fixed occasionally. The syndrome is ascribed to combined damage to the striatum (nucleus caudatus and putamen) and the outer part of the pallidum, and is occasionally caused by damage to the pallidum alone.

Dystonic syndrome: A motor disorder similar to athetosis but principally appearing only in the proximal muscles. Its result is that neck and trunk stiffen, becoming fixed in torsion spasm, slowly turning. Muscles contract convulsively, increasingly resistant to passive stretching and if this stretching stops suddenly, recoil like a spring into the original posture. Dystonic patients may be capable of surprisingly complex activities. They can ride bicycles for example and are able to make considerable efforts. Dystonia is related to damage to the putamen.

Myoclonic syndrome: This is characterized by rapid convulsive arhythmical undulatory movements of the muscles. Damage is usually localized in the nucleus ruber, the nucleus dentatus, the olives, or tractus tegmentalis. There is also a myoclonic syndrome in which convulsions occur only in the musculature of the floor of the mouth or as convulsive yawns. In these cases damage has affected the striatum.

The hypokinetic-rigid group of symptoms include Parkinson's disease (Parkinsonism) and it is worth discussing this in a little more detail because it illustrates the complex conditions of extrapyramidal motor disorders very well.

The most striking thing about Parkinson patients is the absence of spontaneous movements which may even reach a point where they lack motivation, just sit hunched up, not even wiping away saliva trickling from their mouths, even though they are completely aware of what is happening. The patient's muscular rigidity is characterized by the fact that when he lies down his head often does not touch the pillow but stays lifted up.

Once he does start to move, his paralysis does not stop him from running up and down stairs or even catching a bus. Martin described how some patients usually unable to walk can do so quite well on the white stripes of a pedestrian crossing. Parkinson patients may even be able to dance to the rhythm of music. Emotion quickens response too.

Although Parkinson's disease is referred to as a motor disability it is accompanied by vegetative symptoms. The function of the salivary glands is increased and facial skin is greasy.

In addition there may be both static tremor and a very odd postural disorder. Sufferers from Parkinson's disease sometimes stiffen like statues for fairly long periods in positions which look unbelievably uncomfortable and this kind of preposterous statuesque posture is found in only one other illness, one which no one would classify with motor disabilities and indeed is generally thought of as being very far removed from them, namely the catatonic form of schizophrenia.

We might think that it is merely a question of a superficial resemblance between Parkinson's disease and schizophrenia, but the connection must be deeper than that, because symptoms of real mental disorder are associated sometimes with postural symptoms in Parkinson patients.

The cause of Parkinson's disease is said to be damage to the cells of the substantia nigra; this view, however, is not generally accepted. We have given only Jung and Hassler's opinion. Any attempt at localization should be viewed with caution! As early as 1817 when Parkinson described the clinical picture, he noted a case in which the patient's tremor ceased with the appearance of a hemiplegia after subsequent cerebral damage. In another case the disappearance of hemiplegic symptoms might be associated with the appearance of Parkinson tremor.

Experiences like these conflict with attempts at localization, indicating rather the role of feedback circuits discussed earlier. Denny-Brown[19] attributes extrapyramidal disorders to damage to the basal ganglia and explains their symptoms by liberation of vestibular influence or postural control from the effect of visual and tactile information. According to Martin's data the situation is even more complicated. Parkinson symptoms may be increased to a surprising extent by blindfolding the patient's eyes in conditions when no one would otherwise have supposed the regulation in question to be influenced by vision.

Complicated situations in the highest storeys of nervous-system

19   Denny-Brown, D. (1964) 'Symposium on skeletal muscle hypertonia', *Clinical Pharmacology and Therapeutics*, 5/6(2).

regulation and conceptual insistence on the existence of the extra-pyramidal system would explain Jung and Hassler's closing words of their major article in *Neurophysiology*:

The sum of the many observations and experiments brought together in the preceding pages is disillusioning. It is difficult to draw general physiological conclusions from the various experiments and clinical facts relating to the extrapyramidal system for three reasons. First, because the contrived ana-tomical definition of the extrapyramidal motor system as the system of the basal ganglia confines the motor connections within an excessively narrow circle. Secondly, a distinct diver-gence can be perceived between the symptomatology of human extrapyramidal disorders and the symptoms experi-mentally produced in animals. And finally there is consid-erable danger in drawing conclusions from data derived from injuring, stimulating and electrically registering circumscribed areas. . . . In spite of the extensive literature we must admit that we know astonishingly little about the essential physio-logical mechanisms of the extrapyramidal motor system or about their functioning or the coordinating activity of their components.

We have surveyed basically the circle of regulatory systems usually comprised by motorium now and perhaps made it clear that any attempt to draw a sharp distinction between voluntary and involuntary movements conflicts with the functioning of the nervous system and that there is just as little possibility of distin-guishing between movement and 'sensation', motorium and sensorium. However, so far very little reference has been made to the sensory system, so now we will review the afferent, information-receiving, input side of the nervous system.

6 Sensorium

The Sensory Unit

The concept of a motor unit on the output side of the nervous system is matched on its input side by the concept of a 'sensory unit', the name given to the receptor or receptors linking with an afferent axon, the two-directional axon of the 'pseudobipolar cell', which runs between that receptor and other nerve cells.[1] The assembly point for receptor information to an afferent fibre is an area known as the 'receptive field'. On a cat's skin the size of this field may be as large as $9 \times 5\text{cm}^2$ but may also be limited to a single end organ. Adjacent fields usually overlap. Reciprocal relationships form through their contact, and neurophysiologists consider these to be the basis for information on discrimination.

We have seen that the motor unit is a link in a feedback circuit for which afferent peripheral information is crucially important. Consequently both output and input connections influence the unit's functioning. Conversely might input processes be influenced similarly by output regulation in the sensory units?

From the receptor excitation processes of a sensory unit impulses can be recorded on ascendant, afferent pathways of the spinal cord. Hagbarth and Kerr registered action potentials after electrically stimulating a cat's leg. Then they repeated this stimulation, stimulating the cerebellar or cerebral cortex, for instance. When upper 'storeys' of the nervous system were stimulated, the number of impulses recorded on ascending fibres of the spinal cord decreased although the peripheral stimuli remained the same. So even at the lowest level, sensory function is already subject to output and influence directed from the centre towards the periphery.

---

1 (1959/60) *Handbook of Physiology: Neurophysiology*, Washington, DC: American Physiology Society.

Receptive fields of sensory units vary in size and interconnect. It has been shown (for example by Hartline) that the centre and periphery of the retina's receptive fields have opposing effects of excitation and inhibition. For instance, if two points of light shine at the same time on the centre and periphery of a field, they suppress each other's effects. Moreover there are nerve cells which are stimulated by the beginning of excitatory processes (on-effect) and others when they stop (off-effect) so offering a physiological interpretation (by Granit and Kuffler) of observed temporal variations. For vision Hubel and Wiesel succeeded in tracing the neurological and neurophysiological afferentation of spatial direction and movement to the cerebral cortex.

Receptor adaptation

The initial stage of input processes is formed by the functioning of the receptors. Receptors respond to the influences affecting them (that is to stimuli) when an excitational process, by producing a generator potential which gives rise to the action potential of the afferent axon.

A universal characteristic of any receptor's function is adaptation, which is, in principle, the same phenomenon as the change in an axon's stimulus threshold when a stimulus, which is a little above the threshold, loses its effect on repetition.

Every receptor's stimulus threshold is in a constant state of fluctuation. If for example a muscle is subjected to a load and a record taken of the number of impulses on the afferent fibre connecting with that muscle spindle, it will be proportional to the size of the load and decrease progressively. This decrease can be regarded as a change in the effect of a stimulus of constant size through repetition, that is as a raising of the stimulus threshold. The stimulus threshold of a receptor rises proportionally to any increase in the strength or frequency of repetition of a stimulus, while decrease or an ending of a stimulus lowers the stimulus threshold.

Adaptation and habituation

The physiologist sees receptor adaptation by comparing the physical magnitude of a stimulus with the number of impulses travelling along an afferent fibre. Adaptation can take place also if constant repetition of a stimulus affects the axon itself and not the receptor, so that there is a rise in the axon's own stimulus threshold. But if the response of the effector organ diminishes with the repetition of the constant stimulus then this is known as 'habituation'.

So habituation is a change in a stimulus–response relationship. This relationship may be inherited or acquired (learned). The stimulus of an acquired relation repeated without 'reinforcement' gradually becomes ineffective. Pavlov called this 'extinction' and explained it by the build-up of an inhibitory process.

Spence, Thompson, and Neilson (1964) stimulated at constant strength and rate the centripetal stump of an afferent nerve which had been severed recording the impulses on the central stump of the efferent nerve similarly severed. Habituation was shown by a drop in the number of impulses.

From this they deduced that the locus for this process was the link between nerve cells. They gained the impression from their experiments that habituation may be connected with the 'intermediary' cells of the spinal cord and therefore has to do with the functioning of the lowest level of the nervous system.

Adaptation, habituation, extinctional inhibition, and even fatigue share many similar features and habituation may be regarded as a form of learning in the gradual elimination of response to stimuli with no biological significance (negative learning).

Do these different terms refer to the same process? Many would argue so, at any rate in some cases.

Subjective and objective modes of description

So far our description of the functioning of the nervous system has been consistently objective. The reflex principle was traced through from a stimulus affecting the receptor with the excitation of that receptor, signals originating from this, arriving finally at the functioning of an effector organ. In discussing feedback circuits the quality of automatism in the link between receptor and effector was stressed and the importance of the central adjustment of the receptor was pointed out too. These processes can be traced by electrophysiological methods within the structure itself or by a black-box method comparing stimulus and response.

For the sensory unit data acquired by electrophysiological methods were presented in essentially the same way as for the motor unit except that the input side was examined in the case of the sensory unit and the output side for the motor unit.

The functioning of the human nervous system may yet be described in a totally different way from the objective form of description used so far. Man is able to communicate verbally the information arriving through his receptors, or, to use the usual expression, man 'perceives' these stimuli.

For the sake of simplicity, we will not concern ourselves here with other living beings but with man alone and to be consistent confine the term 'feeling' to what man communicates. Communication in which the contents are known only from the words of the person speaking them is 'subjective description' and this has an extraordinary advantage in the simplicity of its language over the technical complexity of objective description. But on the other hand a difficulty arises when we want to check the validity of subjective description, because it can be altered intentionally or unintentionally and as far as the contents of the communication are concerned we are in the hands of an informant whose veracity cannot be checked.

So science steers clear of subjective data, but let us look at the question more closely.

An identical experimental process will be reviewed on the basis of both objective and subjective modes of description. By introducing an electrode into the spinal cord of a cat, Wall[2] was able to register the impulses along the axon of a single afferent nerve cell whenever the cat's hind leg received an electric shock. The same number of impulses were always recorded for shocks of constant strength. But when later he surrounded the point stimulated by the current with a vibrating copper sheet, the number of impulses obtained from the same electric shock diminished. This is an objective description of the reciprocal influence of two different stimuli applied simultaneously at almost the same place: vibration diminished the effect of the electric shock.

The cat could not talk about its experiences during the

2   Melzack, R. (1961) *Scientific American*, 204(2).

experiment and so only objective description was possible. But it is a different matter when a similar experiment is carried out on a human being.

A man's skin was stimulated by an electric shock which he said (subjective evidence) was slightly painful. Then the point where the shock was given was surrounded with a vibrating sheet of copper and the previous shock repeated exactly. The subject reported that the second shock, objectively as strong as the first, caused no pain. So subjective evidence and objective result agreed. It could be objected that a comparison between the two experiments is not altogether consistent since objective results noted in the cat's case have been compared with results subjectively experienced by the man. So let us be more consistent! If any skin nerve is separated out on a human being and then all but one of its fibres severed, it will be possible to register the afferent impulses electrophysiologically on the one axon remaining intact. These impulses are produced by touching a defined skin area. When the skin is touched, the individual tells us that he has felt the touch and at the same time afferent signals passing along the axon can be registered objectively. The gentler the touch on the skin surface, objectively the fewer impulses will pass along the axon, and subjectively the lighter the individual will feel the touch to be. In the end, the mechanical stimulus applied (pressure) is diminished until only a single action potential can be registered on the afferent fibre. The individual can still feel this, but any smaller stimulus produces no response at all electrophysiologically or subjectively (Bowman 1960).

So subjective and objective data change in parallel and dependably so even for the slightest stimulation. With maximum adaptation, the lower limit of visual perception is one or two photons, and for hearing it is of the order of magnitude of the Brown molecular movements of air.

So not only is subjective description acceptable but also may sometimes be even more sensitive than an objective approach. Békésy[3] writes: 'My respect for psychological observation was further enhanced when I learned that in some situations, as in the detection of weak stimuli, the sense organs often exhibit greater sensitivity than can be demonstrated by any purely physical

3   Békésy, G. von (1967) *Sensory Inhibition*, Princeton, N.J.: Princeton University Press.

procedure.' However, the objective mode of description can give further evidence not obtainable subjectively.

Directional perception of a sound source is highly sensitive and Stenger, a German physician of the 1900s, was the first to notice that it can also be triggered by a procedure which in a peculiar way is completely inappropriate. For if the same sound is transmitted through earphones to both ears at the same time but with different intensities only one sound is heard and this seems to come from the side with the louder sound. Ordinarily the directional quality comes from the fact that the air vibration from a sound-source (perceived as sound) does not reach both ears at exactly the same time and the perception of direction is caused by the slight delay with which the sound stimulus reaches the further ear. This is easily verified experimentally. If we transmit a short sound vibration of equal intensity and frequency to both earphones with a time interval between them of 0.0002 seconds, then the listener would hear only one sound as coming from the same side as the ear which the sound reached first. So the directional quality of the sound depends on that slight discrepancy in time between the two sounds. Then why does a difference in intensity also lead to perception of a directional kind?

Subjective description is of no help here but Rosenzweig[4] clarified the problem objectively using a physiological method. He implanted electrodes in a cat's auditory pathways on both sides. The physical sound stimulus affected the hair cells of the Corti organ in the auditory receptor and the generator potential of excitation of these cells set off action potentials on the fibres of the auditory nerve, which end on the nuclei cochleares of the medulla from which two auditory pathways originate. It can be demonstrated anatomically too that the auditory pathways on each side connect with the Corti organs on both sides. Whichever ear is affected by the sound, a response always appears on both auditory pathways because both ears are linked with them. Yet whichever ear was affected by the sound, the stronger response appears on the auditory pathway on the opposite side.

Next Rosenzweig transmitted the same short sound to both ears of a cat through earphones with a delay of 0.0002 seconds. Electrodes implanted in the two auditory pathways did not

4   Rosenzweig, M.R. (1961) *Scientific American*, 205(4).

record identical responses on both sides this time, but registered the same electrical activity as from a sound reaching only one ear. This result can be explained by the fact that the excitation of the first sound alters conditions for excitability in such a way that a second stimulus has no effect. He also obtained the same result when the same sound reached both ears at once but with greater intensity for one than the other and then the response was more pronounced on the opposite side. This threw light on the physiology of directional quality. The objective picture matched exactly with the subjective evidence on directional quality and at the same time these experiments formed the basis for an explanation of perception. The same neurophysiological result is obtained either when one ear is stimulated by two identical auditory signals at an interval of 0.0002 seconds or two sounds of different intensities are transmitted simultaneously. Directional quality depends on the asymmetry of signals travelling simultaneously along the two auditory pathways. This asymmetry may be caused by stimuli on one side, by a slight difference in time between stimuli on the two sides (the after-effect of the first signal on the second), or by a difference in their intensity.

So in testing the validity of subjective evidence neurophysiology was able to explain the correlation. Both methods of description may be equally trustworthy. However, subjective data are concerned primarily with orientation within an environment, referring only incidentally to neurophysiological facts. Its explicit contents refer to the environment but implicitly include important information about the functioning of receptors and the nervous system. Yet subjective and objective descriptions are not simply interchangeable. Subjective description can often be satisfactorily explained only by referring to objective data. But on the other hand, subjective description may play an important part in learning about some functional processes which would be inaccessible otherwise.

The role of movement in perception

If we look into an evenly lit, completely isochromatic hemisphere within minutes its colour will seem to fade. This is the subjective perception of a process of adaptation occurring only if the surface seen is completely homogeneous, that is if it contains no contours.

Evidently there must be a mechanism which inhibits this adaptation where there are contours. What does this mechanism consist of?

In the 1950s Riggs and Ditchburn first demonstrated that the eyeball vibrated delicately with a frequency of about 150 per second. If by some means this vibration is eliminated from the process of seeing, adaptation will even extend to pictures with contours so that they gradually vanish. For example, the eyeball's vibration can be neutralized experimentally by placing a contact lens over it which naturally vibrates with it but which carries a tiny projector sending a motionless picture into the interior of the eye. At first the picture is sharply defined but it fades quickly and finally disappears. (It is worth noticing that individual details in the picture will not be adapted at the same rate. We shall return to this later.)

The picture sent by the projector attached to the contact lens differs from pictures normally seen in that the same details constantly fall on identically specific receptor areas in the retina. Normally as a result of the vibration on the eyeball, separate finer details reach different adjacent receptive fields in turn. (In the sphere of vision, unlike other input processes, zero change can be registered – an indication of the biological significance of shape discrimination.) It is movement which impedes this pictorial form of visual adaptation, the vibration of the eyeball exerting its influence even at the simplest level of sensory nerve-function, receptor adaptation.

To look at another experiment, Held and Hein (1963) put twin kittens in exactly the same visual environment. They were either in complete darkness or one sat in a little cart and the other pulled it. The environment was visually identical for the two small animals whether they looked at it while sitting or pulling the little cart, but from the point of view of movement there was a fundamental difference, the same visual information coming to one 'at work' and to the other when 'taking time off'.

After a certain period both kittens were given optical tests. It was found that the active kitten did considerably better than the passive one in seeing (distinguishing) both form and depth.

The experiment was repeated with the two kittens taking it in turns to pull each other. They always had one eye blindfolded when active and the other eye when in the passive position, so that they had one eye associated with active, and the other eye with passive behaviour. Obviously the same visual signals were received by both eyes of both animals. Yet one-eye experiments resulted in both kittens' vision of the eye associated with active movement being very much better than that of the eye associated with passive behaviour.

In these experiments, the influence of movement on vision took effect at a higher level than in those concerned with vibration of the eyeballs. However, even by using the most recent neurophysiological methods, Hubel and Wiesel[5] could not find any explanation for these differences, either in visual pathways or in the visual cortex, in their research into the neurophysiology of vision.

From experiments performed objectively on animals let us turn to the results of experiments carried out on human beings who gave subjective data.

By repeating them on his colleagues Erismann developed the experiments which Stratton had done on himself around the turn of the century. Reversing spectacles turned the picture of the world upside down and the experimental subject wore them continuously for ten days. Erismann described (objectively) the experimental person's behaviour and compared this objective description with the subjective data reported by the subject.

At first the disturbance of visual information was on such a scale that it made any activity on the subject's part practically impossible. He stumbled into every obstacle and dropped everything he carried. However, he slowly got the knack of walking and carrying out various simple activities. During this time subjectively everything he saw looked topsyturvy.

After that stage, objective observation showed that the subject was able to get about and act more and more easily. The special spectacles impeded him less and less over the range of what he attempted to do.

Seen subjectively, the results are much more exciting. In the stage that followed the first period of stumbling and dropping everything, for example Erismann noted that the subject told him that when a little girl rode towards him in the street on a tricycle,

---

5   Hubel, F. and Wiesel, A. (1966) *Brain and Conscious Experience*, Berlin: Springer-Verlag.

she, the tricycle, the entire street were upside down. She reached the subject who touched her. Then, as though by magic the girl and her tricycle turned the right way up and the entire world turned with them. The new, natural situation (despite wearing the reversing spectacles!) lasted only as long as the subject's hand was touching the girl. When he let go of her everything turned upside down again, passing through 180 degrees. This was an instance of the peculiar rivalry of visual and tactile information, in which touch dominates. After that it steadily became easier to make this reversal by touching people or things. Later it was enough for him to take a stick and touch something with the end of it for the scene to turn immediately the right way up. Later still, merely lighting a candle achieved this result. When the flame appeared it turned into its normal position, pulling his picture of the world with it. The correction increased steadily in frequency and duration.

'Quite obviously', Erismann[6] wrote,

movement had a great influence on gradual visual adaptation to the severely distorted information. And the more comprehensive the activities which the subject was compelled to undertake, so, objectively did his movements become surer, while subjectively he reported that the picture he saw was turning the right way up for longer periods.

Erismann's experiment has been repeated but this time the subject had to remain passive. He was given varied visual information but not allowed to move about during that period. Instead he was taken about in a small cart and in these circumstances the picture never turned the right way up, proving the crucial role of activity (Held[7]).

This shows that the brain does not just take in passively the information coming to it from receptors, but reworks it thoroughly primarily on the basis of further information coming through movement.

Starkiewicz[8] emphasized that vision is inseparable from

---

6 Erismann, T., Pamphlet for the film *Die Umkehrbrille und das Aufrechte Sehen*, Innsbruck.
7 Held, R. (1965) *Scientific American*, 213(5).
8 Starkiewicz, W. (1963) *Die Rolle des Muskelsystems in der Pathogenese und Therapie des Schielens*, Leipzig.

movement. A patient who has had an operation to correct a squint sees objects in the wrong direction to begin with. If he sits down to practise picking up objects with his hand, using only the eye operated on, after a time he will see them in their correct positions. But if he stands up then and walks about in the room still using only the eye operated on, for a time he will again locate what he sees incorrectly. 'His "manual vision" is accurate already but not as yet his "foot vision" ', says Starkiewicz and by this he means that seeing is not just a matter of using one's eyes but is also influenced by movements of the hands and feet in different ways.

Reafferentation

The nervous system does not elaborate the functional systems it commands simply on the basis of information from receptors but on its own expectations and extrapolation from the information received. It prepares in advance for the reception of both actual and probable information from the receptors and this further influences their excitability. For example, Tinbergen demonstrated that a moth is colour blind when sexually active and seeking a mate, but that it can distinguish colour differences when looking for food.

The regulatory organization of the nervous system prepares actively for the information it anticipates. Holst and Mittelstaedt (1950) called this the 'principle of reafferentation' and Anochin (1935) 'centripetal afferentation'.

According to the reafferentation principle, information from receptors is assigned a primarily endorsing or correcting role, monitoring through feedback the functioning which leads to command by the nervous system.

Movement is of fundamental importance for reafferentation. Since the brain regularly prepares itself ('action acceptor' – Anochin) for likely information and incoming information endorses or modifies this cerebral anticipation (reafferentation), perhaps we may infer that it is through the addition of movement that the brain is able to verify and supplement the information reaching the receptors. To take a very simple case, we turn our heads to watch a moving target, correct direction in hearing, and so on. Through movement the brain is enriched with newer, and by no means merely proprioceptive, information which it can exploit reafferentatively to check and correct its commands for actions. Sufferers from tabes, for example, become incapable of walking because of damage to the afferent fibres running from the legs to the spinal cord and carrying proprioceptive information. Yet these patients can become able to walk again by learning to replace lost internal information with visual cues. This, however, is only a very simple example. Any form of action constantly increases the scope of reafferentative control routes for feedback. It broadens the variety of possibilities for ensuring successful action to a quite extra-ordinary extent and so cerebral functioning becomes less and less dependent on inherited connections or on anatomically stable pathways, but relies increasingly on an amazingly diversified informational system built up through experience.

The integration of information

For almost three weeks, Kohler (1953), Erismann's colleague and later his successor, wore spectacles which shifted the light-rays entering his eyes from right to left horizontally, affecting his visual field. He had essentially the same experiences as the people who wore the topsyturvy reversing spectacles. His distorted picture of the world eventually reverted to normal vision and he could then go about all his daily activities without any difficulty while still wearing the experimental spectacles.

Some of Kohler's[9] subjective observations reveal a very great deal about the processes going on in his brain during this time. He described how he was already getting about in the street normally and confidently. Houses were in their right places, traffic was moving normally. But then the letters on the number plate of a car coming towards him still read back-to-front as in mirror writing. Kohler wrote:

> This is optically impossible! The side of the street and every-thing else ought to shift round with the number. And if one were to perform the irksome task of somehow transliterating the number plate into mirror writing, then the order of the digits would reverse itself. But that is what happened. The subject can indeed locate correctly two sides of a figure 3, for

9 Kohler, I. (1953) *Die Pyramide*, 5,6,7.

example, (open on the left and bulging on the right) yet still sees it in mirror writing! What we have here beside perception of the new right and left situation coming from the kinaesthetic area is the survival of previous memories of the shapes of letters and numbers.

Perhaps we could put all this in a different way by saying that the brain actively assembles its consistent picture from a great number of partial solutions. In exceptional cases in this process of integration it could happen that competing partial solutions produce an ill-fitting overall picture.

Erismann's subject whose view was inverted had an interesting experience in the transitional period before it finally turned the right way up. Two people were standing talking in front of him. He told Erismann about them and said that he saw them standing on their heads like everything else. Then one of them lit a cigarette. As the flame from the match appeared it instantaneously turned over into its normal position, 'pulling with it' the person lighting the cigarette. But yet this corrective effect did not extend to the other man who was still seen as standing on his head! So the subject's view corresponded neither with the physical stimulus presented by the reversing spectacles nor with experience but reformed into a hybrid.

The possibility of the details' relative independence gives some insight into the mechanism of the integrative process which combines partial results into a unity. It is conceivable that particular difficulties are not resolved at a uniform speed and that in particularly complex conditions contradictions can remain in the overall picture.

This may also explain the subjective experience of the disappearing picture seen by attaching a projector to a contact lens neutralizing ocular vibrations. The picture goes, breaking up into mosaic-like details, the individual details fading out at different speeds (Pritchard).

One can hardly miss the analogy with top-level regulatory disturbances in the motor system, also relatively circumscribed and occurring in many different forms.

Finally we will mention one other important observation made by Erismann and Kohler. After the brain had completely compensated for disturbance from information distorted by wearing the experimental spectacles, they were taken off but compensation still continued even though it was unnecessary or even harmful at that point. So a certain time is needed for adjusting the compensatory effect and it may be assumed that this is just the time during which the brain projects forward the information earlier experience has led it to expect.

Under experimental conditions this anticipatory activity may show itself in a very peculiar way. In one case Kohler[10] used spectacles through which there seemed to be a rainbow coloured stripe around everything he looked at. After a certain lapse of time his brain cancelled out this distortion and the rainbow disappeared. When he took off the distorting spectacles, for a time an inverted rainbow outlined the things he saw.

'Dynamic stereotype' was the name given by Pavlov to that property of the cerebral cortex shown by its capacity for learning the structural system of a given series of stimuli. Anochin[11] published this account of an experiment performed by Semenienko. A man was exposed for a relatively long time to a sequence of bell, light, horn, bell, light, horn, bell, light, etc. An electroencephalogram (EEG) taken from the occipital region showed the characteristic desynchronization following the flash of light. Then an extra ring of the bell was substituted at the point where a light signal would have followed. The EEG showed a regular light effect! This means that the excitational process did not correspond to the actual stimulus but to expectation stemming from the dynamic stereotype.

From what has been said a new kind of picture begins to appear of the sensory function forming the basis for subjective processes. The brain not only acquires information through receptors, but becomes increasingly flexible in anticipating the probable information on which to base the justification for the measures it will take. Motor measures are put into effect in this way, organized reafferentatively through sensory measures. Detailed items of information are combined and integrated.

Cerebral function is facilitated when motor and sensory systems mesh reafferentatively but inhibited when expectations are proved unjustified in the event.

10 Kohler, I. (1962) *Scientific American*, 206(5).
11 Anochin, P.K. (1967) *Das funktionelle System als Grundlage der physiologischen Architektur des Verhaltensaktes*, Jena.

The two kinds of physiological approach

We have already pointed out that science actually approaches an understanding of nervous system function in two different ways, one attempting to clarify structural details while the other treats the structure as a 'black box', studying the relations of input and output. The two purposes are not mutually exclusive; sometimes their results coincide and on other occasions they can complement one another.

The Sherrington school made some very valuable discoveries about the structural details and functions of both motor and sensory systems – the two cannot be sharply separated, of course. Their research results, based on objective description, fit in quite strikingly with a great deal of subjective evidence. However, the higher we go up the storeys of the nervous system's regulation, the harder it is to trace the structural details of processes. So research based on the black box system acquires a correspondingly greater significance.

The Pavlovian approach

Pavlov's research characteristically followed the black box method. His starting-point was the real Archimedean fulcrum of cerebral functioning.

Pavlov devoted several decades to his Nobel prize-winning investigation into the functioning of the glands of the alimentary canal. In the course of these experiments he noticed something about salivary gland function which at first sight does not seem to be particularly interesting. His work showed that the composition of the secretion of the most diverse digestive glands changes according to the characteristics of the food. This was true of salivary glands too, but surprisingly both the change in the composition of salivary gland fluid and in general the onset of function began before the food reached the mouth, and so also preceded the excitation of the receptors in the oral mucous membrane. Pavlov was astounded since this appeared to refute the reflex principle and he had based his conclusions strictly on that. Pavlov was quite clear that conceptual problems like this are always very significant scientifically.

Indeed, according to the reflex principle, a stimulus always precedes and triggers a response. The functioning of the salivary glands is regulated by 'vegetative nerves' to which excitation is transmitted when receptors in the mouth are stimulated by food. If the salivary gland of an experimental animal begins to function already when, for instance, the animal hears the footsteps of the person who regularly brings its food, it could be regarded as biologically expedient but not considered to be a reflex in the physiological sense.

It was precisely in the course of distinguishing between the concepts of expedience and necessity in physiology that the reflex principle became clearly defined. Pavlov was an adherent of the reflex principle and therefore could not accept the view that what was happening was expedient and not reflexive. He was still less inclined to exchange objective description for 'subjective' data by saying that the dog remembered the sound of its feeder's footsteps and knew that he was bringing food, so that its saliva began to flow at the thought of food. According to Pavlov this was not a physiological description but the inadmissibly anthropomorphic extension to an animal of subjective evidence of a kind appropriate only to humans and then only with proper controls. He looked for a form of description which would not overstep the bounds of the stimulus–response process.

He explained it like this. Salivary glandular functions are regulated by the excitation of receptors in the mouth according to inherited neural connections. Or, to put it another way, receptors are excited by the stimulus (food), which takes effect in an inherited manner and this excitation triggers the appropriate functioning of the salivary glands by means of the system of connections corresponding with the inherited reflex arc. However, if a physiologically effective receptor stimulus is preceded immediately by the stimulation of another receptor, a peculiar connection forms between the two different excitations and it is a permanent one. When this happens the non-specific stimulus becomes a trigger mechanism for a reflex otherwise triggered only by a specific stimulus. So in fact, this is a stimulus-response type of connection, which is not unconditioned (that is inherited) but conditioned (that is learned).

This description belongs completely to the sphere of the black box. It does not refer to structural connections which form the basis for this process but is expressed simply in terms of input-output relationships. In his subsequent research Pavlov examined very thoroughly variations in the response obtained, comparing them with the stimulus and the conditions under which it was administered. This was the way in which he discovered important principles underlying the functioning of the black box.

His basic experiment was very simple. He devised a way of measuring salivary gland function exactly from the quantity of saliva produced over a defined period of time. (His method was to divert the duct of, say, one parotid out on to the skin of the cheek and collect the drops of saliva in a calibrated glass cylinder.)

If, for instance, a dilute acid solution was poured into an animal's mouth a certain volume of saliva would be produced by the gland. For a given quantity of acid solution the same quantity of saliva resulted each time. The experiment was repeated several times under identical conditions. If a tuning-fork was struck at the same time as the acid solution was given and repeated several times, ultimately just striking the tuning-fork would produce the same quantity of saliva as the acid solution had previously.

This regular connection, so simple to measure, was an extremely productive research tool in Pavlov's hands. It became possible to examine the similarity of stimuli and to measure the degree of their similarity or difference. The conditioned reflexes produced made it possible to pinpoint the inhibitions able to prevent their formation, results obtained could be put on to time co-ordinates, comparing for instance the quantities of saliva obtained during a series of five-minute reflexive responses. So an insight into the way in which excitational processes developed became feasible. Finally, from the study of a simple conditioned salivation reflex came a whole hierarchy of principles relating to the functioning of the nervous system.

Hereditary reflexes (regulations) have to be seen as a result of evolution in the Darwinian sense. In the course of the adaptation of the species (natural selection) the favourable stimulus–response connections were stabilized and the unfavourable discarded.

The Pavlovian conditioned reflexes (regulations) complement inherited biological adaptation with the stimulus–response connections acquired (learned) in an individual's lifetime.

Research into structural functions is supplemented by Pavlov's black box-type investigations. There is no justification whatever for regarding the two kinds of approach in physiological research as antagonistic. At the same time it is important for us to see what the relationship is between physiological and psychological methods of description. The psychological method relates to a behaviour or to a communication according to whether an objective or a subjective procedure is followed. (As we said earlier, Pavlov never doubted the significance of subjective data in relation to man but protested against the results of human self-observation's anthropomorphic extension to an animal. A man may know subjectively that when the waiter appears from the kitchen door he will soon have food in his mouth, but we have no right to assume that a dog 'knows' in exactly the same way that it will soon receive food when it hears its feeder's footsteps. We can assume this in the man's case only because we can ask him and he can tell us about it. This is not splitting hairs but an important distinction.) A physiologist can never use a psychological explanation however self-evident it may appear but has to find a physiological answer to a physiological question. The physiological approach to the problem and its result do serve to explain human psychological question and response. (One instance here would be the connection between directional hearing and a sound reaching both ears with different intensities.) For psychology, physiology is metalanguage.

Since Pavlov's train of thought conflicts with a view which seems self-evident, customary, and consequently natural, it is difficult to accept. Newton had to contend with fairly similar difficulties in his day, too. 'It is very easy for us today,' writes Carnap,[12]

> to remark how strange it was that it never occurred to anyone before Newton that the same force could cause an apple to drop and the moon to go around the earth. In fact, this was not a thought likely to occur to anyone. It is not so much that the *answer* was so difficult to give; it is that nobody had asked the *question*. This is a vital point. No one had asked: 'What is the relation between the forces that heavenly bodies exert upon each other and on terrestrial forces that cause objects to fall to the ground?' Even to speak in such terms as 'terrestrial' and

12 Carnap, R. (1966) *Philosophical Foundations of Physics*, New York: Basic Books, p. 246.

'heavenly' is to make a bipartition, to cut nature into two fundamentally different regions. It was Newton's great insight to break away from this division, to assert that there is no such fundamental cleavage. There is one nature, one world. Newton's universal law of gravitation was the theoretical law that explained for the first time both the fall of an apple and Kepler's laws for the movements of planets. In Newton's day, it was a psychologically difficult, extremely daring adventure to think in such general terms.

Pavlov had to overcome a similar psychological difficulty when he was disinclined to accept the opinion (which still seems natural today) that for some questions the constraints of consistent physiological description must be dispensed with in favour of psychological description. In other words, there is no need to draw a sharp distinction between the two descriptive methods and ideational systems. Although it seemed clumsier than psychological description, Pavlov's account based on the black box held both the proof of its consistency and a great capacity for further develop ment.

In so far as salivary gland functioning is triggered by a stimulus which excites a receptor, it must be possible for a complicated connection to exist within the nervous system, comprising the arrival of the feeder, or the striking of a tuning-fork, and integrating these varying and occasional conditions with the regulation of the salivary gland function. Pavlov asked how a contingent stimulus could become a physiological stimulus.

The answer lies in the definition of a conditioned reflex given earlier. A new way for investigation was opened. What could generally become a stimulus in a specific case? What is a subliminal stimulus? What are the internal conditions for the production of a reflex? (Food is not a stimulus for a satiated organism.) He demonstrated the effectiveness of similar stimuli (generalization), the fact of inhibition and its different forms. He described how both excitatory and inhibitory processes are mobile, subject to irradiation and concentration and capable of varying degrees of intensity and mobility. Inhibitory processes are more vulnerable than excitatory processes and inhibition of an inhibition results in excitation. In this way, through Pavlov's decades of work a highly detailed picture of cerebral functioning emerged without any clarification of the precise location within the brain of the various phenomena he described.

Pavlov applied the collective term 'analyser' to the receptors and the cerebral structures connected with them. Through the activity of analysers the brain first of all separates and systematizes its items of information in order to integrate them subsequently and formulate its output measures. The vast mass of information originating from receptors is ultimately analyzed and synthesized in the cerebral cortex, where most of the nerve cells are to be found. Excitatory and inhibitory processes combine to form connective systems which Pavlov called 'dynamic stereotypes'. The nervous system continuously systematizes the connection between environment and organism. Every stimulus comes in to existing systems, strengthens some stereotypes, and weakens others. Many different rival connectional systems vie with one another until the dominant system ultimately becomes a basis for action.

All this research shows the highest level of nervous system control to be a dynamically changing, extraordinarily flexible, and adaptable system in which analysis and synthesis form a unity and no sharply defined boundary can be drawn between motor and sensory systems (Pavlov[13]).

The vegetative nervous system

We have seen what a distorting influence the psychological distinction between volitional and non-volitional characteristics had on physiological conceptions of the functioning of the nervous system. A similar factor lay behind the assumption that 'animal' and 'vegetative' functions must have different regulations. Mobility was regarded as animal; growth, reproduction, digestion, excretion, respiration, and blood circulation as vegetative. The regulation of vegetative functions was believed to be autonomic, that is, independent of animal functions.

True, such conceptions were supported by observations of various kinds. Even in the eighteenth century it was noticed that certain organs regularly work in collaboration. In running, for example, the heart beats more rapidly and respiratory activity of

13   (1956) *Pawlowsche Mittwochkolloquien*, Berlin.

the lungs also increases. Running is volitional and cardiac function is not. In accordance with the terminology of the time, the collaboration of heart and lungs was explained by a 'sympathy' between them and called a 'sympathetic' function. Later the internal organs, 'viscera', were found to be connected with the chain of ganglia running along both sides of the spinal cord, so this part of the nervous system was called 'visceral' or 'vegetative' and also the 'sympathetic nervous system'. It became clear subsequently, too, that the nervous regulation of these organs may be in opposition in stimulating or inhibiting and an anatomical basis for this was sought and found. Nerves with influences contrary to those of the sympathetic nerves run in to these organs from other parts of the nervous system, from the spinal cord end of the brainstem and from the lowest segments of the spinal cord. Since these flank the sympathetic nervous system with the help of the Greek prefix 'para' (alongside), they were called collectively 'the parasympathetic nervous system'.

And, as happens so often in the history of the sciences, at first proofs of the antithetical position of the sympathetic and para-sympathetic nervous systems came thick and fast. But later the picture began to look more complicated.

Here is an example taken from Hess (1948) of contradictions inherent in the situation. An artery is constricted by a sympathe-tic nerve and dilated by a parasympathetic one. (The opposite is also possible.) The constriction is effected through the stimulation of the artery's own musculature. The parasympathetic nerve relaxes it inhibiting the contraction. But this particular artery assures the blood supply to a gland. Arterial constriction hampers glandular function whereas dilation of the artery stimulates it by causing plenty of blood to flow through. So the same nerve which stimulates the arterial musculature inhibits the functioning of the organ supplied by that artery and on the other hand the influence inhibiting the arterial musculature stimulates the gland. Sympathetic and parasympathetic nerves cannot be charac-terized as being in general either excitatory or inhibitory nerves. Their opposition seems rather to have harmonizing effects. For example, the bladder empties if one section of the para-sympathetic nerves relaxes the muscles which close the sphincter and another section stimulates contraction of the detrusor muscu-lature. The two contrasting functions are as one for the organ and in this example both responses are caused by parasympathetic excitation.

Sympathetic and parasympathetic are not two systems exerting opposing influences – their 'opposition' is only relative. The whole thesis of the autonomy of the vegetative nervous system was abandoned long ago. The 'storeys' of the increasingly comprehensive regulation of the nervous system always contain measures relating to visceral functions. Hess showed that large units of vegetative regulation are represented in the hypothalamus and described both energy-mobilizing (ergotropic) and energy-storing (trophotropic) forms of regulation.

But the hypothalamus is not to be seen as some kind of vegetative centre. The cerebellum also participates in the regulation of the 'autonomic' functions, and the part played by the cerebral cortex was clearly proved by Pavlov's fundamental experiment on the conditioned reflex of salivary glands.

Hess[14] also emphasized that

The formation of the function of the vegetative nervous system is not to be understood as a rigid structure. Actually it is a system of regulatory processes, in which individual processes constantly alter position around their centre of equilibrium. Consequently the 'centre' is a concept which should be always understood in a dynamic and relative sense and cannot be described unambiguously but only by referring to a certain zone of varying performance. This variability applies particularly to the time factor.

The concept of a 'functional system' referred to earlier at neural cell level obviously keeps coming up with an ever-widening and multifaceted significance. Implications for nervous system function become correspondingly more complex.

And here again we have to consider another widespread belief. The vegetative nervous system is thought to be 'older' and 'stronger', as compared with 'more delicate' and 'fragile' higher regulations. But in fact the vigour of 'vegetative' functions varies according to how high the level is of the storeys which regulate them.

14   Hess, W.H. (1948) *Die functionelle Organisation des vegetativen Nervensystems*, Basel.

Under physical stress the maximum breathing rate is 120 litres per minute but with volitional hyperventilation can reach as much as 200 litres per minute (Donhoffer[15]). Straub, Ripley, and Wolf[16] measured abdominal pressure when coughing and pressing down and it never rose above 20 cm of water, but it rose above 80 cm from elicited anxiety.

From this survey evidently the vegetative nervous system cannot be functionally distinguished from other parts of the nervous system, any more than one can separate motor and sensory systems, draw any line between volitional and non-volitional functions, or between those of the pyramidal tract and the extrapyramidal system. So what is the explanation for this stubborn persistence of belief in the autonomy of the vegetative nervous system?

It persists not only from inertia, a disinclination to change opinions and concepts, but also from ideas on the nature of consciousness. True, vegetative functions are subconscious to a significant extent, that is to say unavailable for discussion on the basis of subjective verbal description. For a long time the opinion was strenuously maintained that anything that happened in the organization of the forebrain, especially in the cerebral cortex, was *ipso facto* conscious and based on this the completely unfounded opinion that unconscious vegetative neural regulation could be thought independent of the cerebrum.

However consciousness is not necessarily entirely separate from vegetative functional regulation and this is practically a truism since, after all, urination and defecation are two of the processes which are conscious in normal circumstances.

But light is shed directly on a connection between 'autonomous' functions and the hemispheres and consciousness by the following experiences.

For therapeutic reasons epileptic patients have had their corpus callosum severed, cutting the principal link between the two hemispheres. Although this intervention is extraordinarily brutal in terms of the number of neurones affected, there is no noticeable effect. Predictably from the results of experiments with monkeys, there is no disturbance in function. More precisely

15   Donhoffer, Sz. (1957) *Kórélettan (Pathophysiology)*, Budapest.
16   Straub, L.R., Ripley, H.S., and Wolf, S.A. (1950) *Association for Research into Nervous and Mental Diseases Proceedings*, 29 (1019).

it did have effects, as Sperry[17] pointed out in some very fine psychological studies, but they could be demonstrated only with great difficulty. His results showed that the two hemispheres function separately in nearly all areas and if the corpus callosum is cut through they somehow become quite independent, two personalities, sometimes with irritating results. For instance, one patient said that she buttoned up her coat with her right hand and 'against my will' her left hand unbuttoned it.

Sperry demonstrated, for example, that patients whose corpus callosum had been severed, even when blindfolded would still be able to use an object, a comb for instance, placed in front of them in the left hand (controlled by the right hemisphere), but at the same time, although they had no speech problems, could not name the object.

Again, they could place an object on a table quite skilfully and pick it out among the others. If they were allowed to touch it with the right hand (left hemisphere controlled) while holding it in their left, they could name it straight away. The left hemisphere played the principal role in organizing the patients' speech – a fact known for a long time. But from the experiments themselves it is evident that the right hemisphere, too, understands verbal commands. (The eyes had to be blindfolded of course because both eyes connect with both hemispheres.)

Now let us turn to the relationship between the hemispheres, the vegetative nervous system and consciousness. Using a special device, Sperry projected an obscene picture on to the left visual field of one patient. This is connected with the right, non-speaking, hemisphere. The patient could not say anything about the picture consciously. Yet at the same time, she was disturbed and blushed. This vegetative response showed that the 'non-speech' hemisphere (the only one receiving the picture) was affected by its contents. So the hemisphere's influence over the 'autonomic' system, notably on the basis of picture recognition, could be noted objectively from a vegetative response but not subjectively from a conscious report. Therefore both hemispheres are capable of achieving a connection between vegetative regulation and visual identification, but conscious recognition proved to be a function only of the 'speech' hemisphere.

17 Sperry (1960) *Brain and Conscious Experience*, Berlin: Springer Verlag.

And this inevitably raises the question of the origin of consciousness.

Speech and consciousness

In exploring nervous system function, there have been almost grotesque repetitions of similar turning-points. First of all researchers assume the existence of certain defined functions and then attempt to support their hypotheses. Initially results justify their expectations, indicating that illusions outweigh facts at the outset. But gradually facts obstinately prove more and more disturbing. Details do not fit into the predefined theoretical structure by any means and finally the illusion is shattered. It is only at this stage that sober thought is given to compiling the facts and realistic concepts can begin to take shape.

From the start studies looking into questions of speech divided speech almost naturally into motor and sensory functions. It was assumed, and even believed proved, that motor and sensory 'speech centres' can be clearly distinguished from each other and located. Speech disorders were grouped as forms of aphasia on this assumption.

The siting of speech areas in the nervous system developed at first as a replacement for the then dominant views on the soul (spirit or psyche). The relationship between body and soul was at the centre of the debate on location in aphasiology.

Broca was the first to establish that the seat of speech is in the left frontal lobe of the brain and came under 'spiritualist' cross-fire. They regarded as utterly degrading his assertion that speech (for them a 'psychic' or 'spiritual' activity) was nothing more than the functioning of a certain cerebral area. Materialists opposed the spiritualists and stood by Broca. At the height of the debate, anyone opposing Broca's views on aphasias was not only called a 'spiritualist' but also declared to be an enemy of the French Republic! It is interesting that Marie wrote in 1906 that Broca himself would have liked to modify his first conceptions while all this was going on, because he had realized that the question of aphasia was more complicated than he had supposed at first, but he felt helpless, asking how anyone could betray colleagues who had supported him so splendidly in the debate.

Of course, in time, argument subsided. Theories of speech

localization collapsed not because the spiritualists won the day, but because an increasing number of aphasic symptoms were found to be sited in many more centres. From the baffling multiplicity of such 'centres' Hughlings Jackson was eventually acknowledged to be right when he had said in 1864, at a time completely unready for it, that it is impossible to draw a sharp distinction between voluntary and involuntary movements. He pointed out that description of speech symptoms was being confused unjustifiably with the concepts designed to explain them. Jackson's contemporaries took no notice of his views and even at the beginning of the twentieth century there was great confusion and a great deal of muddled discussion on speech disorders. As Sir Henry Head said, this conceptual confusion 'was the result of a wish to explain the aphasias on the basis of non-existent elementary functions.'

Today with our knowledge of feedback circuits there is nothing at all surprising in the impossibility of drawing lines between the various speech disorders or in the fact that damage to different parts of those circuits produces very varied symptoms. Some deficiencies are not total or only seen under certain conditions.

In everyday life, too, when we are excited we can often be 'at a loss for words'. In pathological cases the opposite can also be true. The 'dumb' (patients unable to speak at will) may start to speak again if strongly agitated. Denny-Brown[18] points out that behind speech disorders there may lie a conflict between different afferent processes (perceptions). The astonishing variety of aphasic symptoms is generally attributed to the well-known fact that increasing difficulty disturbs the integration of many specialized control systems, causing certain disorders. (Consider Kohler and his car with the mirror writing on the number-plate.) Sometimes a patient can only read the numbers on a clockface backwards. Some can name only inanimate objects, while others can write their own names only in mirror writing. (Reading and writing belong naturally to the sphere of speech.) The more closely we look into speech disorders the more impossible it becomes to fit them into a logical framework. Some aphasic patients cannot find certain words or are unable to fill in a section missing from a simple drawing – for example a mouth in a

---

18   In (1963) *Proceedings of Conference on Problems of Dynamic Neurology*, Jerusalem.

face – until they name it (Bay[19]). (A disarthric athetoid made a mistake in writing a word and when his error was corrected through Conductive Education, his speech improved, too.)

The variety of speech disorders reveals as many fine differences as the wide variability in motor disorders. Monrad-Krohn,[20] for example, described a speech disorder restricted to stress and rhythm affecting prosody which he called 'dysprosody'.

Dysprosody is very instructive from several points of view. For one thing, although the melody of speech has deteriorated, general musical ability is unaffected. This brings new evidence to support what was known, that apparently single cerebral functions are composed of finer partial features. In different contexts the same components can be present or absent.

At the same time dysprosody serves to clarify an otherwise obscure property of speech conspicuous by its absence (Monrad-Krohn). Dysprosody robs a dysprosodic patient's silence of its attentive quality when someone else is speaking to him. Monrad-Krohn describes very silent people who are generally thought to be good listeners because of their making murmured responsive sounds from time to time in an appropriate tone. So prosodic elements play an important role in the reafferentative connection between speaker and listener. When we are talking to someone, even if there is no explicit reply, we need those cues given by grunts or murmurs.

Where this reafferentative link is broken, that is where the listener is dysprosodic, there are strange results. A patient with Parkinson's disease, for instance, becomes incapable of making these appropriate sounds. He was always silent and so his family and friends accused him quite groundlessly of being indifferent and uninterested, even of being deranged. Parkinson patients can also lose the capacity for facial expression. Both dysprosody and lack of emotional expression can break the reafferentative link and cause Parkinson patients to be disliked by the people around them.

It can be seen that, for the brain, verbal communication conveys a richer informational content than that conscious part expressed in words. That is why a poem has quite a different

19 and 20 In (1963) *Proceedings of Conference on Problems of Dynamic Neurology*, Jerusalem.

effect merely read from when heard skilfully recited. Speech communicates more than mere words for it reveals attention, sympathy, emotion, or dislike, malice and so on. So the brain interprets the informational content with many more nuances and at far more levels than the words themselves express. Only items of verbal information, the linguistic content, become conscious primarily, but apparently incidental circumstances can also have an effect. Minkowski[21] published case histories of aphasic people in Switzerland who spoke more than one language, their most interesting feature being that aphasia following cerebral injury extended to one language only, but the use of the other language improved or deteriorated according to whether it was facilitated or inhibited by current relationships with a spouse speaking that language.

With all these indications, we cannot look on speech as a circumscribed cerebral function, but in many ways rather as embedded in the complex regulatory systems at the level of the top storey of the nervous system.

The origin and significance of consciousness

Speech differs in a sense significantly from every other activity regulated by the nervous system. Verbal communication resembles other forms of action in being purposive movement. It also gives information and co-ordinates a response, so its effect strictly speaking is realized outside the communicator. The speaker uses relatively little energy himself in talking but mobilizes much more effort in the other people stimulated to comply. Speech feedback circuits are completed reafferentatively not by the result of a simple impact on the environment, but by the actions of the people spoken to. All this indicates that speech input–output connections are more complex than other contexts discussed so far.

On the input side speech is a collection of sounds which convey information but only to someone who has learned that language. Pavlov explained language acquisition by conditioned reflexes. In every conditioned reflex, an initially neutral stimulus comes to take the place of an inherently effective stimulus, to become a

---

21 In (1963) *Proceedings of Conference on Problems of Dynamic Neurology*, Jerusalem.

signal for it. Life's experiences produce a whole store of conditioned stimuli which set up a 'primary' signal system.

Words too are signals and the most usual substitutes for the primary signals of conditioned reflexes and so languages become the second signalling system. Animals also have a first signal system but a second signal system is unique to the human nervous system. The acquisition of the second signal system is a specific quality in man's biological potential for adaptation. The first signal system is built up from man's life experiences but the second signal system requires language formed in the course of socio-historical development. Language development is determined by a need to communicate, requisite to the traditional forms of co-operation of any given society.

On the output side, speech as utterance and articulation is muscular movement, and as communicator informant and mobilizer of co-operation. This last must not be viewed too simplistically for to speak at all implies co-operation. Children are often punished by not talking to them – withdrawing co-operation. If someone says 'I refuse to co-operate with you in any way', that is a form of co-operation because the statement establishes a verbal link. The contents communicated give us significant information about what can be expected from the speaker.

Speech is the only phenomenon essentially the same on output and input sides of the human nervous system. Generally, input as stimulus bears no resemblance at all to output as response. Where, for instance, input might be food (sight, taste, smell), output would be the functioning of salivary glands, chewing and swallowing. But verbal exchange seems to be uniform as both output and input.

In fact this uniformity is completed by reafferentation. Spoken or heard, as words travel through the air they have an identical stimulus character, reaching someone or originating from him. Yet in the reafferentative feedback circuit one's own speech returns as input and there is scarcely any difference between words spoken by oneself or someone else's. In this respect output and input coincide almost completely.

For the moment we will leave this on one side. At the lowest level of the nervous system, input speech dysfunction may be total deafness if there is serious damage to both receptors or both auricular nerves. For output, serious damage might take the form of an inability to produce sounds and articulate. There are many forms of finer output disorders at a higher organizational level, like singsong speech, stammering, stuttering, gabbling, and these are usually accompanied by vegetative disorders.

The spoken word (output) has a feedback type of reafferentative regulation with input like every activity. The temporal relationship between input and output in this reafferentative circuit is shown by the fact that if the sounds made are fed back through earphones to the person speaking and there is a slight delay of 0.07 to 0.10 seconds, he stammers and shows vegetative disturbances (Lee). Relationships are further complicated by the fact that there is a vestigial form of speech, 'internal' speech. Earlier than the turn of the century, Lehmann demonstrated that even in silent verbal thought vestiges of speech are present as a muscular activity and this has since been confirmed electromyographically.

So motor speech is much more than what we hear.

Biologically, silent (inner) speech would seem to be nonsense, a tool for co-operation that achieves nothing. But physiologically it has an important function. Luria[22] and Vigotsky reported in 1929 the case of a child between 4 and 5 years old who always answered loudly whenever he was given something relatively difficult to do, because this was the only way he could work it out. His speech reflected both the circumstances and his previous experiences. Putting circumstances into words visibly helped him to structure the situation and so eventually he could sort out his problems. Luria considered this example to be generally characteristic of children around that age: their problem-solving has quite a loud audible verbal accompaniment. As time goes on, it grows quieter, down to a whisper, and then becomes 'inner speech'.

Speech, both spoken and tacit, as energizer can significantly facilitate or inhibit activity according to circumstances.

The input–output reafferentative feedback processes of speech ensure that the relationships forming the activity, that is not only the items of information of motor speech coming in as input, are received but inevitably the linguistic content too. So the speaker becomes a recipient of his own spoken information (output). Through this circuit the speaker informs himself and this is

22   Luria, A.R. (1956) *Pawlow Zeitschrift für höhere Nerventätigkeit*, 6(5).

precisely the way that the mechanism by which consciousness originates (Ákos,[23] Ákos[24]). Consciousness begins therefore in a feedback circuit in which inner speech is output and is fed back to become reafferentative input.

The content of output speech becoming input would seem to be a redundant informational process. An individual tells himself what he already knows! Yet the effective control becoming established is not only motor in form. At any given moment verbal items of information belonging to the second signal system are added to information from the receptors as primary signals, co-operating in the formation of dispositions to action. These items of information are summoned up from memory but only become effective in cerebral control systems through inner speech.

The only computer-type entry to the brain is from the input side. Originally speech was an output activity which served co-operation. A speaker informs others and so influences their actions, a fact of decisive significance biologically determined for both speaker and audience. Through the content, 'sensory' reafferentation, of internal speech a speaker has access to the communal-linguistic experiences stored in his own memory, in the same way as if they were being told him by someone else.

Co-operation obtained by speech is not restricted merely to simple forms of common activity but can give the complex information characteristic of a given society's development. In this sense all education is guidance for working together and one of the first forms of teaching common to all human societies is their language. Through speech we are tuned in to receive items of information from the human beings living around us and are able to inform them too.

Linguistic information about details of the environment can be called into consciousness without external prompting. By acquiring a language a community's informative influence is incorporated into its members and manifests as consciousness. Internal primary signals conjure up secondary signals. In the output-input circuits secondary linguistic items of information are compared with the relevant primary signals, giving them a communal-linguistic significance. This not only puts our problems in perspective but also encourages us to tackle them!

23   Ákos, K. (1952) 'Origin of Consciousness', *Természeit és Technika*, 111 (10).
24   Ákos, K. (1962) in *Science and Humanity*, Moscow.

Luria[25] drew attention to the fact that new connections formed in the human nervous system are frequently effective in a linguistic form initially but only affect any other activity subsequently. It is hopeless to try to get a 2-year-old child to squeeze a bulb to switch off a light just by telling him to do so, but he will learn to do it if the lamp goes out again after he has squeezed the bulb. Reafferentation comes from the concrete effect itself. A 3-year-old child could carry out the verbal instruction quite easily, but if told to squeeze the rubber bulb twice when the lamp lights up cannot do so, yet if he is told to say 'One, two' each time he squeezes it, he will be able to do it. Number sequencing is a particularly effective speech pattern. Bringing in this verbal pattern will facilitate cerebral control of an otherwise difficult task. A general precondition for a child to sort out a relatively complex action is often to put it into words. Luria says: 'All this shows that in the early stages of development the simplest model of voluntary motor activity goes into the control by way of speech.'

Verbal connections facilitate activity for physically handicapped people too. Luria[26] describes how a Parkinson patient was asked to press a rubber bulb repeatedly and the pressure strength was recorded by a kymograph. The patient was told to go on pressing the bulb as long as he could. The weakening successive pressings were recorded until they eventually ceased altogether. Then he asked the patient to count up to eight, for instance, and with each number a strong pressure was exerted once again.

Speech can improve perception to a large extent, too. Every painter knows that the secret of painting is not manual dexterity but how to look and that anyone can be taught to see in this way by explaining it verbally. As we have discussed, words make the looking conscious.

Speech is acquired through auditory receptors but there is a general cerebral capacity for transferring systems acquired through a particular receptor (that is the functional patterns of one analyser) to the territory of another. Essentially this transfer plays a role in learning to read and write. Reading and writing broadly means connecting visual analysis with verbal patterns. It

25   Luria, A.R. (1960) (ed. J. Tizard) *The Role of Speech in the Regulation of Normal and Abnormal Behaviour*, Oxford: Pergamon.
26   Luria, A.R. (1960) *The Nature of Human Conflicts*, New York.

is true that consciousness is built up through objective physio-logical processes but it is achieved through the verbal identi-fication of stimuli. So we can know about it only through an individual's words, subjectively.

The socio-historical precondition for speech is language. Experiences acquired through life link with the influence of social editing in brain function through learning a language and so an individual's direct relationships become associated with those stemming from general indirect communal experience.

To sum up, we have now surveyed the way in which cerebral activity unites motor and sensory systems. Unity is established in cerebral functioning through the reafferentative type of integration of a colossal amount of information by a huge number of specialist control systems. Through language this encapsulates the system of social information and speech can gain the practical co-operation of people around.

It is primarily through the experiences of brain-damaged patients that we are able to build up a picture of the effects of injury to these complex relationships.

7 Cerebral lesions

When animals are the subject of physiological experimentation the effects of cerebral lesions can be described only objectively from observation, but injured human beings can add subjective data to this. It might be useful to draw attention to some general features of observations from brain-damaged patients.

Perhaps we might note first of all that the effects of cerebral lesions are never restricted singly to motor, sensory, vegetative, or psychological symptoms but affect all of these together, though not all to the same degree (Birkmayer[1]). The decisive factor is not the local damage, but the integrative effects.

Another general and characteristic peculiarity of brain-damaged patients is that they are slowed down. This does not affect their simpler forms of reaction so much as the time they take to carry out particular tasks. To be able to recognize and size up a situation they need either more time or more intensive stimulation. Weizsäcker considers 'they need more time, magnitude of shape and degree of intensity to achieve normal standards of fusion, adaptation, visual acuity, after-images and orientation' (reported in Walther-Brüel[2]). Slowing down leaves insufficient time at their disposal to finish things and helps to explain why brain-damaged people, as though protecting themselves against overloading, withdraw from events around them and from the impatience so often shown towards them, their interest dying away. (We should note here that athetoids are not decelerated but rather accelerated in their perceptions and inferences.)

Information is received, processed, collated by the brain, and cerebral control systems are activated through connections previously established, all this taking place very rapidly in normal circumstances. For instance, if we slip, cerebral

1 Birkmayer, W. (1951) *Hirnverletzungen*, Wien: Springer Verlag.
2 Walther-Bruël, H. (1951) *Die Psychiatrie der Hirngeschwülste und die cerebralen Gründlagen psychischer Vorzëuge* Vienna: Springer Verlag.

functional tolerance lasts a surprisingly short time. We regain our balance very quickly by making the appropriate movements. From a height of 170 cm, gravity allows only 0.58 seconds for the head to reach the ground and within this time the brain must receive and process all its information about that slip, decide on the measures to be taken, and finally see to it that the relevant muscles carry them out.

From experience we all know that this space of time is long enough for the necessary action but not for us to become aware of taking it.

Afterwards, it is astonishing to discover how quickly we have regained our balance before even realizing that we had slipped. This is just one indication that conscious awareness is realized through more complex regulatory processes and needs more time than a simple action.

Old people are generally considered to be more clumsy, in that they often fall and have slowed down in a way rather similar to people with brain damage.

Some idea of the speed of cerebral functioning can be formed by taking slipping as an example – an excellent one because the force of gravity is the general structure for everything we do. For man only a few tenths of a second are allowed to compensate for the effects of gravity and acceleration. At the same time fastest muscle contractions take tenths of a second. It follows that if information is to be received and processed and instructions given for action, processes involved must have a velocity of less than tenths of a second. We know that the propagation time for axon discharge is hundredths of a second and that synaptic excitatory processes last at most for thousandths of a second, so clearly neural systems really do work faster than muscular processes.

Throughout the whole cerebral system it seems that events can move even faster. We mentioned that in directional hearing the same sound reaches both ears at an interval of 10^{-4} secs and it has been possible to demonstrate this time difference neurophysiologically. At the threshold of perception of fusion of flickering light or at the critical flicker frequency an interval of at least 10^{-5} seconds can be differentiated. This has been established psychochronographically (Ákos and Ákos[3]).

3 Ákos, K. and Ákos, M. (1966) *The Critical Flicker Frequency Series Effect*, Budapest: Hungarian Academy of Sciences.

Currently we do not know how the brain uses the brief time interval at its disposal, but it seems probable that it functions in a way similar to that described by Carnap[4] in a different context, by successive approximation. We may assume that regulatory systems, capable of forming on the basis of similar items of information are being sifted through again very rapidly in reafferentation and that while this is happening the regulation that finally leads to decision on a course of action is gaining strength. If necessary the course of action can be modified and further corrected en route as a result of new feedback data. So the first 'crudely formulated' measure is progressively refined and specialized in detail. For example, if we follow the movement of someone who slips, right through from the crude initial swaying about like a pendulum to regaining perfect balance, the establishment of this progressive control system becomes clear.

Carnap characterizes this process in connection with a question of the accuracy of measurements which might seem to have very little relevance.

A perplexing problem arises concerning both primitive and derived magnitudes. To make it clear, imagine two magnitudes M^1 and M^2. When we examine the definition of M^1 or the rules that tell us how to measure it, we find that magnitude M^2 is involved. When we turn to the definition of rules for M^2, we find M^1 is involved. At first this gives the appearance of circularity in the procedures, but the circle is easily avoided by applying what is called the method of successive approximation. You will recall in the previous chapter we considered the equation that defines the length of a measuring stick. In that equation a correction factor for thermal expansion occurs; in other words temperature is involved in the set of rules used for measuring length. On the other hand, you will remember that on our rules for measuring temperature, we referred to length, or rather, to the volume of a certain test liquid used in the thermometer; but, of course, volume is determined with the help of length. So it seems that here we have two magnitudes, length and temperature, each dependent on the

4 Carnap, R. (1966) *Philosophical Foundations of Physics*, New York: Basic Books, pp. 98–9.

other for its definition. It appears to be a vicious circle, but, in fact, it is not.

One way out is as follows. First we introduce the concept of length without considering the correction factor for thermal expansion. This concept will not give us measurements of great precision but will do well enough if great precision is not demanded. For instance, if an iron rod is used for measurement, the thermal expansion, under normal conditions, is so small that measurements will still be fairly precise. This provides a first concept, L^1, of spatial length. We can now make use of this concept for the construction of a thermometer. With the aid of the iron measuring stick, we mark a scale alongside the tube containing our test liquid. Since we can construct this scale with fair precision, we also obtain a fair precision when we measure temperature on this scale. In such a way we introduce our first concept of temperature, T^1. Now we can use T^1 for establishing a refined concept of length. L^2 (corrected for the thermal expansion of the iron rod) is now available for constructing a more precise scale for our thermometer. This leads, of course, to T^2, a refined concept of temperature.

In the case of length and temperature, the procedure just described will refine both concepts to the point at which errors are extremely minute. In other cases, it may be necessary to shuttle back and forth several times before successive refinements lead to measurement precise enough for our purposes. It must be admitted that we never reach an absolutely perfect method of measuring either concept. We can say, however, that the more we repeat this procedure – starting with two rough concepts and then refining each with the help of the other – the more precise our measurements will become. By this technique of successive approximations we escape from what seems, at first, to be the vicious circle.

This in-depth description of Carnap's is similar in many respects to the way in which feedback circuits taking shape in the brain gradually adapt to the items of information available to them. Items of information received during this process give rise to expectations and the selected anticipation grows in strength as newer information is received to the point of giving directions for action. This action in turn is a source of further reafferentative information and if necessary its course is modified accordingly.

We must assume that these successive approximations take place very rapidly compared with the tempo of the action. However, pathological cases slow down, brain-damaged patients for example, and this shows straight away in whatever they do. In other cases, integration leading to a direction for action may include inappropriate elements (errors), like the mirror-writing number plate Kohler saw.

The fact that cerebral injury can affect any given partial control system in a fairly isolated way may be attributed to their relative independence. If one of these independent systems recovers to take part again in the joint activity, quite abrupt changes may follow. Writing about war brain-damaged patients, Birkmayer described how

the recovery from central paralysis is not achieved through a gradual functional improvement, but on the contrary what happens is that the function stagnates at the same pathological level of performance for a long time. Then suddenly there is what seems to be a revolutionary change and it leaps up overnight to a higher level of performance, then with some slight unevenness steadies down again. This process of improving by leaps, or stagnating as though blocked off by lock-gates from the restoration of function, looks as though it must be a manifestation of some biological regulation. . . . This revolutionary character of the recovery of function is found not only in connection with motor recovery but also perceptional disorders and generally in the thinking and learning of brain-damaged patients.

Again, the abrupt changes in performance described here are not exclusively characteristic of improvement after cerebral injury. There are similar features in the development of children, each new capability usually appearing quite unexpectedly. This phenomenon has been described as a plateau on the curve of learning ability. It seems as though suddenly a new system of regulation is becoming dominant and is somehow connected with the degree to which energy builds up within the feedback circuits.

This description is of course an analogy, just imagining how the black box might function. We assume that in the cerebral 'computer' feedback circuits and systems are built up in a way rather similar to the technique of successive approximation. The precision of the informational link increases and so ultimately the system of control is strengthened, with perhaps a role played by the intensity of those items of information or indeed simply by their quantity. For example, Fortuyn noticed that one of his non-ambulant patients once happened to knock his head against something and could then take a few steps. Martin's Parkinson patient could not walk in the ordinary way but could walk quite well crossing white lines painted on the floor, presumably under the influence of the association of rhythmically repeated stereo-type visual stimuli. It is possible that this is also the reason why Parkinson patients climb stairs easily. Luria[5] found with one of his brain-damaged patients that placing a small tight-fitting ring over his fingers enabled him to move them more easily. The patient noticed this himself and said his fingers seemed 'real' again to him as a result of the additional stimulation.

Another fact that may be connected with energy available is that brain-damaged patients are quickly exhausted by any unfamiliar task and a similar situation can be seen during the convalescent phase in relatively serious illnesses and 'nerve' patients.

Speaking of the motor unit, we mentioned that motor neurones exert a trophic influence on muscle fibres. It is conceivable that the nerve cells also have some trophic energizing effect on each other. It is true that after a transverse lesion has severed communication in the spinal cord the uninjured and merely isolated part remains unable to function for some weeks. This phenomenon was called 'spinal shock' (diaschysis by Monakow), and while its effect lasts it seems as if 'there were a diminution in the support which facilitates the processes of the spinal cord' (Denny-Brown[6]). He saw the principal element in this as loss of function of the stimulating and facilitatory tracts.

Now let us complete this objective description of brain-damaged patients with subjective data.

5 Luria, A.R. (1963) *Restoration of Function after Brain Injury* (trans. B. Haigh and ed. O.L. Zangwill)Oxford: Pergamon.
6 Denny-Brown, D. (1959/60) *Handbook of Physiology: Neurophysiology*, Washington, DC: American Physiological Society.

On this score up to now we have emphasized the extent to which subjective evidence has coincided with objective neuro-physiological observations and indeed, from certain points of view, richly amplified them. But now we will explore an area which inevitably raises doubts about whether subjective data can be trusted.

For instance, after cerebral lesions very large discrepancies can occur between objectively demonstrable disorders and their subjective perception. Investigations of the visual field have shown that quite considerable defects (scotomas) can be demonstrated which the patients know nothing at all about. They can be virtually blind and yet do not become conscious of this (Birkmayer, Goldstein, Teuber, etc).

In healthy conditions, every one of us has a scotoma extending over the area of the intra-ocular origin of the optic nerve on the fundus of the eye which is insensitive to light because there are no receptors there. The gap in our vision can be demonstrated only under certain conditions but otherwise we are completely unaware of it. Visual processes somehow fill out the gap in what we see.

Quite large areas of damage to the visual field can also fill out subjectively. Similarly, in the Korsakov syndrome, for example, attributed to damage in the 'lymbic system' (Brion[7]), patients are totally disorientated about their actual conditions but not disturbed about it. They fill out gaps in their memories with fantasy, confabulate, and have no idea how disorientated they are.

Abercrombie demonstrated very serious disorders of perception in children with cerebral palsy of which the otherwise intelligent youngsters had no idea. Luria met similar disturbances in adult patients with cerebral injuries. Subjective complaints stemming from brain damage are often surprisingly odd. Hemiplegics may complain that a stranger is lying beside them on the bed and this is because the paralysed half of their bodies feels strange to them. Damage to the thalamus is sometimes accompanied by complaints that the patient feels one side of him is sad.

So it is quite understandable if subjective observations like

7 Brion, in (1969) *The Pathology of Memory* (eds G.A. Talland and N.C. Waugh, New York: Academic Press.

these bring the validity of subjective data into disrepute generally. Yet a distinction must be drawn between the explicit informational content of subjective data with its occasional unreality and its significance when referring to physiological processes.

Every subjective inference, every conscious experience, may be faulty either because it has been based on incorrect informational cues or perhaps from the functional effects of brain damage. Widely varied output functions can be damaged as a result of cerebral lesions causing dysfunctions in the processing of items of information. The effect is shown sometimes by motor and sometimes by vegetative symptoms. Frequently distortions of items of speech information are the most prominent.

Disorders in the regulatory sphere of speech can supply very valuable information on lesions which affect their conscious functioning.

At the same time, conscious processes are generally resistant to the effects of cerebral lesions and disturbances in consciousness are usually the first of the aspects affected to readjust.

Not only is conscious data a valuable source of information symptomatically but also cerebral feedback circuits can be influenced by conscious processes, including those which become evident through action. We will touch on this aspect briefly on the basis of one of Luria's experiments.

Because of a wounded elbow a patient could raise his arm only to a limited extent. He was told to lift it as high as he could. The height was marked on the wall behind his back. Then they turned him to face the wall and showed him how high it was. They asked him again to lift his arm as high as he could and he lifted it seven degrees higher. In the first instance the motive for lifting had been a verbal request. In the second, an associated visual reafferentation was added to the verbal directive.

Next they marked a point on the wall higher up than the wounded man had reached the second time. They asked him to raise his hand to that point and he lifted his arm thirteen degrees higher than on his first attempt. On this third occasion visual reafferentation was supplemented by the intensifying influence of having a set goal to reach.

Finally they altered the instruction, replacing their previous abstract request to lift his arm by making it part of a targeted practical activity. They hung up an object and asked him to touch it. At this he raised his hand eighteen degrees higher than on the first occasion.

A goal consciously defined and embedded in targeted activity has a particularly powerful energizing effect on cerebral control systems.

To conclude we should note that in practically every case impatience and an inclination to depression are among the symptoms caused by cerebral lesions, often with outbreaks of rage and frequent weeping. These symptoms are usually called 'emotional lability'.

Emotion and motivation

Subjectively characterized, emotions are processes known primarily to ourselves but accompanied by a number of objective signs (weeping, blushing, turning pale, increase in blood pressure, a rapid or slow pulse, and so on). Modern physiology has made great efforts to clarify emotional mechanisms in the nervous system. The hypothalamus, thalamus, and lymbic system have all been considered to be emotional centres at different times, but investigations of their claims have always led to contradictory results.

It seems that it is rather the case that if positive emotions are channelled through reafferentative systems activity is incited and if it is disturbed from the absence of the result expected (frustration), or being pressed for time, negative emotions arise.

Positive emotions like happiness and good humour are associated with intensified activity, whereas negative emotions like sadness and depression with passivity sometimes to a point of apathy. When contrasting activity with passivity we refer to motivation or lack of it.

By stimulating areas of the brain (using implanted electrodes) forms of motivation may be directed differentially, intensified, or diminished, including quite complicated motivations like hunger and thirst, or even the prompting of complex activity. Delgado[8] for instance, conducted this experiment with a group of Rhesus monkeys. He implanted an electrode into one of the basal

8 Delgado, J.M.R. (1968) *New Outlooks in Psychology*, New York: Philosophical Library.

ganglia, the nucleus caudatus, of the dominant male in the group. Rhesus monkeys are aggressive and the dominant male particularly so. When Delgado stimulated the nucleus caudatus for 5 seconds per minute with a current of 1.5 m/A the animal became completely docile. When the stimulation ceased, after a good 10 minutes the animal became its old self again. While he was docile the others observed the customary distance less and less, but after the end of the period of stimulation, he made them keep their distances again. Continuing this experiment Delgado placed a push button in the monkey's cage. Pressing it stimulated the dominant male's brain. His companions quickly learned that they could calm down his aggressive behaviour by pressing the button.

Delgado also emphasizes that in the brain there are no designated areas forming centres for specific activities but that direction is linked together into a complex functional network, according to circumstances at any given time. The action which happens to be gaining strength will be the one most strongly motivated.

8 Dysfunction and neurophysiology

This has been an attempt at a brief survey of research results primarily in neurophysiology which bring the understanding of dysfunction a little nearer. From this we would like to stress two inferences primarily.

Anochin[1] who was the first to draw attention to anticipation in cerebral control systems, that is the taking into account in advance of events which can be expected to affect cerebral function through stimulation of the receptors (afferentation). He called this preparation by the black box for information to be expected as a result of the measures taken 'action receptor'. This idea was taken up later by others, Pribram (TOTE) for example. This conception sees the brain as not only receiving items of information but also actively anticipating them. Divergence between anticipated and experienced input data form the foundation for cerebral control systems.

This view highlights the role of activity in adaptive cerebral function. Consequently, in the functioning of input, perceptual disturbances must be stressed as having the highest importance for dysfunctionals.

The second inference concerns those concepts employed by experimental researchers. Our general survey has shown how concepts can play a decisive role either in the valid development of scientific views or in following false trails.

We have noticed that the meaning of some concepts differs in biology from those in physiology. In comparing the different concepts of movement and action, both orthofunction and dysfunction can be seen to raise questions on adaptation in such a way that physiology cannot clarify them altogether and their investigation must extend to biology as well. So this requires a careful scrutiny as to how the concepts are used.

1 Anochin, P.K. (1963) *Fiziológia és kibernetika*. Budapest.

Neurophysiology is certainly essential in any attempt to understand dysfunctionals' problems but boundaries have to be crossed. It might seem that this step could be taken by consulting clinical medical science. But we shall see that this is not enough either.

9 Cerebral dysfunctions

Usually in medical science 'cerebral dysfunctions' is taken to mean that group of dysfunctions arising from brain damage in which motor disabilities are the most conspicuous. Cases in this category are usually divided into several large groups and a number of subgroups. The basis for these classifications is justified primarily by traditional pathographies. In order to find our bearings in this fairly labyrinthine range of concepts, a survey of the best-known groups of conditions will be attempted with their principal problems.

Cerebral palsy

Keats's[1] note may be considered typical of the literature of cerebral palsy: 'The definition of cerebral palsy is given by the most varied authors in the most diverse ways.'

It is usually quite helpful in that case to trace the historical development of the concept.

At the end of the last century Freud[2] wrote several works about cerebral paralysis in childhood. He considered that Cazauvielh's book (1827) showed the way for scientific literature on this noso-logical unity as Cazauvielh was the first to set out a relevant patho-graphy to include clinical and pathological anatomical data. Nineteenth-century medical opinion considered the establishment of pathological–anatomical pathographies to be its lode star and Freud considered Cazauvielh's investigations on childhood cerebral palsy to be pioneering.

He saw these characteristic features from Cazauvielh's work as

1 Keats, S. (1965) *Cerebral Palsy*, Springfield, Ill.: Thomas.
2 Freud, S. (1891) *Klinische Studie über die halbseitige Cerebrallähmung der Kinder*, Wien; (1893) *Zur Kenntniss der Cerebralen Diplegien des Kindesalters*, Wien; (1897) *Die infantile Cerebrallähmung*, in ed. Nothnagel, *Spezielle Pathologie und Therapie*, Band IX, Th. III.

'affording the most exact and fairly comprehensive picture of infantile cerebral palsy in the literature':

- the paralysis appears immediately on or not long after birth;
- is less common in boys than girls;
- is more common on the right-hand side than the left;
- neither the trunk nor the intestines are affected, although the limbs and, to a lesser extent, the facial muscles are affected;
- the paralysed limbs are crippled, their bones are shorter and thinner though this can be concealed by accumulation of subcutaneous adipose tissue;
- the movement of the affected limbs is restricted, but paralysis is scarcely ever complete;
- the symptoms are more pronounced in the upper than in the lower limbs. Muscular spasms often stiffen the arms in peculiar positions yet at other times involuntary movements can be seen in them;
- the fingers are frequently hyperextended;
- sensitivity of the paralysed limbs differs only rarely from the normal, although sometimes the patient complains of severe pain;
- the intelligence of the patient is below average, sometimes extending to idiocy;
- epilepsy can also occur but does not belong to the picture.

Cazauvielh assembled this list of clinical symptoms on the basis of six of his own post-mortem cases and attributed it to two kinds of cerebral deformity. The first he called *agénésie primitive*, developmental inhibition of the hemispheres, primary deformation of the brain. The second he attributed to pathological processes which, as a secondary deformity, created cysts in the brain – *agénésie secondaire*.

Then a violent argument began on the significance of developmental inhibition and pathological processes. Dugés ascribed the clinical symptoms to encephalitis, Breschet to developmental inhibition, Lallemand again to encephalitis, and so on.

The debate ended when Gotard recognized the significance of both factors. The facts on the cerebral lesions were generally accepted but it was not possible to clarify the anatomical and histological position.

Meanwhile an aetiological approach became increasingly

prominent in medical thinking. The forerunner of this change was Little[3] who was recognized in England in his own day and who ascribed the symptoms (not described in any great detail) to damage at birth. Little himself was cerebromotorially dysfunctional. He had a left club foot (equino varus). Strohmayer performed the first subcutaneous tenotomy on him. In gratitude Little had his son christened 'Louis Strohmayer Little'. However his enthusiasm for the surgical method waned later.

As regards cerebromotor dysfunctions Little combined the spastic contractures into one class. He stressed the 'scissoring of the legs', the general muscle spasticity, and added the 'intellectual capacities are sometimes completely sound. In the majority of cases however the degree of intelligence is diminished, extending from extremely slight damage to complete imbecility.' For aetiology he pointed to the significance of premature, difficult birth and neonatal asphyxia.

Little quoted Shakespeare who bears witness to the aetiological significance of premature birth in the words of the Duke of Gloucester who is later to become King Richard III:

I, that am curtail'd of this fair proportion,
Cheated of feature by dissembling Nature,
Deform'd, unfinish'd, sent before my time
Into this breathing world scarce half made up
And that so lamely and unfashionable,
That dogs bark at me as I halt by them;

(I, i.)

At the end of the nineteenth century there was another debate similar to the earlier one on the anatomical basis, this time about the triggering cause. Freud's reports were very factual on this point too but he did not know Little's work. This debate also ended in the compromise of a polycausal standpoint put forward by Marie in 1886.

Since neither the pathological nor the aetiological endeavour led to any success in the quest to clarify the circumstances of cerebral infantile paralysis, attention turned to describing clinical symptoms and grouping them. Freud did pioneer work here and his clinical classification is still regarded as definitive by some.

3 Little, W.J. (1853) *On the Nature and Treatment of the Deformities of the Human Frame*, London.

Freud set up these groups:

- spastic hemiplegia;
- general rigidity (characteristics: extended posture, spasticity, involuntary movements);
- paraplegic rigidity (now paraplegic rigid hypertonia);
- paraplegic paralysis (characterized by spastic heightened tonus which, if very pronounced, verges on rigidity);
- bilateral hemiplegia (two forms: spastic double hemiplegia more pronounced in the arms; tetraplegia accentuated in the legs);
- general chorea or athetosis (characteristics: uncoordinated involuntary movements in the limbs, trunk, and parts served by the cerebral nerves. Tonus swings between hyper- and hypotonus. There is neither clonus nor Babinski reflex, grimacing and dysarthria are seen);
- bilateral athetosis.

Freud attached some significant comments to these clinical classifications which however were not recognized as important for decades. He emphasized that the whole classification is not restricted to the motorium and quoted Charcot who had noted earlier that motor disorders are frequently accompanied by sensory disturbances. Moreover there are many mixed and transitional forms and symptoms can interchange. Freud quoted Weir Mitchell who demonstrated that the younger a patient is the more certainly one can count on chorea appearing on previously paralysed limbs once the hemiplegia has subsided.

The turn of the century brought with it a steep upswing of surgery through the introduction of anaesthesia and asepsis. This led to the application of surgical orthopaedic procedures to the treatment of cerebro-motor dysfunctions. It was in this way that Phelps started to concern himself with cerebro-motor dysfunction. He it was who established the term 'cerebral palsy' in the specialist literature, a name which had been used first by Osler in 1889. Phelps[4] redrew the clinical classification of the disease considering it to be characteristic of the groups he formed that they were static and not progressive and defined five 'dyskineses'.

---

4   Phelps, W.M. (1932) *Journal of Bone and Joint Surgery.*

The five groups are:

1 Spasticity or the hyperirritability of the muscles. Muscles are extremely sensitive to every contractile stimulus and in volitional contraction the antagonists also contract.
2 Athetosis, the superimposing on to voluntary contractions of contractions arising in muscles not pertinent to the intended action.
3 Synkinesis, involuntary movement following attempted voluntary. For example the patient moves his hands when trying to move his legs. This can occur sometimes in healthy conditions, for example sticking out one's tongue when writing.
4 Incoordination or ataxia, associated with involuntary movement, loss of tone or balance.
5 Tremor, a rhythmic dyskinesis, which can be fine or crude, intentional or not.

Apart from these five forms of dyskinesis, Phelps further distinguished chorea, tic, and convulsions. As the diagnostic method he primarily used slow-motion film. He supplemented these motor symptoms with the result of investigation into intellectual capacity.

Following Phelps, opinion on cerebral palsy went through this development. Experiences from operative procedures restricted the initial enthusiasm, then conservative methods of treatment became preferred to surgical ones. Efforts became intensified to make the classification rather more accurate in order to distinguish whether or not cases were suitable for treatment.

The picture of cerebral palsy was still not clear enough however. Perlstein,[5] the paediatrician, in 1957 introduced a description of cerebral palsy like this: 'A great confusion predominates thinking on cerebral palsy.' To clarify it he first established that there were many different forms of paralysis (palsy) in which the only common feature was motor disability.

Apart from cerebral paralysis there are several other forms which all lead to paralysis, resulting from spinal or peripheral (nervous) damage to the organs of movement (organic) or to the disturbance in metabolism. The loss may be caused by a fall in

5 Perlstein, M.A. (1957) *The Journal of the South Carolina Medical Association*, 53(7).

the level of calcium or potassium, for instance. According to Perlstein the fact that so many different origins of paralysis are possible is an indication that in this field customary medical specialization cannot apply.

Even cerebral palsy itself can be classified in many different ways. In principle it should be possible to do so in terms of pathological anatomy but we still do not know enough about it for that. (The pathological anatomists also agreed with Perlstein here. Christensen and Melchior,[6] for example, wrote: 'Cerebral palsy is not an independent unit aetiologically, clinically or neuropathologically.') Perlstein preferred a clinical classification. 'The clinical classification which takes the qualitative character of the motor defect as its basis is more reliable and more useful', he wrote; in essence he was following Phelps here. Perlstein also distinguished a spastic group, seeking the cause of the spasticity in the intensified nature of stretch reflexes. Voluntary functioning of the agonists triggers an intensified stretch reflex in the antagonists and he attributed spasticity to this. He said that the resting tone of the muscles can also be a diminished one.

A second group is formed by dyskinesis. Both muscle reflexes and electromyogram are normal but movements are in part involuntary, undirected, and unexpected and during movement the muscle tone is abnormal. Involuntary movement with normal tone is rapid and jerky, that is chorea-like in form. If muscle tone is a little intensified, involuntary movements slow down and in this way athetosis sets in. Ultimately muscle tone can be intensified to such an extent that involuntary movement becomes impossible and is seen only as spasm. This is dystonia.

In tremor alternative movements of agonists and antagonists can be seen taking place with predictable regularity.

Functional muscle disorder set off not by a rapid stretch reflex but by slow movement was called 'rigidity' by Perlstein who looked on it as an extrapyramidal motor disorder. The limb bends as though it were a lead pipe or as though there were a cog wheel in the joint. According to Perlstein, this rigidity manifests itself principally in antigravitational muscles, in contrast to spasticity localized in gravitational muscles. (For example, the gastro-

6 Christensen, E. and Melchior, J. (1967) *Cerebral Palsy – A Clinical and Neuropathological Study*, London: Spastics Society.

cnemius is an antigravitational muscle, and the quadriceps femoris gravitational.)

Finally, Perlstein applied the term 'ataxia' to incoordination, loss of dexterity and balance.

According to Perlstein 90 per cent of cerebral palsy cases are spastic or athetoid, two-thirds of these cases being spastic in proportion to one-quarter athetoid.

The clinical classification given above can be supplemented topographically. Where symptoms are restricted solely to the legs we talk of paraplegia and the majority of paraplegics are found among spastics. If symptoms in the legs are accompanied by mild symptoms in the arms then it is diplegia, also a characteristic of spastics principally. If all four limbs are affected then the patient is quadriplegic (or tetraplegic). Among these, paralysis more marked in the legs is characteristic of spastics and of athetoids in the arms.

Paralysis restricted to one-half of the body is hemiplegia and here the arm is affected more severely than the leg. The majority of hemiplegics are spastic and one-third of cerebral palsy cases are hemiplegic.

Paralysis of three limbs is triplegia, hemiplegia combined with paraplegia. Two of the three limbs are always the legs and again triplegics generally are spastic.

Paralysis of one limb is monoplegia. True monoplegia is extremely rare but more usually is paraplegia accentuated on one side or a hemiplegia more marked in one of the limbs.

Double hemiplegia is a quadriplegia where the symptoms are more severe in both arms than in the legs but found in spastic patients more often than in athetoids. It is rare.

Clinical classification can be amplified by a third approach noting general muscle tone. From this a patient may be an atonic spastic diplegic for instance, or a hypertonic athetoid quadraplegic, and so on.

A fourth clinical viewpoint takes account of the severity of the case. According to Perlstein, 25 per cent of cases are mild, patients who do not require treatment, another 25 per cent are serious, untreatable cases, and 50 per cent are of medium severity who can be treated. So this classification has a prognostic character, too.

Perlstein also supplemented this classificatory approach by registering the time of inception, namely, prenatal, natal, and postnatal cases. If aetiological data are known, these can be included in the classification too.

According to Ingram[7] all these can be comprised as shown in Table 21.

Table 21　Perlstein's classification (1952)

Clinical symptoms	*Topography*	*Muscular tonus*	*Severity*	*Aetiology*
spastic	paraplegia	isotonia	mild	A *Prenatal*
dyskinesis	diplegia	hypertonia	medium	(1) *hereditary*
chorea	quadriplegia	hypotonia	severe	static
athetosis	hemiplegia			progressive
tremor	triplegia			(2) *acquired in*
rigidity	monoplegia			*the womb*
ataxia	double			infection
	hemiplegia			anoxia
				cerebral
				haemorr-
				hage
				Rh-factor
				metabolic
				disorder
				gonad
				irradia-
				tion
				B *Natal*
				anoxia
				cerebral
				haemorr-
				hage
				trauma
				pressure
				change
				C *Postnatal*
				trauma
				infection
				toxic
				vascular
				anoxia
				tumour
				develop-
				mental
				disorder

7　Ingram, T.T.S. (1964) *Paediatric Aspects of Cerebral Palsy*, Edinburgh: Livingstone.

It can be seen that Perlstein broadened the range of the term 'cerebral palsy' to an extraordinary extent and included forms of a progressive nature. Amplification and the delineation of subgroups had begun even earlier. Some specialists distinguished between forms of athetosis. 'Tensional' or 'contract' athetosis occurs where tension masks movement. 'Flailing' is that movement as though throwing a ball ('ballismus') characterized by violent movements in shoulders or hips, beginning in childhood and progressing. 'Shaking' has movements like shivering with cold. They distinguish between athetosis characterized by tremor and turning athetosis. There is a form, cerebellar deliberational athetosis, where an intensified attempt is made to maintain balance. One side of the body affected is known as hemiathetosis. Athetosis consequent on Rh incompatibility is deaf athetosis, although loss of hearing need not be absolute. There is an emotional deliberational form, where outbursts of laughter, weeping, or rage may be triggered by insignificant stimuli.

One of the most detailed classifications was that accepted by the American Academy for Cerebral Palsy in 1956 on the basis of Minear's[8] elaboration, as follows:

I **Physiologically (motor)**
  A   spasticity
  B   athetosis
      (1) tensional
      (2) non-tensional
      (3) distonic
      (4) with tremor
  C   rigidity
  D   ataxia
  E   tremor
  F   atonia (rare)
  G   mixed
  H   unclassifiable

II **Topographically**
  A   monoplegia: affects one limb;
  B   paraplegia: affects only the legs (usually spastic or rigid);
  C   hemiplegia: affects one half of the body; in general of a spastic type, sometimes athetoid;

8   Minear, W.G. (1956) *Paediatrics*, 18 (841).

D triplegia: affects three limbs, usually two legs and one arm; in general spastic;

E quadriplegia (tetraplegia); affects all four limbs. If chiefly in the legs generally spastic, if chiefly in arms generally dyskinetic, also includes athetosis;

F diplegia: paralysis affecting both halves uniformly, bilateral paralysis;

G double hemiplegia; affecting all four limbs but the arms in a more marked way than the legs, generally of a spastic type.

III **Aetiologically**

A *prenatal*

(1) hereditary – genetic

(2) acquired in the womb

(a) prenatal infection – toxoplasmosis, rubella, and so on

(b) prenatal anoxia; from carbon monoxide poisoning, stifling, anaemia, or hypotension of the mother, placenta infarct, detachment of the placenta, prolapse of the umbilical cord, and so on;

(c) prenatal cerebral haemorrhage, for example as a result of toxaemia, trauma, or bleeding diathesis of the mother;

(d) Rh factor, nuclear icterus;

(e) metabolic disturbance, diabetes;

(f) breech delivery;

(g) poor maternal nutrition.

B *Natal*

(1) anoxia

(a) mechanical closure of the air duct;

(b) atelectasia;

(c) birth narcosis;

(d) detaching of the placenta or placenta praevia;

(e) maternal anoxia or hypotension;

(f) breech delivery;

(g) bleeding in the first three months of pregnancy.

C *Postnatal*
   (1) trauma, subdural haematoma fracture of the skull, brain injury, contusio cerebri;
   (2) infection (meningitis, encephalitis, cerebral abscess);
   (3) toxicosis;
   (4) vascular damage (rupture, thrombosis, embolism);
   (5) anoxia;
   (6) tumour; developmental disorder.

IV **Incidental factors**
A *diagnosed by psychological examination*
   (1) mental handicap if exists.

B *physical state*
   (1) size of body;
   (2) stage of development (e.g. according to Gesell);
   (3) time of ossification;
   (4) contractures;

C *convulsions*

D *postural and locomotor forms*

E *eye and hand movements*
   (1) eye dominance;
   (2) eye movements;
   (3) eye position;
   (4) fixation;
   (5) convergence;
   (6) approximation to grasping;
   (7) grasping;
   (8) manipulating;
   (9) hand dominance.

F *visual state*
   (1) sensory
      (a) amblyopia
      (b) defects in the field of vision

    (2) motor
        (a) conjugated deviation
        (b) fixational disorders
        (c) fixed spasm
        (d) esotropia
        (e) exotropia
        (f) hypertropia
        (g) hypotropia
        (h) nystagmus
        (i) pseudoparalysis of the mm externorum rectorum.

G *auditory state*
    (1) loss of pitch of sound;
    (2) loss of decibels.

H *speech disorders*

V **Functional capacity** (degree of severity)
I–IV

VI **Therapeutic state**
A–D

Increasingly detailed classifications indicate that brain lesions have a very wide variety of consequences and so sharply defined categories cannot be established. As Freud emphasized in his day and Ingram in ours, individual cases are not static either. Again, the picture can change in the course of development (maturation) even from one day to the next (for example, the general muscle tonus). The future spastic patient may become hypotonic after birth. Different muscles may be simultaneously rigid and spastic. Illingworth[9] wrote,

> One must remember the fact that some children have unexpected lulls in development, followed by normal progress thereafter: and more important still, that even severe retardation in the early weeks may be followed by relatively normal or completely normal levels of intelligence later.

9 Illingworth, R.S. (1966) *The Development of the Infant and Young Child Normal and Abnormal*, Edinburgh: Livingstone.

Cerebral palsy cases are never restricted just to motor disorders but are accompanied by intellectual, perceptual, cognitive, or other symptoms related to the sensorium system. While among healthy people 4 per cent may be hard of hearing,[10] in cerebral palsy patients there may be as many as 10 per cent, or according to some (Cardwell), even 25–33 per cent. Amblyopia, and in particular squinting, is frequent, too, the last occurring in more than half of cases reported in the literature, Paine,[11] Blazsó and Giesel[12] found general motor organizational injuries in almost 87 per cent of children with strabismus. Abnormal vestibular functioning was seen in one-third of cerebral palsy children (Török and Perlstein,[13]). Gardiner[14] emphasizes a coactive effect between motor and sensory symptoms. Because in any case it was thought to be mentally deficient, a cerebral palsy child was given spectacles only reluctantly, yet when the child's myopia was corrected in this way his school conduct and achievement improved enormously.

Many people have abandoned attempts at classification altogether because of all the argument, turning instead to small-scale description, extremely detailed and recording the particular symptoms like a mosaic, while on the other hand others just keep to a very broad outline. So, for example, in 1959 the British Little Club recommended a grouping which took only motor symptoms into account:

- spastic cerebral palsy
  hemiplegia
  diplegia
  double hemiplegia
- dystonic cerebral palsy
- choreoathetoid cerebral palsy
- mixed
- ataxic
- atonic diplegia.

Finally, it has been shown over and over again that, as Denhoff

10   (1963)*Die Infantilen Zerebralparesen*, Stuttgart.
11   Paine, R.S. (1963) *Visual Disorders and Cerebral Palsy*, London.
12   Blazsó, S. and Giesel, V. (1969) *Szernészet*, 106.
13   Török, N. and Perlstein, M.A. (1962) *Annals of Otology, Rhinology, and Laryngology*, 71 (1).
14   Gardiner, P. (1963) *Visual Disorders and Cerebral Palsy*, London: Spastics Society.

and Robinault[15] emphasized in 1949, cerebral palsy is not a single a unit but a syndrome characteristic of extensive brain damage, one which includes neuromotor dysfunctions, psychological dysfunctions, convulsions, and organic conduct irregularities. Denhoff[16] has pictured the cerebral dysfunction syndrome as a coherent spectrum which can be characterized by a combination of mental and motor symptoms in different proportions. Cerebral palsy stands at one extreme of this spectrum but it is not restricted to motor symptoms.

Parkinson's disease

Parkinsonism has been referred to earlier in connection with the extrapyramidal system. We will return to it now, briefly.

Parkinson patients do form part of cerebral dysfunction cases and defining Parkinson's disease is a problem no less complicated than for cerebral palsy. In 1817 James Parkinson gave the original description of a disease associated principally with a form of tremor that is hyperkinesis, muscular rigidity, and general hypokinesis and he called this rather an odd name 'paralysis agitans' (shaking paralysis).

Paralysis agitans was first regarded as a disease of the elderly but was realized later to have a youthful form too. Then again it became evident that the symptoms listed in original descriptions were not essential. There is, for example, a paralysis agitans, 'sine agitatione', without tremor and there are Parkinson's diseases with which other symptoms are associated in various ways.

Nor has the anatomical pathological basis been clarified satisfactorily. We have mentioned that the symptoms referred to earlier are ascribed to substantia nigra. But patho-histological alterations have been found in the striatum and cortex of Parkinson patients too and yet characteristic Parkinson symptoms have also been found without any pathological basis.

The aetiological picture is no clearer either. Some have applied the name, 'primary Parkinsonism', to cases of unknown aetiology and 'secondary Parkinsonism' to those where a triggering cause is known. But a sharp boundary cannot be drawn between the two,

15 Denhoff, E. and Robinault, J.P. (1960) *Cerebral Palsy and Related Disorders*, New York: McGraw Hill.
16 Denhoff, E. (1967) *Cerebral Palsy: The Preschool Years*, Springfield Ill: Thomas.

although this view is not universally accepted. We agree however with the following:[17] 'The occurrence of this group of symptoms has been observed in a series of illnesses by itself or associated with others.'

'Secondary Parkinsonism' may be caused by a wide range of cerebral injury. It can occur after encephalitis, associated with brain tumour, following injury, linked with vascular diseases, and so on. It is very much worth noting, too, that a characteristic Parkinsonism occurs in some patients treated with phenothiazine derivative tranquilizers, the symptoms ceasing after the medication is stopped, but sometimes only weeks or months later. With the young, symptoms of this medication toxicosis are primarily choreoathetoid in form, whereas in older patients the characteristic symptoms of Parkinsonism are produced. So according to age the same cause sets off symptoms more characteristic either of cerebral palsy or of Parkinson's disease.

The various symptoms do not form a close unity. The propellant symptom (that is the peculiarity of a Parkinson patient not to be able to stop if pushed unless or until he comes up against some obstacle), may be apparent before the appearance of the stoop and muscle rigidity, considered to be characteristic (Wollenberg[18]). Martin mentions that stereotactic operations do not affect the different symptoms uniformly.

There may be a connection between complex cerebral feedback circuits and the peculiar variability of symptoms. After a bus ride of several hours, one of Jacob's patients lost his tremor for one-and-a-half days. Some Parkinson patients are able to move without tremor at night and their speech becomes normal too. (A similar observation has been made about catatonic schizophrenics.)

All this indicates that within cerebral dysfunction variable transitions are possible and that every classification introduces a certain amount of artificiality into the picture.

Despite its motor disorder character, Parkinsonism often affects mental abilities. Fünfgeld[19] quite directly maintains that

---

17 Cecil, R.L. and Loeb, R.F. (1967) *Textbook of Medicine*, ninth edition, Philadelphia.
18 Wollenberg in Jacob, A. (1955) *Wahrnehmungsstörung und Krankheitserleben. Psychopathologie des Parkinsonismus und verstehende Psychologie Bewegungs und Wahrnehmungsgestörter*, Berlin: Springer Verlag.
19 Fünfgeld, E.W. (1967) *Psychopathologie und Klinik des Parkinsonismus vor und nach stereotaktischen Operationen*, Heidelberg.

Parkinson patients are always psychologically deformed. Jacob cites many examples of the kind of peculiar subjective complaints connected with 'motor' dysfunctions. The patients feel as if their limbs were becoming independent of them, their movements seeming automatic. In fact, their complaints sometimes take on such a bizarre character as to be quite reminiscent of the statements of schizophrenics. For example, one Parkinson patient said about his gaze spasm that 'demons were pulling my eyes up.'

We have also pointed out that Parkinsonism may be accompanied by vegetative symptoms similar to those found in some athetoids.

Hemiplegia

In the ninth edition of Cecil and Loeb's well-known manual, Hausman[20] still said on hemiplegia, 'the expression hemiplegia is synonymous with a one-sided suprasegmental paralysis of the limbs and of the lower part of the face', but this definition is not used in the twelfth edition.

Seen as a topographical concept, that is to say, one which describes the site of symptoms, hemiplegia comes within the sphere of cerebral palsy but usually in adult patients hemiplegics are sharply distinguished while not forming a symptomatically coherent picture either. On the basis of their symptomatic differences 'crossed hemiplegias' are distinguished as a separate group from those stemming from injuries to the lowest section of the brainstem, providing neurologists with their best opportunities for diagnosis and localization. However in speaking of hemiplegia in general it usually means principally the injuries arising from vascular diseases in elderly people, located in the forebrain. It is more difficult to ascertain the precise site of the damage and symptoms are very varied, too. Marshall,[21] for example, states that:

Hemiplegia can arise from obstruction of the anterior artery of the brain close to the Heubner artery, from obstruction of the arteria cerebri media at its commencement, from obstruction of the striary side branches of the cerebra media and from obstruction extending to the perforating branches of the arteria

20   Cecil, R.L. and Loeb, R.F. (ninth edition) *Textbook of Medicine*, Philadelphia.
21   Marshall, J. (1965) *The Management of Cerebrovascular Disease*, London: Churchill.

cerebri posterior, or along the paramedian branches of the arteria basilaris.

From this it can be seen that the pathological anatomical foundations of hemiplegia as a nosological unit are fairly difficult to define. The same is true of aetiological relations as not only vascular diseases, obstructions, or haemorrhages may become a cause of hemiplegia in old age, but also a tumour may possibly do so.

In the literature on hemiplegia authors pass on to each other, as though taking part in a relay race, opinions relating to the pyramidal tract and cortical localization, while often simply disregarding critical observations (Walshe[22]).

Hemiplegia is very varied from the motor point of view too, showing spasticity but also flaccidity or even rigidity. The paralyses variously affect proximal or distal parts of legs or arms. Hemiplegic symptoms may be accompanied by Parkinsonian or athetoid symptoms.

Hemiplegia naturally is not restricted to motor, but involves many sensory symptoms as well. Frequently there is loss of part of the visual field (hemianopia) with a disturbance in balance which is more of a postural disturbance, the patient leaning towards the paralysed side. Peculiar subjective complaints also characterize the input effects of injuries and these are sometimes found in mild motor injuries. Even with his eyes closed a healthy person knows if we touch him simultaneously and symmetrically on both sides but a hemiplegic, on the other hand, would only be aware of being touched on his healthy side, even though otherwise he had no loss of sensation. In the feedback circuit on his damaged side signal strength does not build up quickly enough and is suppressed by the rival information.

The patient may not be able to recognize objects put into his paralysed hand although his tactile ability is quite sound (astereognosis). Or a patient may not notice paralysis on one side (anosognosia), feeling one side not to be paralysed but alien: 'Somebody is lying beside me in the bed.' When drawing human figures these patients frequently forget to include the side on which they

22 Walshe, F.M.R. (1948) *Critical Studies in Neurology*, Edinburgh: Livingstone; Walshe, Sir Francis (1965) *Further Critical Studies in Neurology*, Baltimore, MD: Williams & Wilkins.

themselves are paralysed without noticing the deficiency.

Both emotional lability (compulsive outbursts of weeping) and trophic symptoms may also be associated with these motor and sensory disturbances. Muscles waste away, skin sores erupt, joints become distorted, and so on.

Hurwitz[23] writes: 'The disease causing hemiplegia also damages other parts of the brain. There is damage to the intellect, capacity for judgment, discrimination, discernment, control of movements, the understanding of speech and of various sensations in the limbs.'

In discussing cerebral dysfunctions we have referred only to the principal types which figure most often in the literature on this condition and will discuss our own classification separately in a later section.

It can be seen how difficult it is to characterize cerebral dysfunctions according to the points of view discussed clinically so far, yet actually the difficulties are even greater than one might think from what has been said. Injuries to the brain may cause typical spinomotor symptoms. We ourselves have seen a patient who was considered to have multiple sclerosis with regard to paraplegia but later it transpired that the paraplegia was not caused by spinal cord damage but by a brain tumour. (Of course, multiple sclerosis may also have cerebral lesions but in his case the lesion was localized in the spinal cord.)

So, however important it may be not to underestimate the significance of spinal automatisms in encephalization, it is also true that the central problem in dysfunctions is the brain. Yet just like the neurological model, a clinical mode of description has not proved flexible enough for discussing cerebral dysfunctions. Perhaps provisionally disregarding Pavlov's objections, we might follow R. Jung's[24] advice: 'Complicated physiological facts can often be expressed much more graphically in psychological language.'

23   Hurwitz, L.J. (1966) *Physiotherapy*, 52(10).
24   Jung, R. (1967) *Psychiatrie der Gegenwart*, I/1A, Berlin: Springer Verlag.

10 The psychology of brain damage

Injuries to the brain change the entire system of relationships between an individual and his environment. A brain-damaged person becomes a peculiar new personality. Gelb[1] spent several decades in work on brain damage. Originally he collaborated with Goldstein but Gelb died early while Goldstein lived to be over 80 and so scientific memory has dealt less kindly with its recollection of Gelb. Cerebral dysfunctions could not be given a more worthwhile psychological presentation than by quoting Gelb.

Gelb pointed out that some brain-damaged people do not complain, even though for example they may have extensive gaps in the visual field. This had been known earlier but Gelb went further and from careful investigations of the visual field was able to demonstrate that the part which remains has become restructured as though there were a small 'fovea' in the middle of it and is now the locus of highest visual acuity. Not only does this functional fovea not coincide with the retina's anatomical fovea but it has no completely fixed location, in that its site is decided by visual tasks at any given time. In some patients suffering from loss of half the visual field (hemianopics), although its cone density fits it for acute vision the original fovea is significantly inferior to this new functional one where the structure is less favourable anatomically.

Gelb's colleague Fuchs showed that the visual acuity of a functional fovea may exceed by 33 per cent that of the original.

What has happened here? According to Gelb we have to deal with a rearrangement of the entire optical system. This rearrangement means that the structures taking part in vision become a new system. Their function is structurally readjusted to form it.

1 Gelb, A. (1937) *Zur medizinischen Psychologie und philosophischen Anthropologie*, The Haghe.

131

'It is not that particular parts take over function from other parts but a new system forms which determines the functioning of all the individual parts.'

Perhaps the concept of an optical system can be best explained by an experiment.

One of Poppelreuter's hemianopic patients was asked to stare fixedly at a definite point in a picture projected for one-tenth of a second. The fixed point was located in such a way that the picture, a circle, would fall half on the seeing and half on the blind side of his retina. When he was asked what he had seen, the patient said: 'A complete circle.' Why did the patient not see only a semicircle? Poppelreuter repeated the experiment showing the patient only a semicircle which would fall on to the functioning part of his retina. The patient again saw a complete circle! Poppelreuter regarded this as a perceptual disorder, an illusion and therefore subjective, resulting from spontaneous error. But what lies behind the illusion?

If a person with normal vision stares for a rather long time at a red circle, for instance, and looks at a white wall after that, a green circle appears on the wall as a negative after-image. This is usually taken to be related to physiological, and so objective, visual processes. If a hemianopic is asked to look like this at a red semicircle, the after-image is a complete green circle.

So behind the 'illusion' some kind of very concrete objective function combines the details observed, even complementing them and in this sense we have to speak of an 'optical system'.

This system is not brought into being by experience. Indeed, when we consider the question of the completion of truncated visual figures, experimental results show that different forms are affected differently. For example, truncated letters of the alphabet in general do not seem to complete themselves necessarily even though there should be quite enough experience to round out the process. So experiences are connected and integrate in a multilateral way the functional conditions of units established in inherited structures. In cerebral activity we have to hypothesize structures based on functional units of this kind.

The rearrangement of the optical system seems to be a reconstruction of the damaged neural structure so as to continue functioning as a diminished whole. So a functional fovea is created in the eye after the loss of half of the visual field. This rearrangement of the optical system extends totally over the brain-damaged patient's cerebral functioning.

Gelb had a patient who read and wrote without any trouble. However, if he was only given one-tenth of a second to read a word projected by a tachistoscope, he proved to be completely incapable of doing so ('an easy task for a school child of 7 or 8 years'). It transpired that the patient compensated for his reading incapacity by moving his head to follow the lines of letters and so learned to read again. If they stopped this 'motor' reading, for instance by preventing him from moving his head or by shortening his time available to one-tenth of a second, he could not read at all. So by moving his head this patient eliminated a visual functional disorder apparently in a way quite remote from seeing. He compensated for the deficiency in one area by making use of another, and so here, if we may vary Starkiewicz's expression, we are dealing with 'head-vision'. This experience makes it clearer over how wide a range the brain may be able to achieve those results which we call the concept of 'recognition'.

In the final analysis reading is recognition – the letters, so to speak, stand out from their environment. For this patient it was difficult enough to read anyway and Gelb increased the difficulty experimentally. He wrote the patient's own name on a blackboard and crossed part out with thin vertical lines. This was sufficient for the patient to be unable to read it. If he repeated this test with two colours, wrote the name in red and crossed it out in blue, the result was the same: the patient could not read what was written. Then Gelb told him to look just at the red. He immediately read what was written and so it was enough to give just one clue, a facilitating item of information.

Gelb wrote a capital R on the blackboard for a brain-damaged patient. The patient was unable to recognize it, so Gelb underlined the letter and the patient recognized it straight away. Putting a line under the letter made the task more 'concrete'; the R stood out from its surroundings and became recognizable. Perhaps we might describe the process by saying that 'putting it on the line' adds an additional factor to the letter, one which made the task easier to do.

It is not always easy for us to understand how the brain works and consequently to know how we might help it along. For example, Gelb gave a patient a pencil and told him to sit down at a table on which there was a sheet of white paper. He told the patient to write something above the paper in the air. The patient could not do it showing that he had a writing disability. But in putting the pencil to paper the same patient wrote without any trouble. Supposedly the task became easier through reafferentation. Gelb said a concrete task was easier than an abstract one. He pointed out that this was just as true where the symptom is an incapacity for recognition (agnosia) as where its practical execution may become inhibited (apraxia).

If the patient is unable to mime an activity then neurologists say he has 'ideomotor apraxia'. Actually this is a matter of the brain's functional capacity's adapting to broader or narrower conditions. One patient of Gelb's when asked to lift an empty glass to his mouth as though drinking could not do so, but if a little water were poured into the glass, he drank it easily. When he had put down the empty glass again, he could not lift it to his mouth as he had when asked to a moment before. One seriously brain-damaged patient was able to drink only when he was thirsty.

Gelb writes: 'Patients like these, however different their symptoms, are more closely bound to the situation than healthy people are.' This explains the patient's cautious avoidance of new circumstances, ones which deviate from what he is used to. Anything we do is always influenced by the structuring of the concrete circumstances. Gelb also demonstrated this fact in relation to aphasics. It is remarkable that, for the brain, different conditions can affect the level of difficulty for spoken language.

The easiest is speech in the form of reading aloud. Even aphasic patients who are quite unable to speak spontaneously may be able to do that. There are some ways in which speech can be eased in, for example with counting. Occasionally this may be difficult to begin with but becomes fluent later. Speech is also facilitated by emotion. There are aphasics who cannot speak normally but can curse or swear. Speech is easier when replying to questions than when having to expound something continuously.

Contrary to the common conception, it is more difficult to repeat something after someone else than to say it spontaneously. Some aphasics converse quite well but if they are asked to repeat words they used very well in connected speech, they are unable to do so when the words are taken out of context.

Naming particular objects or processes is still more difficult. In everyday life it often happens in practical situations that an expression will not come to mind. If this happens we probably point to the object in question and say: 'I want that thingummy, please.' In concrete situations it is possible to get by with relatively few words.

Words really become necessary when we are not dealing with concrete reality, when it is not a question of controlling things physically, but when we have to assess certain relationships.

This is exactly what patients with brain damage find so difficult. Only with difficulty are they able to distance themselves from the concrete and slot into a more abstract situation. Changing over from one system to the other causes the greatest problem for a brain-damaged person. (From our own experiences this assertion of Gelb's seems somewhat exaggerated.) For example, a patient reads fluently and writes down the name 'Frankfurt'. If we want him to spell it or write it down as separate letters, he is incapable of doing so. A name is more concrete than separate letters or sounds! For some brain-damaged people, it is extremely difficult to tell a deliberate lie. Aphasics with paralysed right hands may not be able to say 'I am writing with my right hand', but can say 'I am writing with my left hand' which is the truth.

Of course, there are several degrees of concrete relationship in cerebral function. For example, there is a difference between practical and conscious localization. If a brain-damaged person's skin itches somewhere he can touch it quite accurately to scratch it, yet might be incapable of putting into words where the itch is or even of intentionally putting his finger on the spot he has just touched.

The difference between a practical activity and locating it verbally is illustrated by the following examples. A brain-damaged patient had to throw a ball alternately into a red bucket 1 metre away and into a green bucket 3 metres away. He did this perfectly but when he was asked which bucket was nearer to him he had to walk the distance first before being able to reply.

Gelb not only drew his inferences from real situations, both experimentally and actual experiences through his patients, but also carefully avoided the fuzzy ambiguities of muddled concepts. He constantly drew attention to interminable repetitions in the literature of concepts like 'attention', 'awareness', 'noting', 'intelligence', and so on. According to Gelb these are unuseable terms in their generality. They talk about a disorder of 'intelligence', of 'attention', of 'apraxia' being present and they assume that because these particular functions are disordered, the patient is totally changed as a person. They generally interpret such concepts as 'intelligence', 'attention', 'noting', in a very arbitrary way and so theoretical unity is impossible.

Our (Gelb's) analysis of behaviour has led to the opposite. It is not that patients have altered basically because their 'attentiveness', their 'awareness', is damaged, but conversely because they have changed fundamentally in so far as they have become less rational, less immediately active people, that they become incapable of certain intellectual performances, for example paying enough attention, and so on. Only from this can it be understood that the same patients can sometimes solve a problem and at other times fail to do so. Here is Gelb's example.

> I say to a patient [with a frontal lobe injury] 'I am going to read something to you. Pay close attention and then tell me what you have heard.' Then I read a short story to the patient, let us say about a storm. The patient listens to it with a vacant facial expression. He is unable to tell me the story in turn. He only reproduces particular words, e.g. storm, and these in a purely motor manner out of context. What is lacking? The patient's capacity for attention? Or does he forget immediately what he has just heard? No! His conduct changes all at once if I do not read the story but tell it as my experience as though it had happened to me the previous day. The patient listens to this in quite a different way. He is quite at home in these events. What is more, when I have finished my account, he tells his companions 'what happened to the Professor yesterday'. Well now, is he in fact incapable of 'paying attention', 'understanding', 'recall'? We do not get far with such conceptual clichés. Why was it that the patient understood the story so well on one occasion but not on another? It

was because on the one occasion it was not necessary for him to change his attitude while on the other case he would have had to achieve an attitude of 'paying attention'. Is it so easy to do this? What is self-explanatory for the healthy person is not so for the patient. In order to pay attention, we have to dis-associate ourselves from the immediate situation. We have to tear ourselves away from reality and tune into something which has no part in that concrete situation. If the 'here and now' character of the situation disappears the patient cannot achieve the attitude necessary for paying attention. For the patient to maintain contact, the story must be told within the context of the concrete situation obtaining and not be implanted as something alien to it.

The inability of brain-damaged people to lie may be understood in the same way. Gelb had an epileptic patient who sometimes had milder and sometimes more severe attacks. After a mild fit Gelb could not get him to write down, 'I have had a severe attack'. The patient left out the 'severe' and when asked to could not put in the word he had omitted.

This illustrates that in cerebral function adaptive biological factors come into play which match a great mass of items of information with a combination of given functional specialities and environmental conditions. Psychological and philosophical concepts used to describe cerebral function are frequently inadequate to explain what actually happens. On this point we have quoted in detail Gelb's statement on 'attention', 'under-standing', 'recalling', and so on. We will bring in here another standard example, namely that, quite logically, a letter is generally considered to be simpler than a word. But the brain finds the word simpler than the letter! It is not easy to formulate concepts to describe adequately either cerebral function or cerebral disorders.

11 The conceptual system of Conductive Education

The Petö system is to educate dysfunctionals to become ortho-functionals. It has taken shape over several decades based on experience with many thousands of individuals and this defines the scope of its conceptual system. Naturally the concepts of Conductive Education are linked more or less closely with those of other fields but cannot be derived from them. At the same time concepts applied in Conductive Education shed new light on matters arising in these other fields. Of course this kind of application is true of any scientific theory. Different methodologies and practices give rise to relatively independent concepts, the various conceptual systems never merging together to form one single universal system free from internal contradictions.

It is important to observe limits when generalizing from particular perceptions and to fail to observe those limits in applying particular opinions or concepts too zealously would be disastrous. The concept of 'appropriateness', for example, is highly useful in biology in the sense of Darwinian adaptation, but in physiology takes on a teleological character and becomes a completely unuseable term. Following Sherrington's brilliant results in neurophysiology, some people mockingly dismissed Pavlov's black box type of physiological research as 'cerebral research without any examination of the brain' because they failed to notice that these methods were applied to two different fields – to lower levels of the nervous system, and, in Pavlov's phrase to 'higher nervous activity'. Many further examples could be cited. Innumerable attempts have been made to force different phenomena into a single concept by giving them all the same name or by referring to essentially the same phenomena by different terminology and treating them as though they belonged to different concepts.

Actually collating experiences gained by different methods does involve crossfertilization (reciprocal conceptual illumination).

This is an important general observation but we will not follow this thread here. But certainly, to understand and learn to use Conductive Education does require a knowledge of its conceptual system, so we will clarify that now.

Concepts are based on generalizing from observations, yet any generalization must be an extrapolation and include hypothetical features. Consequently Conductive Education theory should be looked at like this: the facts, that is the observations, are firmly established, yet the conclusions drawn from them are heuristic in so far as those observations may be related to black box function and to general indications about its current state.

Concepts serve for orientation and guidance only; facts are conclusive. Sometimes the same facts can give rise to both several different conclusions and also frequently more correlations. A teacher can never rely on a few rigid theoretical rules yet will also fail by approaching his work only in a pragmatic way.

This then is how Conductive Education sees the concepts of orthofunction and dysfunction.

12 Orthofunction, dysfunction as personality problems

Orthofunction is that protean capacity involving the entire personality enabling an individual to satisfy the biological (and social) demands made upon him.

These demands differ greatly, first with age and second according to tradition. One biological demand confronting a baby is that it should suck if it has had nothing to eat for three or four hours. A small child has to be house-trained. Mounted herdsmen might expect a child to ride a horse relatively early but not to learn to read and write. At certain ages there are certain general requirements which vary widely with historical and local conditions, but always take the form of the problem-solutions normally open to orthofunctionals.

People with organic deficit cannot fulfil some of the requirements otherwise appropriate to their ages but may become orthofunctional if it is technically possible to provide a substitute. A one-legged man can walk quite well with an artificial leg within the limitations of the prosthesis and a man with no teeth will be able to chew again with artificial dentures, but a dysfunctional may have teeth and yet not be able to chew, or a contracture may be corrected by an orthopaedic surgeon, but instead of walking normally new dysfunctional symptoms appear.

Dysfunction is, therefore, a lack of orthofunction, an incapacity for satisfying all the demands generally fulfilled at a given time of life, which is not substantially relieved by the use of a prosthesis or other appliance.

You can see from this that both concepts, orthofunction and dysfunction, recognize general requirements at a normal level but do not refer to specific concrete activities or the way they are to be done.

The fact that an orthofunctional person is characterized by a high level of capacity for varying the ways of achieving whatever goals he is aiming for points to the great reserves of cerebral function. An almost infinite number of abilities are there to be used. Cerebral lesions usually leave a very considerable residual capacity so that the activities and demands presented by life may still be satisfied. Residual abilities are left to even the most severely dysfunctional people and make it possible to reintegrate them into mainstream society. The very existence of a dysfunction shows that use is not being made of this residual capacity.

Not even orthofunctionals are able to satisfy every demand immediately. They have to learn how to solve certain problems in going about their activities, quite often needing considerable time to become able to wrestle with them. The essential difference between an orthofunctional and a dysfunctional lies not so much in their respective achievements as in how they learn. A brain-stem baby becomes distinctly different from a healthy baby only when some months have elapsed. Dysfunctions develop with time and show up the more sharply in comparison with 'normal' standards the further the process of adaptation or learning has advanced in the case of the 'normal control'.

So to redefine the point: an orthofunctional person is characterized by a general capacity for adaptation or learning which enables him throughout his life to adjust more and more comprehensively to his natural and social environment and on that general capacity his lifelong development depends.

But the general adaptive capacity of dysfunctional people is diminished or has been lost altogether, so that they are incapable in many ways of achieving the adaptation expected of them. They cannot learn to conform with new circumstances. (The term 'adaptation' is being used here in the sense of biological, or social, adjustment, and not either in a physiological sense or as related to maturation.)

Clearly then, dysfunctional symptoms are only secondary. The primary problem is a persistent deterioration or complete loss in the general capacity for adaptation. That capacity is not some special characteristic but a general functional property of the nervous system which covers the most varied forms of activity. Adaptation is shown with respect to different nervous system functions temporarily changing at every level. Sherrington demonstrated with the most simple reflexes that, when stimuli are repeated, the effect of the earlier stimulus creates a new situation for those that follow. Pavlov showed that for the entire black box the character for the organism of a neutral stimulus changes if it is followed straight away by a hereditarily effective one. Adaptation, facilitation, summation, conditioned reflex and inhibition, learning and habituation, pattern of excitation (stereotype); all point to one common basic feature. Each new stimulus affects the functioning of the nervous system, which is constantly attuning to changing conditions, becoming more refined, making the individual's existence more and more secure in changing circumstances as a progressive biological adaptation. It seems that successive approximation is the way in which two components make their growing adjustment. In the infinite vastness of the feedback circuits of the nervous system a permanent change in function in relation to the environment continues from the birth of an individual or more properly from the beginning of his nervous system. Particular regulations continually become more subtle and their interconnections increasingly differentiated. In the course of a continuous reafferentative reorganization relating input and output data the brain as it were incorporates the relationships of its environment.

Stimuli which are for the most part uniformly undifferentiated and meaningless at first increasingly acquire richer informational, that is, biological significance. The environment becomes more and more familiar. On the output side, inherited or acquired movements combine to form widely varying and biologically expedient action patterns. General adaptational development leads to the emergence of an orthofunctional personality.

What causes this process to break down? In other words, how does a person become dysfunctional?

To speak of an 'orthofunctional personality' and trace it back through its general adaptational development implies a certain continuity, in both the concept of that personality and of the process of general adaptational development. Sometimes, of course, a personality may change unexpectedly – well known in connection with brain tumours for instance or extensive cerebral injury in general. A thrombosis in a blood vessel in the brain can transform a loud-mouthed dominant individual overnight into a quiet and gentle person. Personality can change quite rapidly with fundamental changes in environment, as for example, when an individual has been deported or deprived of human dignity by brutal humiliation. We emphasize all this only to make it clear that in the face of efforts to change a personality, its stability, endurance, and resistance are not unlimited.

Accumulated dysfunctional experiences are needed for a dysfunctional personality to emerge, when an individual is incapable of carrying out the tasks facing him; but again, these are only to be thought of in terms of practical biological needs or the social norms generally accepted in his society. So, for instance, drinking water is biologically motivated and in our society to use a glass a socially motivated requirement. In many parts of Spain the custom is to lift a jug high and drink the wine as it pours down in a thin stream and so everyone learns to do it, but not elsewhere.

A task is indissolubly linked with a requirement to deal with it. Every task presents an inescapable challenge and in carrying it out a feedback circuit is set up in which the performance exerts a reafferentative influence. I want to drink some water, the glass is in front of me, I stretch out my hand, and this series of movements ends when I have grasped the glass. As a result of the next series of movements the glass reaches my mouth so that the water can enter it. Each series of movements becomes biologically expedient through the resulting reafferentation.

Energy is wasted if it is invested in a series of movements not ultimately justified reafferentatively. For impulses to movements to become actions they must prove biologically expedient, that is, be justified reafferentatively. (Biological needs and social requirements are not on opposite sides of a coin. If a member of a community contravenes a norm generally accepted there or fails to fulfil a social requirement, his action will not have positive reafferentation – what he has done has not proved socially expedient. The general demands of a community affect its members very strongly.)

Lack of successful achievement, failure, and frustration, affect our general capacity for adaptation and when repeated several times eventually cause adaptive development to slow down or stop altogether. This is exactly what creates a dysfunctional personality.

The influence, then, of successive failures leads to the appearance of a dysfunctional personality. In some cases a great deal of frustration is needed; in others relatively little. In certain cases a series of failures may be limited to a particular range of tasks and then the brain excludes that area from its regulation, the result being a disturbed body-image or perceptual scotoma. The individual is not aware of discomfort but regards one of his limbs as strange, causing him 'difficulties'. For instance, he complains that he is always bumping into the door on one side, or perhaps having car accidents. Dysfunctional personality-change affecting the domain of the highest cerebral control systems is not necessarily associated with symptoms of motor disability, but in the narrower, everyday sense, dysfunctions affect the nervous system's motor control.

So successive failures to succeed in meeting social and biological requirements lie behind dysfunctional personality changes. Dysfunctional symptoms of an everyday kind corresponding to motor disabilities appear when these failures occur at a very early age at the beginning of general adaptive development, or in an adult in relation to the range of regulations for comparatively simple activities too.

The picture sketched out here indicates that, in the gradually widening field of this general adaptive process absolutely everything we do involves a reafferentative adjustment and so the organization of movements leading to that activity comes to be built in to the nervous system circuits. This is the basis for feedback circuits becoming increasingly comprehensive, that is for adaptational development.

Good results achieved are a spur to further achievement. They increase attention span, activity, and perseverance and this is evident objectively. Subjectively success in achievement is accompanied by feelings of cheerfulness and good humour.

Conversely, a series of frustrations leads objectively to low spirits, passivity, occasional outbursts of rage, and vegetative symptoms (sweating, going pale, blushing, intestinal disturbances, and so on). Subjectively these are paralleled by feeling tired, impatient, occasionally apathetic, or infuriated.

We reject the narrow view of dysfunctions as mere motor disabilities and maintain that in an everyday sense the dysfunctions are a part of the manifestations of a general regulatory disorder stemming from a breakdown in general adaptive development and affecting the entire personality.

Orthofunction   therefore   is   linked   with   the   successful performance of tasks relating to the biological and social demand-systems appropriate for a particular age-group. Dysfunction, on the other hand, is linked with successive frustrations in meeting them. In Pavlov's experiments with dogs he engineered their nervous breakdown through conflicting simultaneous demands. Strictly speaking, these dogs found themselves in a situation resembling a state of general dysfunction and this caused them to develop symptoms of motor and vegetative disorder.

So dysfunctional symptoms reflect a general dysfunctional condition. This may be the result of a primary lesion in the brain when because of damage to the regulatory system unsuccessful actions do not achieve their aim and so are not adjusted reafferentatively and the adaptive learning process breaks down. Cameron[1] writes: 'To children with Little's disease as I have already said, the main way to self-education is closed in early childhood, since the small child learns and collects its sense memories chiefly by grasping and touching.' The cause of a dysfunctional personality-change may also lie in particularly unfavourable environmental conditions, as in Pavlov's experiments referred to earlier when any damage to cerebral regulatory systems is secondary.

Biological and social demands grow with age and successive failures affect an increasing variety of activities. So as age increases there is less and less hope of a spontaneous resumption of the process of general adaptation and to achieve its recovery expert guidance or conduction is needed.

Recovery is conditional both on the imposition of all those biological and social demands appropriate to his age and on the dysfunctional's being directed towards carrying out independently the tasks set by those demands.

Perhaps it is clear by now why, despite all the important data collected in physiology, clinical practice, and psychology, in attempts to clarify the problems of cerebral dysfunction, we are still not able to reach the point where we can receive instructions for practical use. It is only biologically, that is, by considering the global relationships between an individual and his environment, that we can begin to understand dysfunctions. This biological

---

1 Cameron, H.C. (1958) *Cerebral Palsy Bulletin*, No. 2.

explanation itself forms a set of instructions. If we translate the biological concept of adaptation into the language of education as concerning social adaptation, then we must speak of 'learning'.

Primarily cerebral dysfunctions damage the plasticity of the personality, affecting its formation by experience, or 'learning'. But the term 'learning' must not be understood in too narrow a sense! On the contrary, its meaning should be extended to include every aspect of the entire personality and because education is concerned with problems of learning, the rehabilitation of dysfunctionals is an educational task, too.

To sum up, Conductive Education simply teaches people how to be orthofunctional, a system ensuring the adaptive, that is the learning, development of the entire dysfunctional personality.

13 The daily schedule

From our conception of orthofunction and dysfunction, the entire personality must be considered within an integrated system of requirements. Accordingly, Conductive Education constitutes an integrated system, and the integral operator of this system is the Conductor. Understanding Conductive Education depends upon understanding the role of the Conductor.

However, to make things clearer we shall not begin our explanation with the Conductor but with an introduction to the life of the Institute itself in almost photographic detail, for it is only by beginning with this very simple description that we can expect to be able to bring out the significance of particular factors, to explain their correlations, and elucidate various aspects of the system.

So we will begin our discussion of the system of Conductive Education by presenting the daily schedule and take as an example a group of athetoid children. Their daily timetable determines every aspect of their lives right through from 6.30 am to 9 pm (illustrated in photographs 1–167).

The group is woken up by the Conductor. The first event on the programme, a seemingly banal one, is 'conditioning' ('toilet-training'), that is accustoming the children to using the pot or WC at set times of the day and in a standard way. (Nappies are not used in the Institute.)

However banal a task this toilet-training may appear to be at first sight, it is no small problem for this athetoid group. The Conductor knows very well that from the point of view of Conductive Education it would be a serious mistake simply to sit the child on the pot. The child must sit down on it, beginning by climbing down from the slat-bed and pulling down its pyjama trousers. If it cannot do all this successfully it is missing an important opportunity for learning. Passing urine and faeces is a biological necessity and movements leading to the clean satisfaction of this need can be learned only through successful independent action.

This brings us to a question which no one can help asking. How can a 3-year-old severely athetoid child be expected to get up by itself from its bed and sit down on a pot? There is in fact a child like this in the group which we have chosen as our example. Let us see what it does.

On the previous day in the course of working through the 'task-series' and with guidance from the Conductor, this child had learned how to turn over on to its stomach. It uses this method and turns over on to its stomach now. In this position it is able to grasp two slats of the bed if the Conductor ensures that its wrists maintain a dorsal-flexion position. The child had also learned in the same way to push itself backwards on its stomach over the end of the slat-bed until its legs are hanging down. Since the child's legs are not long enough to reach down to the floor the Conductor puts a foot stool ready for them. When the soles of its feet reach the stool, knees are kept stretched and the child stands, leaning against the bed. Then the Conductor pushes a chair along to the side of the child, the back of which consists of ladder-like rungs. The child is able to transfer its grasp to a rung of the chair but the Conductor must still check the child's wrist position and so help it to grasp. Having pulled off its trousers already on the bed, by moving its grasp down from one rung to the next, the child is able to sit down on the potty. So it has carried out the tasks given to it and getting the child used to the pot in this way gives the Conductor, too, an opportunity for teaching the way towards orthofunction.

For the Conductor every single item in the daily schedule is part of an educational programme. This programme is geared to achieving serially imposed demands according to the level of performance reached by the group at that point and, within this, to the results achieved by individual children. So the Conductor must know exactly what the group and each individual member of it learned from the previous day's 'task-series', and bring that into use in the daily schedule in the widest variety of items possible. This requires the Conductor to devise an occupational plan which takes stock of the previous day's achievements by the members of her group.

The daily schedule considers every aspect of the life of the group in its system of biological and social demands. The children stand up after their toilet-training and the Conductor sees to it that in doing so they put down their heels as they have learned. They tear off their own lavatory paper and use it. They pull up their trousers and climb back on to their slat-beds, from which the Conductors have cleared away the bedding in the meantime.

This exceedingly detailed description is justified in the case of this athetoid group, because there are children here with such severe dysfunctions that these everyday requirements are often difficult for them to meet. However, they cope with these tasks in ways which they have already learned and sometimes with the help of the Conductor's detailed guidance ('facilitation').

Each child has his or her own chair in front of the bed, with a canvas satchel on it. The children take off their pyjamas, get their towels out of their satchels, and put them on the backs of their chairs. The Conductors now open the windows. 'Training' follows, which has an individual character for each group. The children roll about on their slat-beds, sit up, lie down, breathe in and out, and so on. Then the Conductors close the windows and the children rub themselves down with their towels. Those who are still incapable of doing so for themselves are rubbed briskly by the Conductors.

Next comes dressing. The children's clothes are there in front of them on their chairs, neatly arranged as they had placed them the previous evening. Tidiness with clothes is part of the system of Conductive Education. The schedule assigns time for arranging their clothes after undressing in the evening. Among other things success in teaching rests on arousing a wish to satisfy aesthetic needs and cleanliness.

In every daily schedule independent dressing (and undressing) is required from the beginning. In this group, too, they dress themselves, some lying down and others sitting up, just as they please. Dressing demands the performance of a number of interesting tasks from pulling on socks to finding the hole in a trouser leg and doing up buttons. Some children still need the Conductor's guidance in doing so. The children help the Conductor and each other and in this way friendly relationships are formed. The development of social relationships in a group of dysfunctionals is certainly no less important than it is for orthofunctionals.

After dressing the children slide down from their slat-beds and wash their faces and hands in basins placed on the beds. They take part in distributing the basins, too. There are some who are already able to go out into the bathroom to wash. Their soap-holders are in the satchels mentioned earlier and they take them out, open them, and pick up the soap. They have a nail-brush in the satchel and take that out, too. All these things are tasks to be done and they have to do them successfully, as well as drying themselves, combing their hair after washing, and replacing their washing utensils.

Next the group 'proceeds' to the breakfast room while their bedroom is being cleaned. This procession is an important and very demanding part of the daily schedule so it is dealt with in a special 'traffic' plan, which is dated so that any changes can be traced on review.

This traffic plan mentions every child by name with individual details of how to get there. The aim is for everyone to reach the breakfast table and for each child there is a definite way of going about it. For example, one will go barefoot, so that it is easier for him to watch his own foot position than if he wore shoes, while on the other hand the second child must be given correcting 'boots'. The third walks in shoes and is given a chair, pushing it along and stopping behind it at each step.

Every child takes part in the traffic movement using his own most expedient method of walking, attained by carrying out the previous day's task-series and put into use now. Support needed for walking, like the help given towards reaching this goal, changes every day. However, to put to use what they have learned is an irremissible requirement, so that action patterns previously created become established in the course of moving from place to place. Here once again a question arises. How can it be conceivable that severely dysfunctional individuals can move about of their own accord? Yet movement from place to place is part of the daily schedule from the outset, specifically provided for in the traffic plan. In any given case there will be some who are able to move about independently and others who have to be given various kinds of 'facilitation'. There will also be some that even in this way will take only a few steps in whatever is the most suitable manner for them on that day but, whatever the case, planning takes each of these problems into account. The child who goes most slowly and whose slat-bed is therefore nearest the door takes only a few steps, breakfasting for the time being at the nearest table too. All this calls for group organization and is included in the plan. Those who walk best will start first and those who need most guidance will start last.

One Conductor directs the entire group and sees to it that when the children walk through, they use what they have learned on the previous day with the appropriate verbal intending. The second Conductor gives whatever help is needed to enable individual children to take their place in the group.

The achievement of moving from place to place has great motivational force. For example, in the group we are discussing the 7-year-old L.M. a few mornings ago, with one hand on his slat-bed and supporting himself with his other hand on the back of a chair, excitedly called to his Conductor: 'Auntie Ildi, look I am a walker!' And in fact from that moment he was able to move about by using two chairs as supports.

Traffic planning is complemented by the Conductor's plan as to how the first arrivals in the breakfast room are going to occupy themselves. The children have free time here which must not be taken away from them but, on the contrary, they must be taught, practically without their noticing it, how to use their free time. Some will talk, others take a picture paper from their satchel and look at it, or listen to the radio, and so on. However, there may be some who do not know what to do because they have not yet learned how to play or to busy themselves with something spontaneously and the Conductor is prepared to give them tailor-made help if they need it. Spontaneous play, intelligently used free time, satisfies a biological need and so is very significant in strengthening the patterns learned and exercised as habits.

Breakfast is taken at tables or at slat-beds covered with a plastic sheet. Breakfast is another task! Indeed if we look more closely it is a whole sequence of tasks. Some children help, for example, in laying the tables, handing out the food, and so on.

The Conductors eat with the children, too. Every child must eat and drink independently, although naturally the severely dysfunctional children need many different facilitations to do so.

For example, there is the child who suffers an opisthotonus when using a spoon at lunchtime and intending to raise it to his mouth. A child like this must and can be taught to bend his hips and knees and bend his head forwards. Sometimes at first it is necessary to help him to hold the spoon or even to help in guiding it to his mouth. However, this is usually needed only at the beginning of the meal.

In the course of the meal progressively less and less facilitation has to be given, or it can be limited to supporting the arm in the position it has reached and waiting until the child himself moves it further. It is only necessary to guide the spoon up towards his mouth until it reaches it. However, the child himself must succeed somehow in getting the food in the spoon to his mouth. It is only by carrying out this task that the feedback circuit is completed reafferentatively and it is only in this way that both learning the activity and its progressive improvement can begin. On the other hand carrying out other items included in the daily schedule is a precondition for this performance. While doing the various series of tasks the child has been able to learn to bend his knees and his hips, to bend his head forwards, to stretch his arms, to place the soles of his feet flat on the floor, and so on.

Learning to drink is another task the solution of which may need a lot of preparatory work and to pass through several stages. In a specific case the crucial point may be to hold the head in a median position or to bend it forwards at the moment when the mug reaches the lips. There will be some who learn to drink from a two-handled mug and even this might be only a quarter-filled for them initially. With time the mug can be filled up more until it is possible to change over to a glass. This is a great delight for the child.

A meal not only provides nourishment but also a whole complex of requirements, giving many kinds of opportunities for learning. While children are eating they can learn the names of the various foods (for instance at breakfast at the Institute to say dripping, egg, liver paste, cheese, butter, paprika, and so on). We generally have two kinds of jam at breakfast, yellow apricot and red cherry. In choosing between them the children are learning to distinguish and name two colours as well.

After breakfast their task is to brush their teeth and small basins are handed out for this. Each child brings out his own tooth-brush, wipes his face with a wet flannel, and dries it with his towel.

After breakfast, they go back to their own rooms ('traffic') in the way described above. By the time all the members of this group have assembled and taken their places on their slat-beds it is about nine o'clock. Any child who has dirtied his clothes in feeding himself changes them.

In our group it is time for the first task-series, the 'floor' or lying task-series. This task-series is always to be found in the daily schedule of every group, like the other kinds of task-series and 'traffic' from place to place. Task-series are extremely important, consequently a special plan is prepared for each one of them. But before we describe their structure and significance we will go on briefly with the daily schedule.

The lying task-series has lasted for one hour and next comes 'conditioning' (toilet-training), washing hands, and the 10-o'clock snack. After this a standing-and-walking task-series lasts for one-and-a-half hours, then 'conditioning' again, washing hands, and lunch, for which the schedule allows an hour.

The 10-o'clock snack, lunch, tea, and supper are all taken in the group's own room. This room is the dormitory but when the slat-beds are cleared away against the wall, the space becomes a work room. When some of the beds are covered with formica sheets to use as tables it is a dining room too. None of this is a rigid rule. The children may also take meals sitting round 'tables' (slat-beds) in the corridor outside their room.

After lunch on this particular day the group we are describing has another series of tasks lasting for one hour, followed by 'conditioning' (toileting), washing hands, and tea. In the meantime, before being relieved by the afternoon Conductors, the morning Conductors have written up their observations in the diary. By noting them down they keep the incoming Conductors informed of their most recent findings and with this help education continues as set down in the schedule for the day. Tea is followed by a lying task-series lasting for one hour, then toileting, washing hands, and preparation for supper at 7 pm. After supper the children clean their teeth, wash their feet, or shower or bathe. A Conductor makes up the beds, takes temperatures, and enters her comments in the diary for the use of the morning Conductors, sees to 'conditioning', and lights out at 9 pm. That is what a sample daily routine with this athetoid group looks like.

This routine brings order into the children's lives, accustoming them to a methodical life up to the standard of the requirements for cleanliness and hygiene.

The daily schedule is not a rigid rule but fits into a weekly programme. There are alternating weekly schedules, Week A and Week B, as regards nursery and school activities, in the mornings for Week A and in the afternoons for Week B on every second day. In line with this, the group shown has a different routine on the next day, in that breakfast is followed, not by a lying task-series, but by a hand task-series, and after the 10-o'clock snack a standing-and-walking task-series prepares the way for a nursery activity which will be environmental knowledge and singing according to the schedule. At 3 pm the nursery children have hand task-series to prepare for using pencils, then drawing activities until tea, and a hand task-series at 4.30 is followed by a standing-and-walking task-series at 5.30 pm.

At the same time, from 3 pm to 6.30 pm, the school group has arithmetic, reading, writing, environmental knowledge, and practice in dexterity.

Specific examples like those mentioned never form a rigid or inflexible structure but are adjusted to suit the level of development of a particular group and even of an individual child, keeping always in line with general biological and social requirements. Activities forming the daily schedule are co-ordinated and the order followed by task-series is determined in such a way that members of a group may become able to satisfy the general requirements relevant for their ages. Spastic children, for instance, begin the day with lying task-series, while some athetoid groups start with hand task-series. The various task-series are interconnected in the timetable, complement and build on each other, while their duration varies according to the character and endurance capacity of the group; for example, in one group the standing-and-walking task-series lasts for twenty minutes and in another for an hour and a half. Again, task-series prepare and complement activities in the daily routine; for instance seated tasks are always either preceded or followed by activities involving a greater degree of movement. Consequently before and after seated school or nursery activity the daily schedule sets a lying or standing-and-walking task-series.

Weekly schedules are not rigid systems either. A 'sequel' to certain types of activity is introduced from time to time. School work is interspersed with study excursions, or with activities of topical interest, ceremonies, celebrations like children's birthdays and name-days, visits to football matches, and so on. There are groups for whom special periods are reserved for playing flutes and other musical activities, while other groups have times for letter-writing, and so on. There may be individual differences: for instance in the time allotted for a standing-and-walking task-series, some may process as far as the bathroom, some to other rooms, or even stroll in the street. Then again, some have a daily schedule which gives a great deal of time to work, while others may have special times temporarily allocated for sleeping, resting, or being out in the fresh air.

However varied the daily routines may be, they are all part of a continuous, unhurried, and smooth-flowing way of life from waking up until lights out. Built in to this are both the fulfilment of inescapable biological requirements without which there can be no survival (such as the need to eat), and also social demands according to the child's age, where it is not enough to consume food but certain proprieties must be observed when doing so. Different demands for getting about independently are made on a 3-year-old than on a 13-year-old. Conductive Education totally accepts the general requirements appropriate for each particular age. Indeed it is precisely on these that we base the teaching of procedures leading to their fulfilment.

Then again, Conductive Education does not restrict teaching to particular activities but covers the entire day and all its occupations. Important lessons can be taught even in satisfying the simplest biological needs: for instance, what has been learned earlier about squatting down, standing up, dressing, undressing, can be reinforced in the course of 'conditioning'. In preparing for the activities prescribed in a daily schedule a Conductor takes as her starting point not only the goals of nursery or school teaching schedules, and not only those of task-series but also to the fullest possible extent endeavours to combine the application of all the opportunities for teaching. During school activity she provides exercise for the skills learned in the task-series, for instance, when children put up their hands to answer their names or stand up to answer questions. In the course of a great many other activities that figure in the schedule children can exercise skills learned in school work. Free time is spent usefully, too, when the children are playing but the Conductor has the satisfaction of seeing that they are practising what they have learned in walking, talking, and a thousand other ways.

For instance, a nursery 'literature' lesson follows the same pattern as in other nurseries. The children discuss a poem about Santa Claus, adding appropriate gestures, and acting the part. The Conductor not only prepares for this occupation like a teacher in a nursery school for orthofunctional children, but also carefully plans the integration of various action-patterns developed in the task-series. It is precisely these moments in the tasks that have the greatest effect in stabilizing orthofunctional activity patterns and so each day's schedule becomes smooth-flowing, economical, and productive and the children's increasingly balanced and harmonious lives guarantee their further planned progress.

Then again, while our school's instruction conforms with the curricular requirements obtaining generally, it is not confined within the rigid limits of a school year so that when planning school activities too a Conductor is able to find sufficient time for applying the principles of Conductive Education. The daily schedule enables the children to practise at different times what they have learned from school activities. There are always some children who go for a time across to a general school nearby which co-operates with the Institute, so that they can learn with the children there. They usually acquit themselves well.

By setting standards appropriate to the children's ages and by ensuring at the same time that the children carry out their tasks by their own efforts, the process of orthofunctional general adaptation is initiated quickly even where a child's condition could be described as severely dysfunctional.

This explains the seeming paradox which catches the attention of every visitor to the Institute straight away. They can see in the corridor very severely dysfunctional children who are bustling about good-temperedly, tirelessly, and cheerfully. They might happen to come across, say, a little boy of 7, who moves along pushing a chair and repeating aloud: 'I put my weight on my right foot, I step with my left foot. I put my weight on my left foot, I step with my right foot', counting up to five with each step. If the visitor happens to ask, 'And which room are you from, young man?', the answer will be self-assured, perhaps 'I work in Room 9'. So the daily schedule sets a unified system of requirements which can be characterized, most clearly, in educational terms.

All through there is that regularity in the allocation of time so characteristic of normal life and forming an important educational goal on the way to a dynamic lifestyle. Items in the daily routine are determined by both general and special educational aims. Our general educational aims can be summarized as education for activity, work, and life in the community. In the daily schedule it is vital to ensure that every child becomes self-sufficient, learning to define his aims consciously, seeking out ways of achieving them so as to become independent and, finally, by participating in the mutually co-operative relationships, is able to become an active member of that community.

Our general educational aims do not differ from those prescribed for any other teaching institution, but unless they are consciously pursued no educational system can be fruitful, for they ensure the development of a well-balanced personality. To achieve them our daily schedules need to be planned to promote an appropriate happy atmosphere and this again is in agreement with general teaching principles.

Our special educational goals stem from the nature of dysfunction. Their basic purpose is to develop orthofunctional habits. Their form is determined by the general level of the group and within this by the level of performance of each individual. On attainment of special aims through performing task-series rests the achievement of the general aims incorporated in our daily schedules. Setting these special targets determines the teaching patterns which lead to their achievement.

It will be seen that the various activities of a day's routine form a unified whole from an educational point of view and here we must emphasize what is perhaps the most important feature of Conductive Education, namely that there is no single event in a day which does not serve its general educational purposes. Every activity for our dysfunctionals must be shaped so as to link in with orthofunctional teaching aims and principles.

In the next section we shall see how task-series ensure the learning of performance patterns to lead to the achievement of practical aims in the daily schedule. By satisfying demands considered either unattainable for dysfunctionals or not taken seriously enough as a general rule, these children succeed in acquiring orthofunctional skills and learn to combine lower level elementary skills. They even become capable of mastering a school curriculum, too. About 94 per cent of children discharged from the Institute are able to follow the curriculum of a general school and only 6 per cent of them will require special remedial or extra tuition.

14 The task-series

Task-series have a very significant place in the daily schedule and in order to understand their role we must start with the unimpaired condition.

Carrying out all sorts of activity in normal life seems to represent achievement only at a definite stage or at a particular level. 'Vegetative' functions alone are associated with the monotonous repetition of certain actions, but true orthofunction is as a whole a more dynamically developing and progressive process of adaptation, which encompasses an immense range of actions. In children, this not only means a capacity for endurance which increases with age and for satisfying new biological requirements, but also requires them to master tasks imposed by society to an ever increasing degree. These demands may include the continuing age-related acquisition of information now obligatory in general schools.

School is, properly speaking, only a continuation of those studies which a healthy child seemingly undertakes practically of his own accord and without any special programme. By the time a child enters school he is self-sufficient. He gets about independently and has developed various skills on which his 'fitness for school' depends. This is a stage of development usually lacking to a greater or lesser extent in relatively severe cases of dysfunction. At the usual age for starting school many of them have not yet learned to stand or walk independently or to talk.

Conductive Education's task-series teach the performance of tasks learned spontaneously by healthy children. They can be of help to adults, where many capacities have been lost which were once acquired long ago. In such cases Conductive Education makes it possible to learn them afresh.

Every task-series is constructed out of several tasks. Individually they are not simple exercises nor defined movements in an anatomical or physiological sense, but intentional activities in a biological sense. We referred earlier to the difference between actions made in a biological sense and movements as seen by anatomy or physiology. So now let us look at this question from the point of view of constructing a task-series.

To begin with a practical example – perhaps you are just at this moment leaning on your left elbow reading this, and let us suppose that you are holding a cigarette in your right hand, just flicking off the ash. There is no anatomist alive who could give an exact picture of which of your muscle fibres are contracting or relaxing at this moment. Still less would it be possible to trace the participation of individual nerve cells in organizing these movements by including the impulses travelling along the axons and all the excitatory processes at the synapses.

Biologically, however, all this is quite simple. You are sitting, leaning on one elbow, reading, and smoking. These activities presuppose the co-operation of numerous nerve cells, and based on them, the co-ordinated contractions of appropriate muscles. In fact, nervous-system functions provide the background for biological activity, with a social activity in this case and are even more complicated than we have stated, because the performance of these activities depends on the collaboration of the entire organism, of complex organic systems which maintain your metabolism, and so on.

The complicated organizing function of your nervous system at this moment is serving one principal aim – to read. Incidentally you are also sitting and smoking a cigarette, but biologically your principal aim is to read and the two minor aims of sitting and smoking are subordinate to that. As far as the functioning of your nervous system is concerned the most comprehensive circuit in the hierarchy of regulating circuits is taking care of that reading. For the moment sitting and smoking may be subordinate but this subordination is not permanent. You could also read standing up, walking, or lying down, while smoking is merely a completely incidental and indeed harmful activity, only associated with reading by chance.

Let us take it that at this moment you are sitting down. This activity includes, for example, a particular positioning of the head which in turn determines the functioning of a number of neck muscles and the fibres contracting within them.

We may speak in this sense of systems accomplishing fairly

comprehensive purposes or, bearing in mind your intention, of actions. You intend both the action realized through the most comprehensive circuit and some of the less comprehensive ones subordinate to that. The lower we go towards the finer details included here the more varied these may be and the less aware of them you will be.

Again, you could tell me how your feet are placed for instance but only if you start to pay attention to them. We sit in various positions and change them almost continuously without bothering about them. Actions realized through comprehensive control systems have this kind of orthofunctional ease precisely because so wide a variety of possibilities is open for them.

Every action serves a particular biological purpose. In the case of a new-born baby, action leading to the goal of nutrition is comparatively simple: to suck. With a little imagination we can trace how in the course of time obtaining food, using eating utensils, cooking, and even producing food were all built up on one another by the goal of nutrition.

For dysfunctionals, however, even subordinate goals such as sitting, so easy to do for orthofunctionals, can often be such complicated targets as to seem as good as impossible. Very often a dysfunctional person cannot even cope successfully with tasks on a still lower level, of which orthofunctionals would not even be conscious. Monrad-Krohn quite rightly emphasized that some details often become significant when they are not there. It is the fact that they are lacking which points up their existence.

In constructing a task-series it is essential to go down through the hierarchy of goals until we reach an activity consisting of goals achieved already and so then the task-series will build up from actions which each dysfunctional can carry out successfully. These actions form the individual tasks and it is by achieving their stated or 'verbally (rhythmically) intended' aim that a dysfunctional person is able to learn the control leading to that action.

We appear to have strayed into a vicious circle. A dysfunctional learns to carry out tasks which he can do already! But in fact his ability is only potential and he will need the Conductor's guidance to be able to understand exactly what that action is and how best to do it. When the Conductor is constructing a task-series she adjusts it to the group's performance level and by taking into account the differences between individuals sees to it that everybody achieves the target set. It is precisely through this process of ensuring that a task is understood and carried out successfully that it becomes possible to learn that action and carry it out in a fully orthofunctional way.

This action serves primarily to develop a habit without which a whole sequence of more comprehensive actions could not be realized. Actions of this kind are the general aim in constructing task-series. The goal is generalized in the sense that attention must always be paid to achieving it through a very wide range of movements and this is just what is taught through a task-series. One example of a generalized goal like this might be to learn to grasp with an outstretched arm. This is an action in general use in everyday life. You may be stretching your arm out to reach for a cigarette and you would put it down in the same way, or you would stretch out your arm to pick up a pen in order to write a note. Such habitual activities constantly underlie everything we do. A dysfunctional individual carries them out as his dysfunction permits. He must make it his general aim to learn to do them in an orthofunctional way and so develop orthofunctional habits.

Secondly, the action may serve to achieve some momentary purpose like clasping the hands, supination, grasping as such, sitting, distinguishing right from left, co-ordinating eyes and hands, or putting a hand on one's neck, and so on. Learning partial actions like these, varying with the dysfunction, leads to the mastery of many much more comprehensive goals.

In constructing a task-series, again it is always essential to start by considering the character of the group. According to the type of dysfunction orthofunctions must be developed which represent defined general goals.

As an example let us consider a group of children characterized by dystonic twisting of the trunk and head, large involuntary movements in arms and legs, alternating upward jerks of legs and feet, and a peculiarity that stretching the legs volitionally is followed by adduction and an inward rotating increase of tone. The general aim of the task-series must be for every child to be able to lie straight, to be capable of controlling the involuntary movements of hands and arms, to stretch and part his legs and keep them abducted. In another dysfunctional group the general aim of a task-series is that the child should be able to sustain the dorsal-flexion position of his wrists. Keeping the feet straight might be another general goal of this kind.

For instance, a diplegic child learns as a general aim to keep his outstretched legs abducted in every position. In the following detail taken from his task-series he has to achieve it during and after turning over on to his stomach. At this point the entire group is lying supine, legs stretched and abducted. The children intend verbally:

'I stretch my right hand back.' The Conductor is teaching this particular child that he has done this correctly only when his arm is stretched back beside his ear, his elbow and fingers staying straight and his legs which he has previously stretched and parted, remain in that position.

After this the children's next partial task is:

'I stretch it down again', then:

'I stretch my left hand back.'
'I stretch both my hands back.'

'I clap my hands.' Before the handclapping, the Conductor shows them how to clap hands behind the head by demonstrating that the hands must be held apart behind the head before bringing them together to clap. While these partial tasks are being done, it is essential to ensure all the way through that legs and feet are stretched and maintaining an abducted position.

The sequence of tasks continues by raising first the right foot, then the left, introduced with verbal intending and rhythmic counting. The child we have chosen as an example is not yet able to keep his raised leg stretched out and so, by way of facilitation, the Conductor places a small chair on the slat-bed. The child puts his heel on this, now intending, 'I stretch it out.' His knee straightens out.

Next he has to take his outstretched leg down from the chair, slowly, and replace it on the bed, taking care that his legs remain stretched out and apart, while his feet are held pointing upwards. Meanwhile, every member of the group stretches arms, hands, and fingers.

Now every child in the group stretches one arm backwards while raising and stretching the leg on the same side. The little boy mentioned earlier puts his heel on the small chair. Then they have to bring that arm down to the side, at the same time replacing the raised leg on the slat-bed, legs still stretched and abducted. Keeping the legs apart is very important as a general goal, too, so now the children intend aloud, 'I put my legs down, keeping my legs apart.'

After raising one arm and leg together, they learn to turn on to one side or on to their stomachs and in fact the general purpose of this task-series was to teach the group of children to hold their legs stretched and abducted while also turning on to their stomachs.

The goal of the part of the task-series introduced here was not to turn on to the stomach (although the children have arrived at this point) but to learn how to keep their legs stretched and abducted while they did so. This task-series includes many other partial tasks, such as gripping, hand co-ordination, sitting, and ultimately standing. And from all these the general goal is that they all in any circumstances shall be able to put into practice the intention of stretching and abducting their legs. With this the way opens up to a whole series of goals which had been blocked previously from their lack of these particular orthofunctions.

The same partial tasks acquire a different meaning with any difference in their general aim. For instance, to turn on to the stomach can be a preparation for the child's gripping with out-stretched arms the rung of a ladderback chair which has been placed in front of him. In this case the general goal would be to learn how to grasp with an outstretched arm in many different contexts.

So you can see that the individual details, identical elements, of a task-series can have different significance in different contexts and that a general goal is merely one factor in constructing it. Each of these task-series is composed algorithmically in the sense that each partial task facilitates the performance of the next and so leads on, step by step, to a goal not immediately within the capability of patients with a specific dysfunction.

What is this goal? Where does a task-series end? What daily result does it have?

There could be no greater mistake than to suppose that a task-series slowly progresses over weeks or months towards separate goals to meet biological and social necessities like independent eating, standing, walking, even activities towards learning to write. In fact the opposite is true. Each day task-series facilitate the satisfaction of all the social and biological requirements comprised in the daily schedule. Day by day the level of achievement required by the schedule rises and indeed is bound to do so when task-series are worked through. This is their justification.

We have seen that the daily schedule encompasses the simplest biological needs, eating, drinking, urinating, and so on, the social requirements that relate to them, and even the educational curriculum of nursery or school programmes appropriate for a child's age.

Through the algorithmic guidance of task-series, ortho-functions develop. They become habitual and so facilitate the carrying out of routine tasks. For example, even to eat independently can be very difficult at first and only possible with a great deal of facilitation in any particular case, but once achieved, the actions leading up to it make it into something learned and established. Subsequent task-series then further the results achieved. This is reinforced by fulfilling social-biological requirements and the process of learning develops reafferentatively in this way.

In this process task-series are the paths leading to ortho-functional activity and their use in the daily schedule consolidates the results, the performance of an understood task.

Therefore within a task-series specific algorithms are always provisional, gaining their significance from being part of a control system (regulation) that leads to a comprehensive goal. The algorithms prepare for the daily schedule to be followed and lead on from satisfying what is, in the broadest sense, a social or biological requirement, to include learning to write, for instance, or nursery school games.

Learning a particular orthofunctional accomplishment is built into our general adaptative processes by shaping, adjusting it to satisfy real demands. In the course of working through the task-series the range grows both of orthofunctional positions and orthofunctional ways of carrying them out. The Conductor does everything she can to bring up these orthofunctional elements in other periods in the daily schedule and slot them into the action. The general level of performance improves in this way and the new accomplishments are reinforced.

We have emphasized so far two aspects of constructing task-series. The first is the general goal, that is teaching some particular orthofunctional habit to replace a dysfunctional one, and the second is how the results gained through task-series can be brought into the activities based on the biological and social requirements of the daily schedule. To put them into practice in the daily schedule appears strictly speaking to be the ultimate goal of the task-series. Their ultimate aim, to accomplish these biological tasks, is met increasingly.

On the other hand defining the task-series general goals means that, through the hierarchical regulatory systems which organize activity, we can arrive at the individual actions used to carry out very many tasks. Previously performed in a dysfunctional way or ineffectually, many very different and more comprehensive actions have been robbed of any success.

To turn now to a third aspect of the task-series: it is a universal characteristic of orthofunctions that very diverse solutions can be used to achieve different goals. Let us take an example at random. We can wash ourselves in a bath, a basin, or under a shower. We have to undress. We have first of all to go to the bathroom, take out the soap, the towel and the more we go into detail the more of these subgoals we can name. They increase in number and variety as we break down the principal goal of washing. This is an important feature of orthofunction. A great number of variations become almost incomprehensible if we analyse them in too great detail. Consider a tennis match. The public registers happily that a player has just returned the ball to his opponent but let us try to describe in simple terms how many possibilities there are for this activity to lead to that result! The security and freedom of orthofunctionals lies precisely in the fact that we have so many possible ways of going about what we have to do and that the organization of the nervous system is capable of using activity patterns (stereotypes) in a most dynamic way. Orthofunctionals are capable of achieving their goals in many very different ways by means which can hardly be calculated in advance. Dysfunctionals have to be taught how to do this.

We bring in this aspect when constructing task-series by linking the separate tasks with the most varied body positions and different functions necessary for achieving the greatest possible wealth of variety. This corresponds to the cerebral functions referred to earlier. Apparently single functions are composed of relatively independent partial functions and when the brain is damaged the same components are present or absent in different contexts. The dysfunctional person has to learn how to carry out every task successfully lying on his back or side, sitting down, while walking, running, and jumping, and so on. Simpler tasks are followed by more complex ones and geared up towards the end of the task-series. And as the level of the problem solving rises we make the task-series increasingly complex and demanding. By combining the particular tasks with speech, song, and so on, a varied association in task accomplishment is created. All this in the end leads to individual partial activities acquiring an extra-ordinarily Protean capacity. Put in another way, the capacity for general co-ordination is greatly strengthened.

This aspect is put into practice in constructing task-series. In a given case perhaps raising the foot would not simply be repeated as an exercise, but would be combined with bending the head forward, sometimes raising the arms, stretching forward, sitting up, turning, and so on. Then subsequent tasks in the task-series are made more difficult, for example by combining raising the foot with stretching the knee. This combination is linked into the activities described already. Advances are made by learning the orthofunctional element given as the general goal in the task-series and by developing a capability for co-ordination. The range of activity extends more and more and the dysfunctionals' operative capacity increases progressively. Consequently, a task-series is never restricted to the same body position. If a lying task-series comes next in the schedule, it will begin with the dysfunc-tionals sitting on the chair and clambering up under their own strength to lie down on their slat-beds. The Conductor never puts them there.

So they stand up from a sitting position and then clamber up on to the slat-bed to lie in a horizontal position. The lying task-series also vary the horizontal lying position itself in as many ways as possible. The dysfunctional children lie on their backs, on their sides, on their stomachs. They roll and turn so that their head comes over to where their feet were just before and crawl. Continuing the lying tasks they get up on to their knees, sit up and finally, sliding down from the slat-bed, stand up. So the lying task series begins and ends with standing up, and, if they have done it correctly, standing up at the end is considerably easier than it was at the beginning. This affects the children. As a motivating force it has a stimulating effect on the whole of their activity.

Similar principles are put into effect in drawing up the sitting task-series. This includes bends, turns, and changes of leg position in great variety and always starts and finishes with standing up, as it begins. Not only does the standing-and-walking task-series include standing and walking, but also sitting down on the ground, standing up and carrying various objects, and so on.

On the basis of all these considerations, just as we have referred to the learning of a capability for general co-ordination as one of the task-series goals, we also stress changes in posture and acquiring the capacity for activity carried out in various bodily positions.

Accordingly task-series must be constructed in such a way that not only must the specified goals be put into effect at the same time and closely linked but also modified practically from day to day, keeping pace with the results already obtaining. This means that more and more elements are built into the task-series which are important for orthofunctional biological or educational requirements. For example, in the lying and hand task-series at this stage tasks are linked which require relatively finely directed actions contributing to larger purposive activities.

In constructing a task-series we emphasize too that due attention is given to the special character of particular groups. In the case of hemiplegics, for instance, accent is placed on abducting the arms, stretching elbows and fingers, grasping, fine finger movements, bending hips and knees, and on the dorsal flexion of feet and hands.

The task-series for diplegics stresses the abduction of the legs in any position, dorsiflexion of the feet, knee stretching, and bending the knees. In the athetoids' task-series very close attention is paid to directed movements and holding a posture.

We mentioned that the daily timetable flows smoothly or in other words the aims of Conductive Education operate even in leisure time. The different occupations harmonize and this continuity of purpose is characteristic of both task-series and daily schedules. Song, music, recitation, conversation, play can be built organically into the task-series. All this is very important for maintaining attention.

Finally, through task-series dysfunctionals learn how to tackle a task in the widest sense. They begin to understand what a task will require and become very persevering both in seeking solutions and goals. This is another factor in considering our general educational aims. Again, task-series in their general co-ordinative capacity can include the broadest possible range of items of information, recognizing any problems that arise, shaping procedures to think it through in finding a solution, matching speech with activity and conscious action.

According to the schedule each particular task-series can last between twenty and ninety minutes. These wide limits show that there is no rigid rule here either. Task-series are allotted about six hours a day. The day is divided up into morning and afternoon and school or nursery school occupations cut in to it, too. Each particular task-series consists of between twenty and thirty partial tasks. The length of time planned both for the separate tasks and for the task-series is determined partly by the group's tempo and partly by its members' attention span.

When a task is still new and there has not been enough practice in learning, carrying out each particular task needs more time. On the other hand the fact that the task is new and difficult to do increases interest and if attention should flag the Conductor has to turn to another task or intercalate a game, or song, for instance. She prepares for this beforehand too and it is not just a matter of reawakening attention but also of seeing that whatever has just been learned is put to practical use.

True, a task-series is designed for the entire group, but in

Conductive Education it will not even remotely resemble the uniform exercises used elsewhere. The common tasks in a task-series simply present the members of a group with similar problems, but the children each achieve an individual solution for them and individual differences may be very great. The important thing for their Conductor is to see that they are all successful in working through the number of tasks originally set out for them. She has to guide them by giving any facilitations they need.

The tasks in a series are completed when a child achieves his goals by conscious effort and experiences the result. The child must realize that he has done it by his own efforts and can do it again whenever he wants to.

The group's working together is an important general condition in Conductive Education and again is planned for. For instance, if a group is working through a task-series in sitting, there will be some who are not capable of sitting. Since the goal here is to do the tasks properly and not sitting as such, these children may be allowed to do the exercise lying on their backs. Or again, slowing the tempo would make it possible for the most severely dysfunctional patients to keep up with the group. To give an example: the detail of a task-series is:

They count 'One . . . to five',   they sit up and clap their
hands behind their heads then
clapping four more times
slowly lie down. They repeat
this several times.

Meanwhile when the group sits up for the first time its most severely handicapped member remains lying and stretches his arms forward with clasped hands. When the group sits up for the second time he sits up with his hands stretched forward. When the group lies down he stretches his arms above his head and lies down with them. The severely handicapped individual executes the group's task at a slow tempo and in a modified form.

This is the way in which the common goal set for a task-series reduces to a common denominator activities which seem very different at first sight. The Conductor is always clear what it is that the group's conscious achievement must be. She makes the group understand this too and it is only when the goal is achieved that a task can be said to be accomplished.

The goal is always an orthofunctional solution. Orthofunction, however, is an ambiguous concept concerned both with satisfying biological (social) requirements and continuing the development of adaptive learning. That is why an orthofunctional solution must always be relative. Achieving a goal must be measured against the level reached by a particular child and yesterday's result for that child is not good enough for today. Each individual in the group has a different level of performance and that is why each child should work out the problem in the best way he can. This is what it means to be orthofunctional.

This aspect makes it possible to form a group from children who have different kinds of dysfunction and use the same task-series for them all. The general purpose for one child in a given case might be to stretch his legs and keep them abducted while turning over, while another's will be to support himself on his hand while turning. The Conductor sets a conscious goal for each child and adjusts both guidance and facilitations accordingly.

Another essential component in constructing a task-series is to plan the positioning of the group beforehand. Children with similar problems and requiring similar help must be put next to one another. A less active child or one who still has difficulty in understanding what is wanted would be put next to an active child or one who understands it very well, so that he can imitate his neighbour, watching him to see the right thing to do. Less attentive children are put among the more attentive. All the facilitational tools should be ready to hand. The Conductor directing the group's work must be placed so as to have a clear view of the group. The other Conductor gets ready any facilitations that will be needed.

Task-series planned with all these considerations in mind are given a title (hand, lying, grasping, and so on) and a date, with an indication of the group (type of dysfunction, age) for which it was designed. The particular task details are noted on the left-hand side, while on the right are notes referring to the ways in which the task can be done, the facilitations and organization of the group. The Conductor gives the children partial tasks as goals and the children verbally intend them in the first person. These intended goals will not coincide with the general and specific goals mentioned in relation to task-series construction. It is the

Conductor's task to define them in several ways, assessing relative individual achievements and occasionally modifying the goal to be intended. But the verbally intended goal must always be completely achieved by the dysfunctionals at whatever their performance level is orthofunctionally. For this the Conductor must arouse interest in the task first of all, then explain it, drawing attention to possible mistakes and finally telling the children what form the verbal intending will have.

Each member of the group intends the task aloud and sets about working it through. This is the first time that this particular activity becomes consciously intendable and on subsequent occasions it is always requisite to introduce the same task solution with planning the activity and thinking it through consciously. Consciousness is linked with the operation of the cerebral hemispheres and this is the same as saying that one is succeeding in building in to the function of the nervous system whatever pattern is necessary for goal attainment, to be controlled by the most effective and comprehensive member of the regulatory hierarchy.

The process of verbal intention can only be understood in relation to reafferentation and the principle of successive approximation. At first verbal characterization of a goal often defines what must be achieved only sketchily or not at all. For instance, it is no advantage for a dysfunctional to repeat after the Conductor the goal characterization 'slant it upwards' when he does not know how to draw a line obliquely upwards – it would be totally unintelligible for him. At most it might indicate dimly some direction. (How many people are there who know that 'bay' is the colour of a horse but do not know what colour it is!)

That is why before the verbal intention the Conductor must get the children to understand the activity in a practical way by demonstration. They still do not understand perceptively what the aim is but by managing to do it successfully after verbally intending it, the children gradually learn both the intention and its meaning. It becomes conscious intending in fact. A verbal goal is characterized in such a way as to prepare for and begin an action at the same time. And as the solution of the task becomes more and more orthofunctional, so the child's consciousness (perception) of it becomes increasingly refined. Correspondingly in the regulatory circuits for verbally intended activity that conscious intention itself becomes more and more defined and the activity increasingly orthofunctional.

It is possible that speech itself can begin in just this way, if a dysfunctional child cannot speak yet and then the sounds which are still unintelligible at the start of intending gradually become clearer.

If a task is not carried out properly because a child still does not understand how to do it correctly the Conductor never blames or rebukes him and especially does not scold him, but she creates circumstances that will help his activity to become effective (facilitation). Then the Conductor makes sure that he notices how successful he has been, perhaps like this: 'Now you are keeping your knees straight and in this way you are going to be able to stand!' The child soon learns to monitor and check up on his own progress.

We emphasized earlier that the daily schedule encompasses the task-series and this has to be kept in mind when drawing them up because the Conductor must see that they fit in with the other activities of the daily schedule. So the Conductor prepares an accomplishment plan each day for the task-series. Apart from the details mentioned already, this plan states the educational goal or goals for a given occupation, how to make it interesting (motivation), lists any equipment necessary, states how results will be evaluated and confirmed biologically, with practical application for the results achieved (that is consolidating what has been learned, for example within the framework of another activity or play). In one case, for instance, a Conductor put a goal attained into practical use by playing the popular 'Shopping Game'. In introducing this game the Conductor referred to what had been learned in the last lesson about the environment and linked it in this way with items of knowledge learned previously. As motivation she said: 'We are going shopping.' She had got various 'purchasable' toys ready for the game, green vegetables, fruit, shopping basket, and discs to serve as money.

At the beginning of the game they used a counting-out rhyme to decide who was to be the seller and who the buyer. Then the group stood up and sang a song about shopping. The shopper, making use of the walking skill he had just mastered, set out 'to shop' and was learning how to behave when shopping, too. Paying, he learned to count from one to five or to ten. Taking out the 'money' he also practised standing without support. In ways like this the children learn to put to very varied use skills learned from task-series. It is quite possible for a child who cannot stand at all well yet outside a contextual situation to stand very well busily counting out money.

The productive result of the task-series within the daily schedule is principally reafferentated and consolidated through being put to practical use. So the degree of facilitation needed grows less from day to day and the execution of the partial tasks quickens up to merge into the more comprehensive goals. Over a period of time it is enough to intend further goals and these can become attainable directly. In this way intermediate goals lose their conscious status becoming automatic. This is a secondary process, however. Automated details can be called into consciousness at any time and intended.

By applying in the daily schedule habits learned through task-series, the individual's sphere of activity widens all the time. This forms the most important motivation in working through task-series and explains the 'indefatigability' of our pupils.

15 Follow-up

Transforming the various kinds of dysfunction into orthofunctions follows its course like any other learning programme. But while more usual teaching programmes strive after educational goals unattainable in themselves if the corresponding educational programme is not completed, the goals in a learning programme for dysfunctionals are both attained spontaneously in any case and universal.

Task-series consequently lower the level of particular educational goals to below those generally pursued while their ultimate purposes coincide.

However there is no difference in principle between learning an orthofunctional activity and acquiring what is taught in schools. Conductive Education differs from education in the usual sense of the word only in extending its teaching goals to orthofunctions as well.

Separate tasks in a task-series are relatively independent units forming the material to be learned, so that in carrying out a task-series the Conductor gets a child to work through the material in the individual units. This working through makes a task familiar to the child so that he is able to find the way to solve it that best suits him. For this purpose task-series can be modified and broken down further in such a way that the separate parts serve to analyse more complex solutions. The result of completing a task-series that the child experiences should be used in new forms of occupation and the daily schedule always gives an opportunity to do so. Results from the task-series are consolidated through new activities and the children become keen to go on to further stages in the programme.

Task-series' results are the formation of orthofunctional skills and skills systems and with them a capacity for using them in combination. The entire orthofunctional learning process takes place in a way well known in education, from understanding a task through thinking it out even better, estimating correctly how consistent it is in relation to the individual's environment, completing it, and monitoring the result.

The same thing applies in Conductive Education task-series as the mathematician Polya[1] recommended for mathematical problems:

1 Define the task
2 Prepare a plan for accomplishing it
3 Carry out your plan
4 Check your result.

As goals are achieved, a given task-series will need to be systematically altered, as the tempo in carrying out the tasks quickens and even becomes automatic. When this happens the goals of the task-series have to be changed to raise the standard, for example, by extending the range of environmental conditions in which they should be achieved. Someone able to walk about quite well on a smooth surface will learn to get about on a rough surface, a staircase, or even on the decks of moving vehicles, and so on.

Again, task-series must be changed from time to time where the learning process has slowed down and the task-series has somehow become a matter of habit. A new task-series will stimulate attention and, while the patterns of solutions learned may be shaken, not only will they return with the achievement of the new goals, but also the learning itself acquires a new impetus.

Task-series must be changed, too, after each set of results arrived at. It is obvious that one must reduce those facilitations which have become superfluous and changes like this happen every day. Task-series have to be reshaped entirely if a group develops enough to change the Conductive goals set in the series, for example by setting a new general goal. To conform with this, because of changes in the lengths of time required and in order to put into use straight away what has been achieved by the task-series, changes have to be made in the daily schedule too.

We know that the daily schedule is a system which meets biological and social requirements and now we would like to point out that the task-series and the daily schedule must link smoothly together. Since the group's progress has meant a change in the task-

1 Polya, G. (1957) *How to Solve it*, Princeton, NJ: Princeton University Press.

series then that must be brought into harmony with the whole of the daily schedule.

A follow-up of this kind is a serious event which group members and Conductor prepare for. Together they assess the results achieved, define the goals as necessary, and look forward to the results that might be expected.

Elements forming a new task-series may deviate from the previous ones in sequence, rhythm, manner of intending, or starting position. New facilitational equipment or methods may be used. There might have to be a change in grouping the children, sometimes in the composition of a group and in the way the room is arranged, too.

On this basis, tasks may evolve that it would have been impossible to manage earlier. Follow-up like this not only raises the group's spirits and stimulates their efforts (energizing), but also is often accompanied by that very sudden progress typical of learning processes. Then success appears 'unexpectedly' for the children and is a strong motivational spur. But in fact these 'unexpected' successes have been prepared for by previous systematic work and the Conductor has been counting on their appearance with sober judgement. This process of follow-up also gives the Conductor significant information, clarifying which elements in the new context are not sufficiently solid yet and so must be given special emphasis in future for their consolidation.

New task-series and daily schedules allow for new forms of study excursions and cultural activities, too, while developing orthofunction also affects educational goals, since, as Conductive Education understands it, biological and social requirements form a single harmonious unit, a unitary educational programme.

In this way follow-up is at once an evaluative assessment and the beginning of learning at a new and higher level.

16 Maintaining attention

Teachers are usually very concerned about holding their pupils' attention, so absolutely necessary for serious work, and they try various ways of arousing it, sometimes indeed enforce it by 'discipline' but quite often unsuccessfully.

There are recognized signs of loss of attention – hands moving restlessly, children fidgeting and beginning to chatter. These are all similar to signs of fatigue and what might be called 'hyperkinesis' (a high degree of fatigue is also accompanied by tremor). Waning attention encourages activities in other directions where fatigue gradually slows them all down. So loss of attention seems to coincide with the onset of fatigue. Inadequate response and mistakes are common features too.

From all this one might suspect that waning attention and fatigue are the result of a functional disturbance, an overload in the central nervous system. If this were true, we would have to assume that these symptoms, appearing in orthofunctionals as well, will present themselves more quickly in dysfunctionals – that the attention of dysfunctionals weakens quickly and they are easily tired.

The literature actually refers to this and sees an 'inability to concentrate' as the most serious problem in the education of dysfunctional children.

Our experience in Conductive Education however does not confirm these reports. Dysfunctionals educated in the Institute are in general lively, attentive, and so pertinacious that they are practically 'indefatigable'. This can be explained by Conductive Education proper with its increasing results.

It seems that decline in interest level like fatigue is not connected with the current state of orthofunction or dysfunction, but with the adaptive-learning process and general orthofunctional condition. The achievements of Conductive Education appear very early because this method is concerned with the support needed to meet biological and social demands as instrumental in teaching. So a reafferentative learning process is evident very quickly, bringing with it an increase in attention and a surprising lack of fatigue. Holding attention therefore is a sensitive index for evaluating the efficiency of Conductive Education, or to put it another way, flagging attention indicates that the adaptive-learning process has slowed down and must be corrected. So next we will give a detailed description of the tools we use.

The daily schedule is realistic. This means that while it has no gaps, it is never over-hasty – it always leaves sufficient time for solution of any problem decisive in meeting biologically–socially justified demands. Its details ensure enough time to allow for the preparation and orthofunctional – and therefore fruitful – execution of every activity, and must never lead to overloading. Order, both of positioning and sequence of activities and free time, can be learned at the same time. Consistency, systematic work, and profitable rest become a habit, even a claim. Maintaining it has a stimulating effect.

The morning 'training' is refreshing, too. Again, short activities of a similar nature can be interposed in the course of the day. They are not even mentioned in the daily schedule. Even dysfunctionals always have a need for movement and satisfying it tends to enhance attention.

Repetition is always bad for attention and consequently even within the task-series we would always rather go back later to a particular task than repeat it immediately it has been done.

The daily schedule itself also provides for constant variety. The different events are always changing, even within the framework of a given activity. Achievement of the real goals, the biological and social requirements, is what matters most, like teaching the children how to write, for instance, which coincides with orthofunctional goals, that is to be able to write also gives increased motivation. There are some athetoid children who can spend one-and-a-half hours joining two dots on a line and this holds their complete attention. By doing this they approach the set goal progressively. The successive approximations are not the achievement of what seems at first sight to be an abstract partial goal but implicit steps in learning to write and so a reinforcement along the way to becoming an orthofunctional.

In schools for orthofunctionals, children often lose sight of any connection between a set task and the fulfilment of the real biological and social requirements. In the case of dysfunctionals, the educational goals, that is to say carrying out the principal scholastic programme, coincides with developing into ortho-functionals. In this way educational tasks are often more realistic within the framework of Conductive Education than in schools for orthofunctional children.

In ordinary schools breaktime interrupts the learning process but not in Conductive Education. The daily schedule has no interruptions as we know and this means that the Conductor, according to plan, is able to bring the spontaneous activities from free time into the educational process. In the intervals between occupational activities a Conductor does not leave the group to its own devices as a primary or secondary school teacher would her class. Breaktime is not a break for the Conductor, but almost imperceptibly she channels the spontaneous activity of the children at play. She includes this in her planning, too, delighted at every spontaneous initiative. Far from stifling their activity she helps them to expand it for the sake of their orthofunctional development. For instance, one group made a puppet show, wrote the parts, and worked the puppets themselves. The Conductor can assist and support this kind of initiative by putting it into the schedule. This is how the individual profiles of the groups take shape. Often spontaneous activities are a great help in educational tasks in the schedule.

For the Conductor lack of attention from any child is an important sign, principally indicating either that the child had not understood the task and so could not intend the goal, or that he cannot distinguish between essential and inessential elements in what he has to do, making him seem inattentive.

When this happens the Conductor has to discover the imme-diate reason for this loss of attention and direct the child so that he can understand what he has to do. Sometimes it helps to inter-calate a goal and at others keep up the intending (by getting him to count from one to five – 'counting'). Interest can be increased by calling the attention of the whole group to what its member has done or by using other (energizing) means attractive to that child. Indirect methods can be very efficient in reinforcing attention. We have mentioned Luria's patient who was able to raise his hand to maximal height when he was not directly asked to do that but to touch an object hung up for him. In this case the preferred goal appeared through association with another goal. Analogously just as here the performance improved as the goal was made more concrete so the situation is the same with attention. Small children are better able to understand that they have to put their hands on their heads if we say to them, 'Now shall we make a hat'.

Possibilities for arousing interest and strengthening attention are almost infinite and we shall return to this in discussing facilitations where personal contact with the Conductor is also particularly significant.

So to be aware when interest is flagging is the central focus of a Conductor's attention and immediately she has to find the most useful way of arousing it appropriately. She interposes a game or leaves a task demanding a great deal of precision to turn to a less detailed one, like singing.

Sometimes she must mention the longer term goal of an occupation. With both group and individuals she must proceed flexibly, without any schematism. Maintaining attention is therefore essential to her role as a teacher and an educational function.

Finally we must add that attention itself is something that can be learned. In the process of Conductive Education richer and richer opportunities appear for a Conductor to stimulate greater attention. As orthofunctional development proceeds the circle of interests grows ever wider. Orientation is behind this or, strictly speaking, adaptation. Aspects of an originally unknown environment are continually being transformed into a storehouse of items which can serve as markers from a biological and social point of view.

17 Conductive (operative) observation

Patients with cerebral injuries always have a considerable residual functional capacity. This is why dysfunctionals can be transformed into orthofunctionals. In other words, they are themselves (re)habitable and their capacity to learn rests on this residual ability, yet except in mild cases they are incapable of making spontaneous use of it. They need guidance that is educational help to learn orthofunction and the Conductor's teaching gives it to them.

Perhaps the most important aspect of the practice of Conduction is 'Conductive observation'. This has many factors, extending over locomotion, dexterity, speech, attention, perception, and satisfying biological and social needs.

For this the Conductor must know the algorithms of the task sequences and how they can lead increasingly to satisfying fully the requirements of the daily schedule. She must understand the ways of promoting human relationships, their importance, the motivation of the human personality, all the educational goals and teaching principles.

The daily schedule as we know consists of a multiplicity of tasks. The various tasks are received by the group as a general formulation but its members nevertheless solve them individually. Conductive observation means ascertaining the conditions necessary for each individual to complete his or her task successfully according to the views of Conductive Education. This form of observation therefore is an operative (active) process.

Whereas a doctor's observation is primarily of a diagnostic nature, looking for symptoms, and the general educationalist's observation is rather an assessment, a Conductor's observation aims at ascertaining the circumstances making it possible to achieve a given goal. In making his examination a doctor sets out from identical standard conditions and looks for any pathological change. Similarly a teacher usually registers performance change under identical circumstances. A Conductor, however, explores the component elements of conditions which will lead to achieving identical goals but vary between individuals. Her goal is to point the way to accomplish the tasks set out generally for the group but in a way which will be appropriate for each individual member. Her observation is continuous because it is directed not at the condition at the time but at bringing the developmental process into being, so it is not just restricted to particular examination periods but is constant, both during occupations and the breaks between them. This observation always embraces the whole group and each of its members and is inseparable from all the Conductor's other activities that continue throughout.

Dysfunctions cannot be ended by any prohibition or using any of the various technical restrictions. They can be eliminated only by learning orthofunctions. For instance, no one can walk safely as long as his feet are in a club-foot position. Club-footed children must first be taught how to put their heels down to take a step and when the child has learned, in the task-series, how to do this, he can then apply it in the various elements of the schedule. The dysfunctions would easily return through habitual inertia at first and so a Conductor must see that a child continuously puts into practice in everyday life the orthofunctional skill he has learned and use her knowledge at the same time to prevent any dysfunctional reactions.

Conductive observation also makes sure that the requirements in the schedule can be met in spite of individual differences and that the greatest possible use is made of individual potential. Superficially we would think that operative observation would load an almost impossible burden on to a Conductor. After all there is every detail of the schedule to be kept to and they leave her no respite. Again, she has to set out a plan for each of the individual points and keep to them. A group of dysfunctionals has been entrusted to her which, anywhere in the world, would probably be regarded as untreatable. How in the midst of all these tasks can she also continue to practise Conductive observation?

There is the point too that while a teacher usually grades his pupils' achievements according to various set classifications, a Conductor is in a much more difficult situation. What she might see as the right solution for one dysfunctional could be quite wrong for another and would have to be remedied straight away. There are as many possible ways of working out how to do identical tasks as there are dysfunctionals in a group. Each individual's performance must be assessed in relation to his own capacity and not as compared with the others'.

To meet all these conditions a Conductor has to be capable of recognizing and noting each child's full potential. Only by applying operative observation is she able to see that every member of her group carries out properly what he has to do and, by giving her maximum attention to individual differences, reach the point at which all the children meet the schedule's requirements.

Let us take an example. The group is sitting down and the task is to stretch out one arm. The Conductor gets one of the children to bend his head forward and so his arm stretches out. Another child manages it by grasping a stick. A third is given a chair and by getting hold of a rung on it is able to stretch his arm out correctly. The fourth child needs more time and while the group is doing the exercise twice he manages to stretch his arm out once. There is likely to be someone who does not understand what he has to do and the Conductor will show him what the goal is. Another child still cannot stretch out his arm while in a sitting position so the Conductor directs him to do so lying down. Conductive observation makes all the relevant 'facilitations' possible and through them a successful outcome.

In all this there is a reafferentative link because both Conductor and her group of dysfunctionals have enjoyed their success. In this educational relationship a dysfunctional achieves his result because he can count on the conductive co-operation of the brain of an adult trained for the purpose and able to help in the functioning of the regulation of his damaged nervous system. ('Conductive' – Latin for 'guiding', corresponding to the Greek 'pedagogic', the origin of which points to the boy 'led'. Translators' note: Conductive Education is *Konduktiv Pedagogia* in Hungarian, where pedagogy and education may be used as synonyms.) The Conductor is able to give her pupil realistic guidance precisely because her goal is that he should succeed and so reafferentatively this seems to be her own result that comes within the range of her biological regulation. So the dysfunctional's completing the task set him by the Conductor closes a regulative circuit reafferentatively in the Conductor herself. This is very important from the point of view of Conductive observation, biologically the most adequate and effective form of observation. The Conductor is not looking for abstract causes. She is not exploring correlations. She never poses questions in the form, 'If I experience this or that irregularity or symptom, what can it be attributed to?' The Conductor's question is, 'How can I see to it that this dysfunctional can do this in this particular concrete case and in the right way?' Put like this observation and intervention (facilitation) coincide and success in a dysfunctional's educational progress serves the Conductor's own adaptive development, maintains her attention, and eliminates her fatigue.

18 Conductive facilitation

In physiology the concept 'facilitation' refers to a favourable influence and mutually intensified effect between stimuli and is explained by the summation of excitational processes in space or time (Exner). Conductive Education uses it in a far more wide-ranging and differentiated sense. The process of facilitation for us has an educational, not a physiological connotation. Facilitation meets every condition necessary for a dysfunctional to be able to carry out an activity through his own efforts. Facilitation is educational help, guidance in the use of methods and techniques for reaching a goal. Facilitation can become organized, built into an activity, but can also remain outside the regulatory circle of a given activity, gradually becoming superfluous with developing orthofunction.

Some facilitations build on the mechanical correspondences pointed out by Foerster, the German neurologist, who took a detailed interest in the relationship to be found between the simultaneous postures of different joints and in the gravitational effect on movements. Through these correspondences and the mechanical elasticity of the muscles, a surprising degree of function can be elicited even in the case of muscles which became paralysed.

For instance, despite the paralysis of finger flexors, flexion and grasping are possible through extending the wrist (dorsiflexion). As a result the paralysed fingers shorten relatively, pressing against the palm and this merely mechanical process can be used for grasping. In the same way it is possible to compensate to a certain extent for the paralysis of the finger extensors by flexion of the wrist (volarflexion), when the retracting paralysed muscles straighten out the fingers.

Despite paralysis, knees can be straightened, remaining extended and supporting the whole weight of the body, if the centre of gravity comes in front of the transverse axis of the knee joint. Where the knee extensors are paralysed the force of gravity can carry the leg forward with a pendulum movement which may prove a help in walking.

A quick active movement of proximal parts of the limbs is followed by a passive swinging movement of distal parts. If the muscles moving a shoulder joint are paralysed, for instance, then using a swinging movement of the trunk and shoulder lifts up the paralysed arm for a moment. It can be held in this position too if the trunk is bent backwards at the same time, bringing the centre of gravity of the arm behind the shoulder joint. This method will even make it possible to put the hand of that paralysed arm on the head.

Mechanical correspondences like these can be used as facilitations over quite a wide range. From our experience in Conductive Education these indirect solutions can be transformed into orthofunctional movements with time.

At first glance this is difficult to understand because our thinking is still often permeated with an obsolete anatomically localized conception of the way the nervous system works. How could it be possible to tie in to the regulation of the nervous system a paralysed muscle when it is deprived of its link with the efferent nerve, paralysing movement at the joint? In fact there is quite a simple answer. The brain can learn reafferentatively to utilize these mechanical relationships better and better as time goes on, increasingly smoothly, making use of them adaptively to perfect those actions. If neurophysiological research had not been hampered by the view that every reafferentation arises solely where it appears (that is exclusively on a direct route from the organs executing a particular action), we would have a clearer picture of movement.

We have mentioned Bernstein's opinion that walking is a form of activity which is perfectly adjusted to even the most uneven ground surfaces. In this reafferentation the brain exploits far more complicated items of information than the 'proprioceptions'. In walking we use not only our legs but also the whole body and obviously many different parts share in the regulatory functions of walking. (Walking is strictly speaking continuously falling and constantly making use of the force of gravity to stay upright.) In stumbling or slipping arms too are lifted and the trunk bent.

Foerster also described what extensive correspondences there are in the positioning of the joints. Flex the elbow and the shoulder joint extends (abduction). Extend the elbow and the shoulder joint flexes (adduction). Extending the knee the hip extends at the same time. These relationships are affected in various ways by the initial position of the limb. It is clear that in the course of organizing all our activities the brain also has the facility for building quite a wide range of these relationships into its control systems.

However it is not only mechanical correspondences which can be exploited reafferentatively. In the case of a transverse lesion of the spinal cord, after the shock caused by the lesion has passed, a number of spinal regulations become 'liberated' from being directly influenced by the brain. But this 'liberation' does not mean that the brain cannot learn to bring that regulation under its control again *indirectly* and build them into actions. In that event the control is to be seen as different from usual: as adaptation. (It is possible to sail either with a favourable or a contrary wind.) It is possible not only to learn to stand on one's feet in spite of paralysed knee extensors but also to build spinal organizations into purposive activities. The Conductor must always see – and this constitutes the essence of operative observation – what special possibilities there are for any particular dysfunctional to work out how to do the tasks set, so that he can be shown the way to achieve his intended goal. It is the prerequisite for the dysfunctional's brain reafferentatively building in varied movements to the organization of actions. Facilitation can create in many cases the special circumstances which make it possible to achieve a set, verbally intended, and apparently unattainable goal.

For example, contractive athetoids have difficulty in coping with tasks in which they have to abduct their arms. If they try, it regularly brings on an adduction spasm. In order to manage it they have to learn to inhibit that adduction after intending, or, in other words, intend in another way, orthofunctionally. This is what would be needed.

As an intercalated guiding task, an athetoid child lies down and intends this task, 'I raise my right arm upwards [to a position above my head]', then from there he can already bring his arm down to the abducted position he had previously planned to achieve. He has avoided what had been a critical factor previously and has found a practical way of achieving the desired position. This too is a facilitation.

There are many possible ways of learning how to stretch arms. On the Conductor's advice the child lies on his back and lets his arm hang down from the slat-bed, where the weight of the arm slowly stretches it out. During this the child intends the action slowly with the words, 'I am stretching out my [left or right] arm'. In this way the child learns to become consciously aware of (feels) the free extension of his spastic arm. In other situations after this he can achieve a repetition of this feeling when intending and he waits until his arm loosens up – the precondition for being active in a number of ways. Facilitation here has led to a learning process through which the child has grown to be consciously aware of the loosening up of his contracture and so he can conjure it up. Later the child will always intend verbally actions extending to the limit of that loosening up. In this way his intending will be effective.

This child's task-series was structured in such a way that eventually he could stretch out his arm in twenty to thirty ways. Through transfer each variant has a favourable influence on the others.

There are many other ways to facilitate arm stretching. For instance, if the child lies down, putting the arm down by his side and turning over on to it will facilitate extending the elbow. With repetition it becomes enough to put the arm down by his side without turning over on to it, then later just intending and the arm stretches out. As a facilitation the sitting child can grasp a chair with bent arms, then slide back from it and maintaining his grasp stretch out the arm. Lying on his back the child reaches backwards with bent elbows and grasps a chair. Then maintaining his grip he slides lower down the slat-bed and so his arms stretch out. With the child lying on his stomach stretching his arms forward can be facilitated by reaching forward to a goal. As a means of facilitation he can manage to raise his arms above his head by intercalating partial tasks: grasping his neck, nose, head. Stretching can be facilitated too by preliminary bending. This is 'successive innervation', the facilitational significance of which was already recognized by Sherrington and particularly emphasized by Kabbat. Facilitation can be achieved too by using body positions as the two Bobaths emphasized. Again, the arms can be stretched by clenching the fists, by grasping a stick, and by turning the head away. The arm stretches out diagonally under the influence of a purposive movement in stretching or lifting the leg. It can be done by lying down and grasping the slat-bed or, squatting down, by holding on to a chair or even by grasping heavier objects. Arms can be stretched with a subtle movement of one of the fingers or in response to a change of rhythm, imitating the movement of yawning, by folding the hands, or by grasping a stick with both hands, in sitting by grasping the ankles, in lying by holding the thighs, and so on.

This extraordinary variety of facilitations does not mean that they can be applied indiscriminately. According to the various dysfunctional conditions, different facilitations are necessary and indeed, within these, for each individual. For dysfunctional types, let us take contractive athetoids as an example once again. They are incapable initially of moving their hands up from their sides to put them on their heads, so they cannot comb their hair for instance. As an example here is a task-series which makes it possible for them to put their hands on their heads as a task achievement. As a facilitational tool for this purpose, a chair is put in front of each member of the group with the back (rungs) facing the child.

The task is to raise one arm and the precondition to be able to stretch it out. First of all the children grasp the next rung as a facilitation and with verbal intending their elbows extend. If they tried to raise their arms quickly at this stage, their elbows would bend again and it would be pointless. The facilitation is to slow down the arm raising so that it becomes a gradual process.

So the athetoid children move up from rung to rung grasping each in turn up the back of the chair, intending each time lifting their arms and extending their elbows. In this way it becomes a gradual movement and every detail of the lifting activity comes under conscious control. The stiffness in the arm diminishes then.

The lifting can be increased only to the extent to which the athetoid children are capable of maintaining the arm in a stretched position. So in time they succeed in lifting it as high as their heads. If they bend their arms inwards now they will touch their heads. The tempo of the intercalated tasks is speeded up until it finally becomes automatic. Then raising a hand can be intended and achieved directly in an orthofunctional way. The ladder chair and the partial tasks interpolated here were the facilitations for achieving the further goal. By working through the task-series these dysfunctionals have learned the pattern to be applied and what they need to do if they want to comb their hair or put on their caps, for example. Activities like these which are part of everyday life are items included in the daily schedule and this reinforces the pattern learned through the task-series.

In this example facilitations were partly the chair (equipment) and partly the task-series itself.

The spectrum of facilitations is extremely broad. Facilitation may be, for example, grasping and gripping a thick stick. This partly encourages development of self control because when involuntary movement of the fingers sets in the stick is dropped. Gripping a stick facilitates arm stretching too, and this in turn stops involuntary movements and also helps in stretching the legs. Presumably there is a general effect in the sense of the Jendrassik technique, increasing energy flow, so that grasping the stick evokes a knee reflex which would not have appeared otherwise. Grasping a stick makes it directly possible for the child to stand erect and balance without his having to clutch at our hands and our having to take away this 'support'. Again, grasping a stick in one hand the child can write easily with his other hand because the disturbing involuntary movements are stilled. The child's speech also becomes more intelligible, louder, and more articulate, when he holds a stick.

Lifting the head up or straightening the trunk also facilitates balance in standing. Yet it would be useless to tell some dysfunctionals to raise their heads before their conscious perception has developed sufficiently for them to be capable of registering what raising the head means. Facilitation in this case would consist in our saying: 'Look up at the ceiling', or 'Clap your hands high in the air'. Looking up, which the child can control, inevitably lifts up the head too and the child stands. So they first intend: 'I look up. I am standing', or 'I clap my hands, I am standing'. In the course of time this becomes simpler: 'I am standing'. So initially looking up or clapping hands above their heads is the intended goal. Later the straight (erect) posture becomes automatic. With this facilitation the child understands what the correct body posture is, not through an abstract explanation but from practical guidance.

Learning to make actions with the help of the arms can often be influenced facilitationally by similar leg activities and vice versa. Right- and left-hand sides also mutually facilitate each other. The way for understanding what a task means for abducting the legs can be prepared by parting the arms. Using the hands while lying prone can be facilitated by bending the outstretched legs at the knee. Position of the limbs is influenced by head position.

The variety of the connected effects which facilitate each other is so substantial that it surprises even the specialists and is constantly taken into account in Conductive observation. A Conductor must recognize the possibilities for facilitation present in an individual, note them down, and apply them consistently.

For instance, it is surprising in how many ways the members of a choreo-athetoid group can learn to sit up. One lies across a slat-bed letting his legs hang over the side between the two beds, stretches out his arms, clasps his hands, and so sits up. Another turns on his side, crosses his legs, sits up, and then uncrosses his legs. A third hooks his hands between the slats of a bed and holding on to the slats, sits up. A fourth has his left thigh pressed down by the Conductor and so is able to hold on with his left hand, grasps a stick with his right hand, and sits up.

In Conductive Education the educational goals set the acceptable level of accomplishment for any given task. For instance, in the group just discussed, that type of facilitation would be useful if the members of the group had never sat up and this was the first time they had done so, or if the sitting up merely facilitates carrying out another task. The Conductor must prepare in advance each day for every single occupation, setting its educational goals, tailoring facilitation and variations in accomplishment to suit the goals. In the choreo-athetoid group we mentioned, for instance, if the general purpose in the task of sitting up had really been to use their hands, then the point of the facilitations would be for them to prop themselves up and grip. In the same task-series if stretching or spreading the legs apart had been the goal then the facilitations would have to be designed to help with that.

In certain cases the Conductive goal may vary between different individuals when the group is working through the same task-series and the biological (social) goal is identical for every child, perhaps sitting up, where one child is learning to grasp, another to stretch his legs, and so on, always towards orthofunction.

However crude a child's initial attempts at a set and intended goal may be it is acceptable at first, because in any case this solution is engaging in the process of adaptation and learning and in this way it will become open to further improvement.

When we speak of the 'crude' attainment of a goal, we mean that it is an approximation, the child can achieve only part of it as yet. If for instance the intended goal is: 'I raise my right arm', initially perhaps all that can be counted on might be stretching or raising the fingers to rest them on something, or lifting the arm just a few centimetres and putting it on a stool. Initially lifting the head and propping oneself up can count as 'sitting up'. (This is a note for the Conductor. The child must intend the full goal and its attainment will be due to complementary facilitation.) The extent or proportion of the task achieved will increase naturally from day to day. If an athetoid child's task is to touch his face with his hand, then at first we might call something like this successful. The child lies on his back and then turns on to his side and so immobilizes the arm which otherwise would be in continuous involuntary movement. Then he brings his head over to his hand until it touches it. The child achieved the goal by his own effort by using this detour. But in the meantime he still has to work towards the general orthofunctional goal the Conductor has set, for instance by keeping his legs extended.

In due course, dysfunctionals learn to make better and better use of facilitations. For example, a child learns that he is sitting securely only when he slides back as far as the back of the chair, but to do so he has to overcome his increasing general hyperextension (opisthotonus) by grasping the seat of the chair with both hands and bending his head forward. It is always what he has learned to do that counts as an achievement and that is why it would be quite wrong to correct the way he sits by holding him or fixing him on the chair with some kind of appliance. If manual assistance is given at all, in general it should only be so that the child would retain a result achieved by himself alone.

The children also learn what facilitational tools they need to carry out the task set them. The Conductor for instance asked a child what he needed to sit up and in this case the child said: 'If I get on a chair on my left side I can sit up.' He got the chair and sat up.

Their companions' success is another important form of facilitation. It stimulates both imitation and greater originality. The algorithmic character of task-series also has a facilitatory effect. In the sequence of component goals fitting into each other, each goal achieved facilitates the next. So stretching the arms is a step towards moving them to the side. Moving the arms to the side helps toward bringing them into the middle line and this is a step towards turning the palms up, and so on.

In preparing for writing, athetoids learn to grasp with both hands, relax their grasp, and reach the goal accurately with their fingers. They learn how to suppress involuntary movements in every situation, to place their palms downwards, make fine finger movements, grasp thicker and then thinner sticks, and then grip with two fingers. They practise all this within a single task-series in one daily schedule. In order to learn to make a dot, they should dip a finger in paint at first and make a dot with it, but the same purpose can be served by sticking a disc on, or in some cases, through a taking-aim goal from the task-series, like pointing a stick at some particular figure in a picture on the desk, on the blackboard, and so on. The facilitations are in many cases in line with what Gelb said about it being easier to recognize and accomplish a problem in a concrete rather than in an abstract situation.

For example, if we want to teach a dysfunctional to turn his wrists round (pronation and supination), we have to guide him in these movements by an action which is a concrete activity. (Pronation and supination are general goals because without them so many activities could not be realized.) Supination often fails because a child does not understand initially what he has to do. We would make his correct wrist position part of a concrete activity like managing to place a stick in a certain way or grasping a tool, and so on. If a child does not know how to turn his palm up, we can put a hammer in his hand and say: 'Hold it with the hammer head up', then he will supinate his hand. Getting him to grasp the rung of a chair from beneath will also supinate his hand. In orthofunctionals, it is often precisely using a tool that teaches the most varied movements, for example knocking in a nail with a hammer, cutting out a shape with scissors, turning on an electric switch, and so on. There are children whom it is useless to ask to dorsiflex their feet, but if we tell them we want them to pretend they are putting their feet on a stool, then they will do so.

Facilitations therefore serve partly to guide dysfunctionals into an orthofunctional way of completing whatever they have to do and partly to ensure that every member of the group keeps pace in working together through the task-series. The facilitations must adapt flexibly according to each individual's current condition.

Separate orthofunctional accomplishments assist the performance of orthofunctional tasks at a higher level. In this sense the facilitations coincide with the task-series proper to some extent. Subordinate goals facilitate the achievement of the ones that follow.

In the task-series, the order of the tasks and their degree of emphasis, the degree of individually determined precision, the material in them to be mastered, the length of time devoted to particular tasks, and even the entire daily schedule are a function of the situation of the group at any particular moment and within this personal facilitations are a function of each individual's position at the time.

The task-series constitutes the most complex form of facilitation, but at the same time sometimes a single word will be enough. For instance, a choreo-athetoid group happens to be learning to sit up by supporting themselves on the palms of their hands. They lie on their stomachs and stretch their arms forwards. The goal is: 'I support myself on the palm of my right hand'. One child's hand is clenched. The Conductor goes to him and calmly makes him repeat: 'I stretch it out'. And that is enough – the child's fist unclenches.

There is no kind of miracle in this. Speech, particularly when we refer to ourselves in the first person, takes part in cerebral regulation as input. Because he had not intended the movement the child could not direct his attention to that hand and open his fist (although obviously he had previously learned to open his fist!).

From this, which only appears to be a most simple facilitation, to doing the most varied work (for example, in the workshop of the Institute, where pieces of furniture and boots, among other things are made), the spectrum of facilitations is extraordinarily wide. However the facilitation is never, in any of its forms, an end in itself.

There are occasions when a facilitation is needed only so as not to lose out on an achieved result. If, for example, a dysfunctional has once sat up by his own effort he must not fall back again and then we may hold him by grasping his clasped hands. If when walking he had succeeded by himself in 'pressing out' his knee, then his leg might be supported in this position for a time. In due course we reduce this support gradually by sliding the hand lower and lower down the leg and finally taking it away altogether. In another case, if a child has succeeded in grasping a handle of a two-handled mug with his right hand, we can support his grip until he has grasped the other handle of the mug with his left.

If the facilitation is equipment of some kind, it is never a complicated prosthetic instrument to which the dysfunctional would become a slave, but a simple object normally at hand. For instance, a chair is an excellent facilitational tool for practising walking. The dysfunctional stands behind the back of the chair and stretching his arms out and straightening his legs, touches its back with two fingers, and then lifts them up. He learns to stand correctly in this way. Equally he is learning to lift his hand from the chair. The Conductor may offer a toy to the child standing behind the chair. She only lets go of the toy (or stick or pencil) when the child is standing securely with his heels on the ground. Other facilitations can be used similarly for bringing into consciousness (a feeling for) standing securely. The child lets go of the supports for a moment and claps his hands above his head. For this he must learn how to keep his balance steadily without wobbling in finding his body's centre of gravity. What he learns here will help to keep up his stability in walking between steps, too. Clapping hands and clasping them is also effective in inhibiting that involuntary flinging apart of the arms, the reactive movement that accompanies, and at the same time reafferentatively characterizes, insecurity. In learning to walk clapping puts that pause in the rhythm necessary for transferring one's weight, or putting the weight of the body on to the standing foot. So clapping hands is a generally useful facilitation when a support is used, since when they clap they let go of the support. The support is used only as a prerequisite for clapping in a negative sense – to let go of it.

So the clapping and walking exercise may be done between two rows of chairs, backs towards each other. But the importance is not in the chairs; it is that they are there, giving security from the fact that they can be grasped. The rows of chairs can be replaced by two ropes giving only an illusory rather than a real support. The difficulty of a task can be increased by making these ropes hang more loosely. There are of course several other possibilities for facilitating the appropriate leg position besides clapping.

If a child has a tendency to walk on his toes, making his balance unstable, he can be taught to step by stamping so that his heels touch the ground or he can control them by intending. The child steps and intends verbally, 'Heel' and first of all puts his heel on the ground, then says 'Sole' and puts down his sole too. Occasionally the intending will only be counting, 'One, two', and the child knows that this stands for the same results. He learns whether he has to turn his foot outwards or inwards. He could also use a chair as facilitation for this purpose. Chairs of different sizes can be used in many different ways for facilitation, turned one way or another, or lifted. The child can learn to get up from the floor by supporting himself on a chair or progress from a small stool to a larger stool and then to a chair. The seat of a chair can be used to support his hands or facilitate stretching one leg by leaning sideways on to it.

The backs of chairs in the Institute are like the rungs of a ladder. We have mentioned how they can be used in raising the hands by putting them on to these rungs and going on upwards. By grasping or touching the rungs involuntary movements can be stopped. One task might be to grasp the rungs from above or below at different heights with the hand, or to touch it with the fingertips, with one finger or more, or even with the toes. Another task might be to place and keep the hand in the spaces between the rungs. The rungs at the back of the chair can continue downwards between the legs of the chair. Lower rungs can be used while sitting on another chair, for 'stepping' the hands down in learning to lean forward. In walking, sitting, or even while lying down the rungs can serve as a goal for lifting a foot or leg. Heel or toes can be placed on a particular rung in prescribed positions. In the task in which one heel has to touch the other knee at each step in walking, a chair rung can be used for the interpolated goal, for instance: 'I put my weight on my left leg. I put my right foot up [on to the second rung]. I turn my knee outwards. I touch my knee with my heel. Then turning my foot outwards. I slide my foot down to the bottom of the chair leg'. Again, squatting can be learned while grasping the chair rung, or dropping down on to all fours and gradually getting up again. Chairs can be set out in rows to facilitate learning to walk and to diminish facilitation we can thin them out.

For patients with ataxia we use four chairs arranged in the form of a cross. They sit on one and then have to stand up and sit on the opposite one, and so on. With chairs arranged in the same way athetoids are given the task of grasping across from one to the other and turning round at the same time.

There are bars across the bottom of the chair legs, sometimes extending beyond them so that the chairs are stable enough for squatting, standing up, and so on while holding on to them. With two chairs one task might be to stand up from one, walk across and sit down on the other and this task can be made more difficult by increasing the distance between them.

Standing up from a chair can be facilitated by making the seat higher. They can be put up on the slat-bed and for example used as a facilitation when a child standing in front of the slat-bed has to straighten up to stand erect. If we want to get the child to learn to lean forward and so bring the weight of his body forward, then we put a chair in front of him with its back facing him, at a distance where he can just reach it. His task then is to stretch his arm to reach the chair with his hand.

Excellent use can be made of slat-beds too for facilitational purposes. The Institute's slat-beds are made of oak or beech and are light and springy. At night covered with bedding they are beds. By day they are easy to stand on end and are quite stable like this. Laid at a mealtime, they become tables. All this is very characteristic of the simple and effective solutions which are generally the mark of the Institute. (The groups sleep at night in the room where they work and eat during the day. Rooms have smooth washable floors and no doorsteps and all this helps in getting about.)

As regards the slat-beds, an extension can be put under the legs to raise their height and so even tall people can easily slide down from them. Pushed together it is possible to roll about on them. Grasping can be learned by putting hands down between the slats. One can crawl backwards and forwards, lie down and sit up, turn on to one side to sit over the edge and to turn round, all on a slat-bed.

For sitting task-series the slat-bed can act as a table and for those who cannot sit very securely, slats can facilitate task-series worked through while sitting down. When standing up to answer in school lesson-times the child can grasp the slats too.

Children can go round a slat-bed sideways, step along in the space between the rows of beds, support themselves on it by the palms of their hands, lie on the ground and place their feet on it, use it as a hand-support when it is up-ended, and climb up and down from the slat-bed, and so on. Finger-stretching can be facilitated if the palm of the hand is turned upwards and the backs of the fingers are pressed on to the slat-bed and if the child then bends his wrist on to his fingers, the grasping of objects can be facilitated.

A stool is placed in front of a bed where a child would have been too small to be able to reach the ground in sliding down from it. There are stools of various heights in the Institute, which can be placed under a foot or elbow or on the seats of chairs. Again, stools can make a step ladder and the chair backs make a side rail or banister for it. Stools can be used in lifting and for other tasks.

The slat-beds, chairs, and stools will all fit inside one another. Conductive Education regularly teaches dysfunctionals the many different ways in which objects can be used in different contingencies. For this, apart from slat-beds, chairs, and stools, we use sticks of various lengths and thicknesses, standard weights, measuring sticks, gauges, jugs, mugs, and eating utensils also. Any piece of equipment can play a role as a facilitational tool. This is precisely the opposite of the situation obtaining between a blind man and his stick or a crippled man with one leg and an artificial limb or crutches. In becoming orthofunctional a dysfunctional must be versatile and free and this could never be achieved by making him into a handicapped person relying on a prosthesis to compensate for his disability. It would not even be realistic to try it. A dysfunctional individual is dysfunctional but not maimed, precisely because in any case he is not able to deal with a prosthesis before he has learned how to learn. At the same time why should any half measures be acceptable in ortho-functional development.

To summarize, the variety of possibilities for facilitation is enormous. They include the force of gravity, motor mechanical interrelationships in the organism, and even the synergisms of brainstem reflexes. The important point most clearly distinguishing Conductive Education is that it teaches how to use all these facilitations for learning consciously. They can be sensory items of information or any kind of influence which gives impetus for effort (energizing). Facilitation can be used before starting a task (energization, arousal of attention), during and after it (consolidating consciously recognizing the results achieved) always with the purpose of increasing reafferentation.

19 Interpersonal facilitation

In our introductory survey we attempted to outline the scientific results from which we might be able to understand the role of the nervous system and its functional conditions. We made no secret of how many gaps may be found in our current knowledge in the shaping of a conceptual system relating to the problems discussed.

Anyone who hunts around in modern psychological literature hoping to find out what kind of interpersonal relationships an individual needs to be orthofunctional or, alternatively, the lack of which would stop his general adaptive development altogether, is in for a bitter disappointment. However important this question may be, the literature on it is extraordinarily meagre.

There are of course some important indications. Pavlov[1] mentions that there are dogs which cannot be used for experiments validly if they are left alone. He called this property 'social reflex', this demand for human company or otherwise they become unmanageable.

Thompson and Melzack[2] raised puppies in almost complete isolation, on food which was entirely adequate in every respect. They grew into neurotic adult animals with peculiar fits of turning round and round.

Similar results were obtained by the husband-and-wife team, the Harlows[3], in their experiments with monkeys.

Schmidt-Kolmer[4] emphasized the significance of human relationships for babies and small children. If young babies with adequate nutrition are not picked up regularly in their mother's arms and breast-fed, their development is retarded and even if they are fed with mother's milk in a bottle, they have less resistance to infection.

1   (1956) *Pawlowsche Mittwochkolloquien*, Berlin.
2   Thompson, W. R. and Melzack, R. (1956) *Science*, 123 (939).
3   Harlow, H. F. and Harlow, M. (1962) *Scientific American*, 207 (5).
4   Schmidt-Kolmer, E. (1961) *Psychiatrie, Neurologie, und Medizinische Psychologie*, 2.

In his Pelican paperback addressed to a general readership, Adcock[5] devoted a lot of attention to this question and quoted H. Bakwin's summary of the horrifying experiences of paediatricians with the high rate of mortality among babies kept in an unfriendly institutional environment. R. A. Spitz[6] discussed this on the basis of careful observation of babies and experimental data and he considered interruption in the dual mother–child relationship explained that depression among hospitalized babies which is sometimes accompanied by an appalling mortality rate. L. J. Yarrow[7] proceeded more cautiously in his survey of the literature to 1964 but drew similar inferences.

Well-known reports on adults have shown that even a short period of complete isolation has sometimes proved to be a quite serious source of stress. In the literature, however, these experiences have not been recognized as a break in interpersonal relations but as a general consequence of lack of stimulation.

There is surprisingly little literature on the effects of deportation, but perhaps here we may assume from the changes in personality which appear almost immediately that being torn out of a familiar interpersonal relationship system has great significance. But greater prominence is given in reports, however, to the role of hunger and other kinds of deprivation or physical torture.

The sociography of group interpersonal relationships was expounded by J. L. Moreno and the significance of groups in psychotherapy is acquiring a larger and larger literature.

All this is mentioned here so that in the next part of our discussion we can point to the interpersonal conditions indispensable for the formation of an orthofunctional personality.

I. V. (see Illustrations 346–50) was put into a Home from the age of 3 months. When he came to us at 5 years old the little boy could not speak or walk, could do nothing at all for himself, and lacked virtually every kind of orthofunction. He was regarded as severely mentally and physically handicapped. In his first week in the Institute he presented a picture of extreme panic and kept his head buried in his arms. Since the first condition for integrating new children is to ensure that they can mix happily with

5   Adcock, C. J. (1967) *Fundamentals of Psychology*, Harmondsworth: Pelican.
6   Spitz, R. A. (1967) *Vom Sängling zum Kleinkind*, Stuttgart.
7   Yarrow, L. J. (1964) *Review of Child Development Research*, New York.

the others I. V.'s integration seemed highly problematic at this point and indeed it was impossible to establish personal contact with him. His attention span was non-existent. He did not focus on anything and he threw away anything given to him to hold.

The Conductor often spoke to him, fed him, put him on the pot, and constantly paid attention to him. In the group the children of more or less the same age surrounded him with the greatest kindness and tenderness. (It is always a great joy for children to follow their teacher's example in concerning themselves with a 'new child' and befriending him.) After three weeks the new child was walking along the corridor and the stairs holding a Conductor by the hand! Everything excited him enormously. He squealed and laughed all the time. He ate with a spoon, undressed independently, and sat on the pot of his own accord. He took part enthusiastically, especially in the walking task-series, but not as yet in the whole daily schedule.

We will give another example of interpersonal relationships of a kind which we might call 'personal facilitation inherent in a Conductor'.

There is a demonstration item in the daily schedule. In these demonstrations the Conductors of other groups are informed on the current position of a particular group, and on the educational procedures being applied. The demonstrations also contribute towards the training programme for the Institute as a large educational unit.

A task-series, beginning with standing up, is being demonstrated. The group sits in the way planned previously. In front of and beside the children the necessary facilitational tools, chairs, and stools have been placed. The Conductor is holding the plan for the task-series and the goal is designated: 'I stand up'.

Some children do so but the rest are unable to stand up in spite of the facilitational tools being provided.

A more fully trained second-year student takes over the group from the first-year student Conductor and recommences the same task-series. And as if some kind of switch had been turned on the sleepy atmosphere of a moment ago vanishes and the general mood becomes cheerful and awake.

What happened?

The second Conductor struck a much more lively and spirited note than the first one. She asked the children a humorous question. She repeated one child's answer loudly and gave it jokingly a kindly interpretation referring to a song that the group knew. A laugh ran through the whole group.

Technically nothing has changed. The children are sitting in the same arrangement as before. Nevertheless, some kind of electric current has run through the air. Faces are flushed, eyes are sparkling, the children who were quiet have become noisy. Their song has wings.

After this, the Conductor repeated the previous goal, 'I stand up', and amazingly all the children stood up one after another. Finally the whole group was on its feet, although they had not had any particular facilitation in doing so.

The second Conductor succeeded in creating a favourable atmosphere for the task. This general effect depended exclusively on the interpersonal relationship. And what did that depend on? Neurophysiologically we do not know. Education, of course, is quite clear as to the significance of this kind of relationship. The personality is inseparable from the relations binding us with our human environment. Through these relationships the Conductor succeeded in changing the mood of the group and creating the right opening. She took into account the range of the children's interests, understood how to find a common note, and that is what ensured the success of the first task.

The success achieved provided further favourable preconditions. The execution of the algorithms in continuing the task-series is motivated precisely by the general orthofunctional effect, building up gradually to success after success. The first step, however, became possible through creating a good interpersonal relationship.

Dysfunctional children admitted to the Institute, even the little ones, come from a family and sometimes from a Home, needing to be integrated into their new microstructure. The seal is set on this integration by the Conductor's creating an adequate relationship between himself and the group as well as among its members.

20 Conductive groups

A group is the principal vehicle for interpersonal relations in Conductive Education. Every activity in the daily schedule is arranged to take place in a group, however severely handicapped its members may be. A group is made up of between twenty and thirty members of both sexes, chosen very carefully. It is never a stop-gap arrangement but the group is seen as an essential part of the practice of Conductive Education.

Groups are not homogeneous in medical diagnoses – indeed medically speaking there is no such thing as homogeneity. No two athetoids or any other kind of dysfunctionals are identical. The groups are not uniform either in length of residence in the Institute or in age – boys and girls of nursery age, school age, and even 15- and 16-year-olds can all be undergoing education in the same group. Nor is group membership always the same – children learning in various school and nursery school classes can be put together temporarily to form a new group. According to the results of their studies, children may go on to different classes and form a group with classmates or with members of a nursery school group. There may be children in the same group who get about ('traffic') easily or with greater difficulty, quickly or more slowly. Bigger boys and girls and adults of either sex live separately but may belong to the same mixed group in the daytime.

Members of a group may sleep, eat, and work in the same room and this would be indicative more of its state of development than of its character. All its members have to wrestle successfully with every orthofunctional requirement right from the start and their place of work and the distance to it will be adjusted to the functional development they make. In due course the time will come for them to walk up and down stairs and then they will spend a considerable part of the day away from the place where they generally work.

This is of course a departure from the usual notion of groups. Nevertheless, the Institute's groups are largely uniform and organized to a high degree. We shall understand this better if we set aside the points of view usually found in the literature on groups, mainly to do with leadership, the problem of 'pecking order', and so on. The specialized nature of a Conductive group stems from the fact that whatever differences there may be between its members the educational aims are the same. The organization and conformity of a group is principally ensured by keeping to the daily schedule. The Institute's daily schedules are self-evident for everyone to follow and even become habitual.

The entire atmosphere is shaped by sharing common goals and tasks, in fact precisely the kind of situation on which the well-known observation about group psychology was made. 'Groups mobilize great forces and these exert an extraordinarily significant influence on the individual' (Kelber[1]).

We will give just one example of the energizing influence of a group. B.A. was a contract-athetoid child of almost 4 years. At the demonstration his Conductor was sitting in such a way that she happened to block his view of the other members of his group. Recently B.A. had come on splendidly and been very active, but there he sat now, slouching, head bowed, thoroughly passive. Then the Conductor moved away and was no longer sitting in front of him. B.A. could see his group again and all at once his conduct changed completely. He joined in the tasks they were doing very actively.

The mood of a group is another important point. The Conductor takes great care that it is favourable and her general influence indirectly affects every group member, facilitating the development of their whole personalities. A group coalesces precisely through adopting a Conductor's tempo, her requirements, and high standards.

The uniformity of a group does not depend on the level of its members' performance but on a series of other factors.

One of these factors is the rhythm of a group. Every group has its own most favourable rhythm to which the 'Rhythmical Intending' is adapted and this is used throughout the schedule. We shall discuss Rhythmical Intending later in more detail.

1 Kelber, M. (1966) *Enzyklopädisches Handbuch der Sonderpädagogik (Gruppenpädagogik)*, Berlin.

In a paradoxical way, the uniformity of a group is also ensured by the way it is structured. This structure does not develop spontaneously but is planned and co-ordinated by the Conductor to fit in with the various sections of the schedule. The requirements for 'traffic' decide, for example, that the children who walk with the greatest difficulty should be nearer the door, so that is where their slat-beds are and that is where they sleep. In planning for a walking task-series, small groups are formed from children needing fairly similar forms of facilitations. Some walk between rows of chairs and others between ropes.

An athetoid group can be our example here. Some of them can already walk so well that they do some of their tasks in the corridor, on the stairs, and in some cases in the garden. They are thoroughly enthusiastic about each change in environment. Just at present they are in the garden, going indefatigably from tree to tree and walking round the house. If one of them forgets to put down his heel in taking a step or to straighten out his knee his companions certainly draw his attention to it. The ones who stayed inside welcome them back with great excitement and overwhelm them with questions about what they have seen and everything that has happened. They in turn naturally pour out all this information and tell their experiences excitedly. Among those who have stayed indoors the rhythm of work steps up. Sooner or later, once again someone else will be able to join the others outside. Ultimately they are all walking in the garden and the structure of the group has been changed constantly towards that end.

The organization of a school class of double hemiplegics meant that at answering time the children only stood up but did not go out to the blackboard. Now that group has been given the task of learning to write on the blackboard for which the prerequisite is that they must be able to go to it.

For this the group had to be seated in such a way that the children who still had difficulty in getting about were put nearest to the blackboard. They had learned to write prior to this. Now the group has been asked who would like to be the first to try to walk to the blackboard. Two have volunteered and gone out each with the help of a chair. Seeing how well they have done, two more have offered to go out and they have also managed it successfully. Noisy excitement reigns. Now the fifth child has stood up and gone out. The noise, if possible, is even louder. Only three are sitting in their places now and in the end they stand up too and go out to the blackboard. That was a few days ago. Since then the first two children have gone outside for the first time (using two sticks for the time being) on to the street in front of the Institute. Another two watch them from the door as they walk up and down out there indefatigably.

The most important factor in the uniformity of a group is to decentralize the work of its Conductor. To promote the unity and organization of a group and the education of the individual dysfunctionals in it, every member takes part as 'Conductor's assistant' in the tasks they share among them and this is regarded as being of paramount importance. Some of them help to lay the tables, others pass round the wash bowls, others hand out and collect working tools, and so on.

It works so well partly because it diminishes tension in the dual relation between a Conductor and individual dysfunctionals. In this way each child has less of a feeling of being the centre of the Conductor's attention and yet it is obvious to every child that the Conductor is paying attention to him and is helping him if necessary. Another reason why it is so important is because through decentralizing the Conductor's work all the group members come to participate in the common activity and dysfunctionals develop a feeling of collective responsibility. Keeping to the schedule, successfully completing a task, and the success of every individual member become matters of general concern and this more than anything else ensures that the group is able to become uniform.

This unity stemming from interpersonal relationships, and so important for personality development, is found both within and between groups, too. There are many different forms of co-operation between groups, for example between the children in nursery school and primary school classes. There are common workshops, one group visiting another, celebrations and excursions which are organized jointly. The Institute has youth groups of 'Venturers', too.

21 Rhythmical intention

Rhythmical intention is another form of facilitation. It has two important factors, firstly, to make activity voluntary and second, rhythm. In practice, rhythmical intention goes like this. The Conductor defines a goal, for example, 'I raise my right arm' or 'I lie down on my back'. The members of the group repeat the statement of the goal and then they carry it out, counting out loud, 'One, two, three, four, five'. The entire group counts together. On walking into the Institute straight away you can hear the sound of the chorus of groups counting.

The significance of verbal intention has been explained previously so the reader understands its role. We know that with the linking of speech and action into feedback reafferentative circuits the achievement of a goal becomes conscious and verbally intendable. Verbal intention prepares the action and starts it off in all its complexity. But does counting add anything?

The many cerebral connective systems taking shape to become more or less stable are usually called 'patterns'. One of the most established of these patterns is ordinal numbers. If we begin counting out loud and stop suddenly, people around us will go on counting involuntarily in their own minds. The sequence of numbers virtually forces itself on us and that is precisely why counting forms a convenient vehicle for rhythm. If we begin counting and get someone to go on saying the numbers he will involuntarily take over our counting rhythm, too. By rhythmical intention a Conductor makes a group set up a rhythm and this rhythm which we know to have such an energizing significance takes effect amplified into a chorus. In flaccid conditions a lively rhythm enhances muscle tone. With spastics slow counting can inhibit pathological synergisms.

Every group has its most favourable rhythm for activity at any particular time. This rhythm can be maintained not only by counting but also by singing, reciting nursery rhymes, or by other

209

movements. At a time when the cerebral organization of an activity leading to a particular goal progresses relatively slowly, counting has a co-ordinating role in filling out the rather lengthy period between verbally intending a task and accomplishing it. This may be such a long interval initially that sometimes it seems to threaten keeping up the intending. At that point counting will allow more time to finish the task.

If counting up to five does not give enough time, the intending and counting must be repeated, possibly several times over.

Both verbal intending and counting make it possible to link into the organization of an action cerebral structures capable of mobilizing intensified energy for its regulation. Concrete activity combines speech with the pattern relating to it in the cortex, as we know from Luria's experiments which we referred to earlier.

Rhythmical verbal intention is the combination of verbal intending and rhythm which can be used to regulate the rhythm of an action. For example, flaccid paraplegics and athetoids have to carry out their tasks with a single impulsion after verbal intention and counting prevents the loss of what they have achieved.

With the stabilization of a regulation counting is discontinued first and activity synchronized with verbal intention. Later, intention is restricted to only the more comprehensive tasks and then inner, silent, intention is enough. Finally even this becomes virtually imperceptible and changes into simply a plan aimed at the action, as it generally is for orthofunctionals.

A counting speech rhythm affects other movements and their rhythm, say of hand movements, affects in turn aphasics' regulation of speech. Counting can be replaced by movements of the mouth or other rhythmic movements for anyone who cannot speak.

Rhythm helps both in registering in words the correlation of components in a task-series and in intending them in an appropriate tempo, as for instance when walking.

Rhythmical intention in chorus also means that the members of a group have to work together and co-operate regularly, however great the differences between them in their level of task accomplishment may be. In this way rhythmical intention facilitates not only the learning of an activity but also the cohesion of the group.

From the point of co-operation within a group, rhythmical intention is important, too, because it facilitates caring for one another. If a child is the last to finish a task, the Conductor may occasionally say to the others who have done it already, 'Let us all count together now for Steve', and then the group counts with him until the attainment of the intended goal, enjoying his success with him. The simplicity of setting a rhythm allows children without speech to join in. They begin to hear their own rhythm and then to produce it by making a sound. In this way rhythmical intention forms an introduction to learning to speak and the first signs of it may appear precisely through rhythmical intention.

22 Fitting into a group and integration

Usually some attempt is made when dealing with dysfunctionals to find out through preliminary examination what results might be expected from various treatments and to exclude 'hopeless' cases. In Conductive Education no such method of preliminary examination is possible whether it lasts for a quarter of an hour, days, or weeks, for drawing this kind of inference. The Institute generally makes progress with precisely those dysfunctionals who on the basis of earlier examinations elsewhere have been graded as unsuitable for any kind of teaching and are being given only whatever therapeutic procedures may be appropriate to their clinical condition. In other words, they are considered to be un(re)habilitable or else, if any attempt is made to teach them, a special course curriculum is worked out for them.

To be accepted for Conductive Education it is not a question of how severe the dysfunction is at the time but whether that individual can integrate with a Conductive group and if so what kind of development he or she is making. Integration means that after an initial period of time when he just watches what the others are doing, he gradually begins to take part in it himself in some way or other. Integration is often a complicated task and sometimes is successful only after repeated attempts.

A child aged less than 2 years or any other child still needing a constant immediate relationship with his mother comes to the Institute with her for a time. We teach the mother how to get the child doing certain tasks at home, making sure that they are done correctly. Later, child and mother together begin to work in a group. If the mother cannot come in daily, she will be able to live in the Institute with her child for one or two weeks.

The mother learns ways of evoking activity and so the child becomes more and more active. Only after this will it be the right moment for the child to integrate into a group without its mother.

Integration consists of taking an active part in every occupation in the daily schedule. To expedite this a group may be given a new task-series, constructed so as to be particularly favourable to the new arrivals.

The 10-year-old T.O. (see Illustrations 309–14) was admitted with opisthotonus, with crossed legs and a luxation of the hip caused by spasm. She had never sat up previously. Initially it was necessary to lie her down because on the basis of her memories about the failure and painfulness of attempts to make her sit, even the thought of sitting made her cry. The group's new task-series gave T.O. an advantage because it began with such tasks as clasping hands in which she turned out to be most skilful.

Her success had a tremendous effect on her and, during the performance of every further task, she tried to maintain the favourable standard, thus approximating to the goal fixed in the task-series better and better, namely to sit up. In the course of a few weeks, she had already learned from lying on her stomach to sit back between her legs, and by grasping the rungs of the ladder-back chair she could sit down too. In eighteen months she could eat sitting down.

Development is not uniform even at the start; it can be rather difficult to attain. For example, A.A., a 10-year-old obese boy with spina bifida, initially developed very slowly and his incontinence could not be controlled quickly. He performed tasks inattentively and appeared to be mentally retarded. All this changed fundamentally after the first successful achievement, teaching the paraplegic boy to stand up independently. With this his personality changed completely. He became attentive and industrious and quickly learned to control his urine. His scholastic attainments improved by leaps and bounds, too.

Both integration and the beginning of development often depend on a correct choice of group. The 5-year-old hemiplegic, B.T., was at first accepted into a group with a relatively slow rhythm, where he was bored and worked through the tasks unenthusiastically. He was transferred to another group with a livelier rhythm. Although this was a group of spastics among whom there were no other hemiplegics and the task-series were relatively difficult, B.T. integrated very well. It turned out later that he had learned how to do a number of the tasks in his first group but these results remained latent and appeared only in his new group.

23 The unity of Conduction and the Conductor

By now it should be absolutely clear that Conductive Education is a unified system and that its concepts form a unitary whole. It has been difficult to discuss particular questions separately precisely because all the concepts tie in together and particular points of view or inferences are valid only in a total context.

This interweaving of concepts corresponds to the functioning of the nervous system and to the complex unified hierarchy of its regulatory circuits. If we were to attempt to isolate the principal features of Conductive Education we would have to point out as the first one that its details can never be separated, for if we neglect any one thing the whole suffers. Conductive Education is directed at the whole, not to improve symptoms merely but the whole personality.

Its results are possible because even a damaged brain always retains a large residual capacity and with the appropriate educational methods this can be mobilized and used even in the case of dysfunctionals where damage to the nervous system is restricted to the spinal cord or to peripheral nerves.

Every dysfunction arrests the cerebral adaptive developmental process even if it were not the brain which was damaged first but, say, the spinal cord. A dysfunction always appears when an individual cannot cope with his biological-social demands. Education for orthofunction is possible only through recognizing and accepting all those demands normally relevant for a given age, by using successful forms of instruction directly applicable to them and by finding orthofunctional methods suitable for the developmental state of each individual. Then the activity will be linked with cerebral regulation through carrying it out successfully and this is the only way in which any residual capacity can be mobilized.

In Conductive Education the system of biological and social requirements is comprised by the daily schedule. Orthofunctional accomplishments are learned through task-series and facilitations and stabilized through the daily schedule.

The group forms the only possible interpersonal condition for Conductive Education.

Through verbally intending the tasks their accomplishment always takes place consciously and through comprehension and achievement each activity can be intended more and more readily.

Every one of the factors explained so far presupposes a Conductor's presence and organizing directive functioning. A Conductor acquires the necessary theoretical and practical training in a four-year course at the college of higher education in the Institute itself.

In each group two or three Conductors (some still students) work harmoniously together at the same time in whatever way is defined by a task at any given time. Conductors relieve each other at midday and pass on to each other their observations verbally and in writing.

From what has been said so far, it is clear that it is the Conductor who has to see to putting into effect the entire system of requirements for living. In everyday life orthofunctionals more or less put up with always having to deal with specialists in a single discipline. Even at school, on relatively common ground, many difficulties are caused by the fact that often the claims of individual teachers are not attuned to each other. Specifically to prevent this happening, in nursery school and the four classes of the primary school, one person actually teaches each class. It is curious that this aspect is so generally ignored with children at a lower standard because of their dysfunctions. It is quite usual for the various problems facing dysfunctionals to be shared out between them by several doctors, educationalists, physiotherapists, nurses, sometimes ten or twelve people.

Conductive Education sees this as the greatest obstacle to the (re)habilitation of dysfunctionals. In hoping that dysfunctionals will learn to apply in practice the knowledge they acquired through task-series, we realize that this rests on the same people seeing to it who taught the task-series too.

The fact that any Conductor is able to take care of all the teaching necessary for both orthofunctional and normal education means that the maximum use can be made of all aspects of set and free activities in the schedule. This requirement on the one hand imposes heavy burdens on Conductors and on the other makes it their direct concern to bring in all the members of their groups towards achieving the common goal. Once again a favourable circuit is established. Establishing group collaboration is an important task in itself and at the same time a prerequisite for a Conductor's being able to cope with the problems which rest on her shoulders.

Not only do the Conductors of one group form a 'team' but also there is close collaboration between all the Conductors in the Institute. By means of demonstrations and the joint enterprises organized between groups, Conductive Education forms a unitary system throughout the Institute. The Conductor's training and function has developed out of the unitary system of Conductive Education.

Summaries

Összefoglalás (Hungarian summary)

Ez a mű Dr. Pető András konduktiv pedagógiájának tudományos összefoglalása. A konduktiv pedagógia a "mozgássérültek" (dysfunctiósok) orthofunctióssá nevelésére, vagyis (re)habilitációjára szolgáló rendszer, amelynek tapasztalatai évtizedek alatt gyűltek össze, és sokezer egyénre vonatkoznak. E rendszer elméletét és gyakorlatát, azok általános elveit és speciális kérdéseit a Mozgássérültek Nevelőképző és Nevelőintézetében tanulják a konduktorok, az Intézet munkatársai. Ez a kötet a konduktiv pedagógia elméletét és gyakorlatának általános elveit tárgyalja. Ezt a speciális rész több kötete fogja követni. Az első kötet tartalmának főkérdései a következők.

A dysfunctiósokkal foglalkozó szakember számára elsődleges fontosságú az eredmények kérdése, a bevezető fejezetet ezért a Pető-rendszer eredményeinek szenteltük. A Pető-intézetben korábban bentlakó és 1950–65. között kibocsátott összes (1002) személyt berendeltük felülvizsgálatra. A felülvizsgálaton 866 fő jelent meg. Ezekre vonatkozóan részletezzük a felvételi, a kibocsátás és az utánvizsgálati (nem egyszer 10–15 évvel a kibocsätäs utáni) helyzetüket jellemző adatokat és statisztikailag általánositjuk. Ilyen módon az Olvasó megismeri a dysfunctiósok minősitének a módját is a konduktiv pedagógiában.

A konduktiv pedagógia fogalomrendszerének megértése érdekében a könyv rövid áttekintést nyújt a dysfunctiók értelmezésében ma átalánosan alkalmazott neurofiziológiai, neuropathológiai, klinikai és psychopathológiai kutatások releváns tényeiről és az ezekre épitett következtetésekről.

A könyv részletesen tárgyalja a konduktiv pedagógia – vagyis a mozgássérültek első teljes mértékben pedagógiai megközelitése – gyakorlatából levonható általánosabb következtetéseket.

217

Az orthofunctio és a dysfunctio fogalmát biológiailag, az egyén általános adaptációs – tanulási folyamatára vezeti vissza. Rámutat, hogy az egyén születésétől kezdve egy sokoldalú, az életkorral is változó, rendkivül széleskörűen értelmezett követelményrendszerrel kerül szembe, amelynek aktív adaptációs fejlődés révén tesz eleget. Ha adaptációs fejlődésében lelassul vagy elakad, dysfunctióssá válik. Ha viszont a dysfunctióst sikerül újra bekapcsolni az adaptációs – tanulási folyamatba, fokozatosan orthofunctióssá alakul. A (re)habilitáció lényege tehát rávezetés a tanulásra, vagyis alapjában véve pedagógiai kérdés. A dysfunctió fogalmát a könyv biológiai és pedagógiai szempontból – s ezen belül a percepció és a tevékenység elválaszthatatlanságából – kiindulva tárgyalja.

A konduktiv pedagógia a dysfunctiós egyénnel szemben mindazokat a követelményeket támasztja, amelyeket az élet vet fel az orthofunctióssal szemben, életkorától függően. Ugyanakkor a konduktor rávezeti a dysfunctióst a követelményeknek megfelelő feladatok egyénileg lehetséges megoldására. A sikeres feladatmegoldás révén, a reális feladatok megoldásának tudatos intendálásával és az eredmény reafferentációjával indul meg a tanulási folyamat, mobilizálódik a dysfunctiós agyának mindig meglevő, csak különben kiaknázatlan residualis kapacitása. Az egyszer eredményhez vezető megoldás a szukcessziv approximáció értelmében fokozatosan tökéletesedik. Így válik a dysfunctiós egyén sokoldalú gyakorlati tevékenység révén orthofunctióssá.

A dysfunctiósok konduktiv nevelése csoportban történik. A közösségi nevelést az Intézetben négyéves elméleti és gyakorlati képzésben résztvett pedagógusok, a konduktorok végzik. A mozgássérültek tanulásának folyamatosságát a napirend sokoldalúan szabályozza. Az egyes tevékenységek programszerű fejlesztését feladatsorok készitik elő. A feladatok céljainak elérését tudatos intendálás előzi meg. A konduktor egyszemélyben irányitja a dysfunctiós egyén minden (higiéniai, önellátási, oktatási stb.) követelményének kielégitésével kapcsolatos foglalkozásokat, s igy biztositja az összes foglalkozás teljes integráltságát, s ugyanakkor hozzájut a csoport eredményes működéséhez szükséges sokoldalú információanyaghoz. A dysfunctiósok minden tevékenysége ily módon egyetlen pedagógiai folyamatba olvad egybe.

Mindez lehetővé teszi, hogy az előzetes vizsgálatokkal megállapithatóan alacsony értelmi szintet mutató dysfunctiós

(mozgássérült) is a konduktive pedagógiai folyamatban gyors
fejlődésnek induljon. A konduktiv pedagógia alkalmazhat-
óságának eldöntésére nincs szükség előzetes tesz-tekre. A cso-
portba való beilleszthetőség és a fejlődés dönti el általában, nevel-
hetőe az adott dysfunctiós az adott csoportban vagy nem. A
beillesztés aktiv, türelmes, sokoldalú folyamat, amely gyakran
lehetővé teszi a konduktiv pedagógia eredményes alkalmazását
kezdetben képezhetetlennek látszó esetekben is.
Az első kötet felépitésének vázlata a következő:

A konduktiv pedagógia alkalmazási köre és eredményei
A mozgássérülések (dysfunctiók) fogalma
Az idegsejtek szintje
Motorium
Sensorium
Dysfunctio és neurofiziológia
Cerebrális dysfunctiók
Az agysérülés pszichológiája
A konduktiv pedagógia fogalomrendszere
Orthofunctio és dysfunctio mint személyiségproblémák
A napirend
A feladatsorok
A továbbvitel
A figyelem fenntartása
A konduktiv (operativ) megfigyelés
A konduktiv facilitáció
A konduktiv csoport
A ritmikus intendálás
Alkalmasság és beilleszkedés
A kondukció egysége és a konduktor
Ábrák

Az ábrák részben kazuisztikai jellegű, az egyes személyek
fejlődését bemutatő, másrészt a rendszer egyes mozzanatait
szemléltető fényképek.
A könyv azoknak a szakembereknek szól, akik a dysfunctiósok
nevelési, oktatási, therápiás és (re)habilitációs kérdéseivel foglal-
koznak, de fontos mondanivalója van minden pedagógus számára
is.

Резюме (Russian summary)

Настоящая работа является научным обобщением «кондуктивной педагогики» д-ра Андраша ПЭТЭ. Кондуктивная педагогика — это система, служащая для перевоспитания дисфункциональных больных, превращая их в ортофункциональных, и в то же время реабилитируя их. Данные для этой системы накапливались в течение десятилетий в обращении со многими тысячами пациентов. Теория и практика этой системы, ее принципы и специальные вопросы изучаются кондукторами, сотрудниками Института для воспитания дисфункциональных и для подготовки педагогического персонала. В настоящем томе рассматриваются теория кондуктивной педагогики и принципы ее практики. За ним последуют дальнейшие тома специальной части. Основные рассмотренные вопросы в первом томе следующие.

Для специалиста, занимающегося с дисфункциональными, первичное значение имеют достигнутые результаты, поэтому вступительная часть посвящена результатам системы ПЭТЭ. Были приглащены все выпущенные в периоде между 1950—1965 гг. воспитанники Института (1002 человека) на контроль. Появилось 866 человек. Относительно этих выпускников в книге подробно рассматриваются данные, характеризирующие их состояние при приеме, выпуске и дополнительном осмотре (состоявшемся нередко по истечении 10—15 лет с выпуска). Эти данные затем статистически обобщаются. Читатель таким образом ознакомляется и с методом классификации дисфункциональных в кондуктивной педагогики.

В интересах лучшего понимания системы понятий кондуктивной педагогики дается краткий обзор о важнейших достижениях неврофизиологических, невропатологических, клинических и психопатологических исследований, применяемых сегодня в истолковании дисфункций, а также о дальнейших заключениях.

Подробно излагаются общие заключения, выводимые из практики кондуктивной педагогики, первого, полностью педагогического подхода к дисфункциональным. Понятие орфофункции и дисфункции возводится биологически к всеобщему адаптационно-учебному процессу индивидуума. Авторы указывают на то, что индивидуум от роду сталкивается с очень сложной и широко интерпретируемой системой требований, изменяющейся и с самим возрастом. Он отвечает этим требованиям своим активным адаптационным развитием. Если его адаптационное развитие замедляется или останавливается, то он будет дисфункциональным. А если удается снова включить дисфункционального в адаптационно-учебный процесс, то он постепенно становится орфофункциональным. Реабилитация в существе имеет задачу привести больного к учебу, то есть является вопросом педагогики. Итак в книге понятие дисфункции разбирается с биологической и педагогической точек зрения, исходя при этом из принципа неотделимости перцепции и деятельности.

К дисфункциональному ставятся все те требования кондуктивной педагогикой, которые ставятся жизнью к орфофункциональному, в зависимости от возраста. В то же время кондуктор наводит дисфункционального на индивидуально возможное решение заданий, отвечающих требованиям. С помощью успешного решения задания, сознательным интендированием решения реальных заданий и реафферентацией результата начинается процесс учения, мобилизируется резидуальная, в частности не используемая, но всегда имеющая налицо в мозге дисфункционального деятельная способность. Раз найден успешный подход, он постепенно усовершенствуется в смысле сукцессивной аппроксимации. Таким образом, путем многосторонней практической деятельности дисфункциональное лицо становится шаг за шагом орфофункциональным.

Кондуктивное воспитание дисфункциональных осуществляется в группах. Коллективное воспитание проводится педагогами-кондукторами, проходившими четырехлетний курс теоретического и практического обучения в самом Институте. Бесперебойная учеба дисфункциональных многосторонне регулируется режимом дня. Программное развитие отдельных видов деятельности подготовляется серией заданий. Достижению целей, намеченных заданиями, предшествует сознательное интендирование. Кондуктор единолично руководит занятиями, связанными с удовлетворением всех требований дисфункционального (гигиенических, по самоснабжению, учебе и т. д.), обеспечивая таким образом полную интегрированность всех занятий, собирая в то же время многосторонний информационный материал, нужный для успешной работы группы. Итак все деятельности дисфункциональных сливаются в единственный педагогический процесс.

Все это позволяет, чтобы дисфункциональный, да показавший при предварительных осмотрах низкий умственный уровень, стал быстро развиваться под действием кондуктивной педагогики. Для решения о применяемости кондуктивной педагогики в данном случае нет необходимости в предварительных тестах. В общем возможность включения в группу и личное развитие решают о том, можно ли дисфункционального воспитывать в данной группе или нет. Включение является активным, терпеливым, многосторонним процессом, который позволяет успешно кондуктивную педагогику и в случаях, казавшихся сначала безнадежными.

Схема построения первого тома следующая:

Область применения и успехи кондуктивной педагогики.
Понятие дисфункций.
Нервная клетка.
Моторий.
Сензорий.
Дисфункция и неврофизиология.
Мозговые дисфункции.
Психология повреждений головного мозга.
Система понятий кондуктивной педагогики.
Орфофункция и дисфункция как проблемы личности.
Режим дня.

Серии заданий.

Продление.

Поддержание внимания.

Кондуктивное (оперативное) наблюдение.

Кондуктивная фацилитация.

Ритмичная интендация.

Кондуктивная группа.

Способность и приспособление.

Единство кондукции и кондуктор.

Рисунки.

Рисунки являются фотоснимками отчасти казуистического характера, показывающими развитие отдельных лиц, отчасти же показывающими отдельные моменты системы.

Книга рассчитана на специалистов, занимающихся вопросами воспитания, обучения, терапии и реабилитации дисфункциональных, но в ней содержатся важные указания и для каждого педагога.

English summary

This book is a scientific account of the system of Conductive Education introduced by Dr András Petö. Conductive Education is a (re)habilitative system which makes people with handicaps (dysfunctions) into orthofunctional individuals and experience has been gathered over several decades and some thousands of people. The theory and practice of this system, its general principles and special features are taught to Conductors at the Petö Institute for Conductive Education of the Motor Disabled and Conductor College in Budapest. The present volume deals with the general principles of the theory and practical application of Conductive Education and will be followed by a number of further volumes on the specific topics involved. The following are the main topics discussed in this first volume.

For professionals working with handicap results are of the utmost importance and so this volume begins with a description of the results obtained by the Petö system. One thousand and two patients with a wide variety of dysfunctional conditions who lived in and were educated by the Institute between 1950 and 1965 were invited to return in 1968 for follow-up, many ten to fifteen years after discharge; 866 were retested and data assessed on their condition on admission, discharge, and reassessment. Statistical results classified according to type of disability are discussed with their implications.

The theoretical background of Conductive Education is then amplified by a review of relevant research in neurophysiology, pathology, clinical medicine, and psychology, followed by a discussion of their results of interest for the treatment of disabilities. Orthofunction and dysfunction are dealt with from the biological aspect always relevant to each individual's capacity for learning and adaptation, to learn to cope from birth with the multilateral demands of life and changing with age. This will be attained by adaptational development. If it slows down or stops dysfunctions develop, but if the adaptational learning process can start again, dysfunction changes gradually into orthofunction. (Re)habilitation is regarded as teaching how to learn and so may be seen as essentially an educational process of the broadest application. Dysfunction is discussed from both biological and educational standpoints, stressing the inseparable nature of perception and action.

Conductive Education sets the same everyday goals and requirements for handicapped as for non-handicapped individuals according to age. Conductors teach dysfunctionals how problems may be overcome always relative to the situation obtaining for each individual. Learning begins with working out how to do a sequence of realistic tasks, verbally intended, going on through reafferentation (neural feedback) by success, so that those residual capacities are mobilized which are always present but otherwise unused. Performance leading to the solution of initial dysfunctions improves gradually through successive approximation. Eventually the whole action becomes smooth and harmonious and in multilateral practical activity a fully orthofunctional personality develops.

The pupils do not work in isolation but in groups. They are taught by Conductors trained in the Institute for four years. Continuity in progress in learning is achieved through a global daily schedule with a comprehensive programme which includes all the forms of activity necessary to satisfy everyday social and biological requirements. The goal for each task within it is initially stated with conscious, verbal rhythmical intention. The Conductor alone controls every aspect of this activity (hygiene, self-sufficiency, kindergarten or school teaching, and so on) and at the same time gives the group an integrated unity while continually receiving the information necessary for its efficiency. In this way each aspect of activity merges to form a single educational process.

All this means that even those handicapped cases who showed a low intellectual level at first quite rapidly begin to improve and develop within the framework of this treatment. Preliminary testing is considered unnecessary because the feasibility of fitting into a group and individual progress within it will show whether or not benefit is likely to result from training within that group. This fitting in is an active, patient, and multilateral process by which Conductive Education has achieved very striking improvements even in cases which had seemed ineducable.

Photographs illustrate some aspects of Conductive Educational practice and case studies show examples of individual progress.

This book is intended primarily for all those concerned with the care, education, training, therapy, or rehabilitation of children and adults handicapped neurally. But in regarding (re)habilitation as 'teaching how to learn' it also offers a great deal of information of value to all educationalists.

Zusammenfassung (German summary)

Die vorliegende Arbeit möchte eine wissenschaftliche Übersicht über die "konduktive Pädagogik" Dr. András Petős bieten. Diese Art von Pädagogik stellt ein Erziehungs- und Bildungssystem zur Förderung der Orthofunktion, d. h. zur (Re)habilitation von Bewegungsversehrten dar, und fusst auf jahrzehntelang gesammelten Erfahrungen, die bei vielen tausenden Personen gewonnen wurden. Die Mitarbeiter der Staatlichen Anstalt für konduktive Erziehung Bewegungsversehrter und des Konduktorseminars werden sowhol theoretisch als praktisch auf dem allgemeinen und Spezialgebiet der konduktiven Erziehung im Institut selbst ausgebildet. Dieser Band behandelt zunächst die Grundprinzipien der konduktiven Pädagogik und ihrer Praxis, die speziellen Bereiche darstellenden Arbeiten folgen in mehreren Bänden. Die Hauptprobleme des ersten Bandes sind folgende:

Für Spezialisten die sich mit den Bewegungsversehrten beschäftigen ist vor allem die Frage des erreichten Erfolges von primärer Wichtigkeit, deshalb ist das einleitende Kapitel den

Rehabilitationserfolgen des Pető-Systems gewidmet. Die im Pető-Institut vor Jahren stationär rehabilitierten und zwischen 1950–65 entlassenen, (insgesamt 1002) Personen wurden im Jahre 1968 zu einer Kontrolluntersuchung einberufen. 866 Personen erschienen. Ihre Befunde, die zur Zeit ihrer Aufnahme, der Entlassung und der Kontrolluntersuchung erhoben wurden, 10–15 Jahre nach der Entlassung werden in diesem Abschnitt dargestellt und statistisch gewertet. Auf diese Weise lernt der Leser – ausser der bezüglichen statistischen Daten – kennen wie die Funktionsfähigkeit in der konduktiven Pädagogik beurteilt werden kann.

Die Übersicht und Zusammenfassung des begrifflichen Systems der konduktiven Erziehung werden auf Grund der Beschreibung und Deutung der Dysfunktionen angewandten neurophysiologischen, neuro-pathologischen, klinischen und physiopathologischen Verfahren und der im Laufe der Forschung gewonnenen Ergebnisse relevanter Daten und der auf diesen stützenden Forgerungen dargestellt.

Die allgemeinen Folgerungen aus der Praxis der konduktiven Pädagogik, d. h. die zum erstenmal konsequent unter pädagogischer Sicht durchgeführte Annäherung zur Frage der dysfunktiven Personen werden in der Folge eingehend behandelt. Die Begriffe "Orthofunktion" und "Dysfunktion" werden biologisch auf die allgemeine Adaptations- und Lernfähigkeit der Einzelnen zurückgeführt. Es wird darauf hingewiesen, dass jedes einzelne Individuum von seiner Geburt an einem ausserordentlich vielseitigen und auch dem Lebensalter nach sich wandelnden überaus weit verzweigten Anforderungssystem gegenübergestellt wird, dem es infolge seiner aktiven Adaptationsentwicklung Genüge leistet. Verlangsamt sich etwa die Entwicklung der Adaptation, oder kommt es gar zu einem Stillstand, dann tritt die "Dysfunktion" ein. Gelingt es die Einzelperson erneut in den Adaptations- und Lernprozess einzuschalten, mag die Orthofunktion allmählich wieder hergestellt werden. Die (Re)habilitation ist daher bezüglich der Dysfunktion ihrem Wesen nach eine "Konduktion", d. h. Erziehung, im Grunde genommen also eine pädagogische Frage. Das Werk behandelt demnach den Begriff der Dysfunktion in biologischer und pädagogischer Sicht aufgrund der untrennbarkeit von Perzeption und Aktivität.

Die konduktive Pädagogik stellt die Bewegungsversehrten vor dieselben Aufgaben und Anforderungen, die dem Gesunden je nach seinem Lebensalter – im normalen Leben gestellt werden. Gleichzeitig führt der Konduktor den Bewegungsversehrten der (ihm individuell möglichen) Lösung der den Ansprüchen entsprechenden Aufgaben heran. Der Lernprozess vollzieht sich eben mit der erfolgreichen Lösung der Aufgabe, mit der bewussten Intendierung und Reafferenz der Lösung reeller Aufgaben, wobei die stets vorhandene, jedoch nicht ausgenutzte residuellen zerebralen Fähigkeiten des Bewegungsversehrten mobilisiert werden. Die in einem Falle sich als erfolgreich erwiesene Lösung vervollkommt sich dann im Sinne der sukzessiven Approximation immer mehr. Auf diese Weise wird im Laufe und infolge der vielseitigen praktischen Aktivität des Bewegungsversehrten, die vorher bestandene Dysfunktion zur Orthofunktion.

Die konduktive Erziehung der Bewegungsversehrten erfolgt gruppenweise. Die Gemeinschaftserziehung wird durch die Konduktoren, d. h. durch Pädagogen durchgeführt, die in der Staatlichen Anstalt für Konduktive Erziehung und im Konduktorseminar eine vierjährige theoretische und praktische Ausbildung erhalten haben. Die Kontinuität des Lernprozesses der Bewegungsversehrten wird durch die Vielseitigkeit der Tagesordnung gesichert und geregelt. Die programmässige Förderung der einzelnen Leistungen erfolgt mit Hilfe von Aufgabenreihen. Der Erreichung der Zielsetzungen bei den einzelnen Aufgaben dient eine vorangehende bewusste Intendierung. Der Konduktor leitet alleinverantwortlich sämtliche Beschäftigungen, die mit den (hygienischen, Selbstversorgungs-, Unterrichts- usw.). Ansprüchen des Bewegungs-versehrten zusammenhängen und sichert auf diesem Wege die vollkommene Integration sämtlicher Beschäftigungen, gelangt zugleich auch zum gesamten Informationsmaterial, das zur erfolgreichen Arbeit der Gruppe erforderlich ist. Dadurch vereinigen sich sämtliche Tätigkeiten der Bewegungsversehrten in einen einzigen, einheitlichen Erziehungsprozess.

Auf diese Weise wird es ermöglicht, dass auch jener Bewegungsversehrte, dessen intellektueller Entwicklungsstand zu Beginn mit Testverfahren als sehr niedrig befunden wurde, durch den konduktiven Erziehungsprozess eine schnelle Entwicklung nimmt. Zur Beurteilung der Bildungsfähigkeit werden keine Tests angewandt. Im allgemeinen lässt sich aufgrund der Eingliederungsfähigkeit und der Entwicklung entscheiden, ob irgendeine dysfunktion aufweisende Person in einer gegebenen Gruppe erzogen werden kann, oder nicht. Die Eingliederung selbst ist ein aktiver, viel Geduld erheischender, komplizierter Prozess, der häufig in zunächst als ganz und gar bildungsunfähig erscheinenden Fällen eine erfolgreiche Anwendung der konduktiven Pädagogik ermöglicht.

Der erste Band des Werkes gliedert sich folgendermassen:

Anwendungskreis der konduktiven Pädagogik und Erfassungs-
    möglichkeiten ihrer Erfolge
Begriff der Dysfunktion
Niveau der Nervenzellen
Motorium
Sensorium
Dysfunktion und Neurophysiologie
Zerebrale Dysfunktionen
Psychologie der Hirnverletzung
Begriffssystem der konduktiven Pädagogik
Orthofunktion und Dysfunktion als Persönlichkeitsprobleme
Tagesordnung
Aufgabenreihen
Neue Phase
Aufrechterhalten der Aufmerksamkeit
Die konduktive (operative) Beobachtung
Die konduktive Fazilitation
Die rhythmische Intendierung
Die konduktive Gruppe
Bildungsfähigkeit und Anpassungsvermögen
Konduktion als einheitliche Führung
Abbildungen

Die Abbildungen sind teils kasuistischer Art und stellen die Entwicklung einzelner Personen dar, teils veranschaulichen sie die einzelnen Phasen des Programms und die verschiedenen Lösungsmölichkeiten der einzelnen Aufgaben.

Das Buch ist zunächst für jene Fachleute bestimmt, die sich mit den Fragen der Erziehung, des Unterrichts, der Therapeutik und der (Re)habilitation von Bewegungsversehrten befassen, es enthält aber auch wichtige Mitteilungen an alle Pädagogen.

Résumé (French summary)

Cet ouvrage présente en résumé la pédagogie conductive du docteur András Pető. La pédagogie conductive est un système d'éducation servant la (ré)habilitation, c'est à dire le développement de l'orthofonction des inadaptés moteurs. Les expériences ont été recueillies pendant des dizaines d'années, au cours de l'application de ce système sur des milliers de personnes. Les éducateurs, nommés conducteurs reçoivent leur formation théorique et pratique à l'Institut d'État pour l'Éducation Conductive des Inadaptés moteurs et École des Hautes Études de l'Éducation Conductive; les futurs conducteurs y sont initiés aux principes généraux et aux problèmes spéciaux de l'éducation conductive. Ce volume traite le théorie de l'éducation conductive et les principes généraux de sa pratique. Ce premier volume sera suivi par plusieurs autres contenant la partie spéciale.

Ce qui intéresse avant tout le spécialiste, c'est de connaître les résultats; c'est pourquoi le premier chapitre est consacré aux résultats obtenus grâce au systéme du Professeur Pető. Tous les anciens pensionnaires de l'Institut qui en sont sortis entre 1950 et 1965 ont été invités à se soumettre à un contrôle en 1968. Sur les 1002 personnes invitées 866 se sont présentées. Concernant ces personnes nous indiquons tous les détails relatifs à leur état au moment où elles ont été admises à l'Institut et au moment où elles en sont sorties confrontés avec leur état constaté de 10 à 15 ans plus tard. Ces renseignements sont complétes par les données catamnéstiques; en généralisant les données caractéristiques, nous en tirons des conclusions statistiques. Ainsi le lecteur sera à même de connaître les procédés d'évaluation de l'éducation conductive.

Pour expliquer les concepts de la pédagogie conductive, le livre passe rapidement en revue les faits importants des recherches – neurophysiologiques, neuropathologiques, cliniques et psychopathologiques – appliquées généralement dans l'interprétation des dysfonctions et les conclusions qui sont tirées de ces faits.

Le livre précise les conclusions générales qui peuvent être tirées de la pratique de la pédagogie conductive, première approche purement pédagogique des infirmes moteurs. Du point de vue biologique, cette méthode ramène les origines de l'orthofonction au processus général de l'adaptation et de l'apprentissage de l'individu. Il souligne que, dès sa naissance, l'homme doit affronter tout un système d'exigences complexe qui change selon l'âge de l'individu aussi; celui-ci doit faire face à ces exigences par son développement d'adaptation active. Si le développement de l'adaptation se ralentit ou s'arrête, l'individu devient handicapé. Par contre, si nous réussissons à rallier le handicapé au processus d'adaptation et d'apprentissage, la dysfonction se transforme progressivement en orthofonction. L'essentiel dans la (ré)habilitation est donc d'amener le handicapé à apprendre, ce qui signifie que le procédé est, au fond, de caractère pédagogique. Par conséquent le livre traite le concept de la dysfonction de points de vue biologique et pédagogique; il part du principe de l'unité inséparable de la perception et de l'activité.

La pédagogie conductive pose les mêmes exigences vis-à-vis des handicapés que la vie elle-même pose vis-à-vis des individus normaux. Le conducteur amène le handicapé à trouver la solution individuelle des problèmes posés par les exigences. Le processus de l'apprentissage commence, et la capacité résiduaire des handicapés – toujours présente, mais généralement laissée inactive – est mobilisée grâce à la solution réussie des problèmes; cette solution est promue à l'aide de l'intention consciente et verbalisée et la réafference de l'exécution des devoirs. La solution qui a déja une fois amené au succès, ne cesse de se perfectionner petit à petit, conformément à l'approximation successive. C'est ainsi que la dysfonction finit par se changer en orthofonction, grâce à la multiplicité d'une activité pratique.

L'éducation conductive des handicapés est une activité collective. Assurée par les conducteurs éducation dont la formation théorique et pratique se fait dans notre Institut et dure quatre ans.

La continuité des études des infirmes moteurs est réglée d'une manière très variée par l'emploi du temps, embrassant toute la journée. Le développement programmé de chaque activité est préparée par une série de tâches. La réalisation du but proposé est précédée par l'expression orale de l'intention. Le conducteur dirige lui-même toutes les activités visant à suffir à tous les besoins (domestiques, hygiéniques, d'apprentissage, etc.) des handicapés. Ainsi le conducteur n'assure pas seulement l'intégration complète de toutes les activités du handicapé, mais lui-même, de sa part, reçoit une série d'informations variées, nécessaires, à l'activité fructueuse du groupe. Ainsi tout ce que le handicapé fait, devient partie intégrante d'un seul processus pédagogique. Tout cela rend possible qu'un handicapé, dont le niveau intellectuel relativement bas avait été constaté par les examens préalables, puisse se mettre à progresser rapidement. Il n'est pas nécessaire de soumettre le handicapé à une série de tests, en général c'est l'intégrabilité et le progrès réalisé qui décident de la question de savoir si le handicapé peut être élevé dans tel ou tel groupe ou non. Le procédé d'intégrer le handicapé est une activité complexe qui nécessite beaucoup de patience; grâce à ce procédé, la pédagogie conductive est applicable avec succès dans le cas des handicapés qui, au début, paraissaient inéducables.

Le premier volume embrasse les chapitres suivants:

La pédagogie conductive; sa sphère d'application et les résultats obtenus
Définition des dysfonctions motrices
Le niveau de neurones
Le motorium
Le sensorium
Dysfonction et neurophysiologie
Dysfonctions cérébrales
La psychologie des lésion cérébrale
Les concepts de la pédagogie conductive
Orthofonction et dysfonction en tant que problèmes de la personnalité
L'emploi du temps de la journée
Les séries d'activités
Introduction à la nouvelle phase
Comment maintenir l'attention
Les observations faites part le conducteur
La facilitation de la part du conducteur
Le rôle du groupe dans la conduction
Aptitude et intégration
L'unité de la conduction
Figures

Les figures servent, d'une part, à présenter des cas, le développement de certains individus, d'autre part à présenter certaines phases du système.

Le livre est destiné aux spécialistes s'occupant des problèmes d'éducation, d'enseignement, de thérapie et de (ré)habilitation des handicapés, mais tous les enseignants trouveront de l'intérêt à le lire.

Illustrations

Daily schedule of an athetoid group

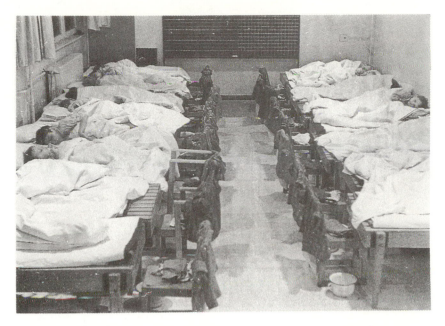

1 The group is still asleep. The orderliness of the room shows the result of the previous day's activities of the group and is a requisite part of the children's education.

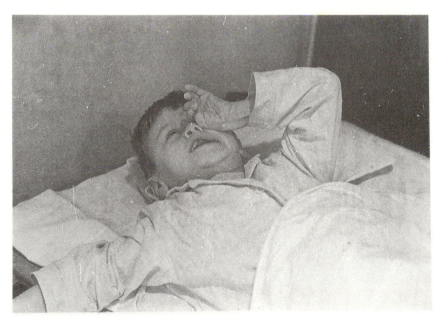

2 Waking up.

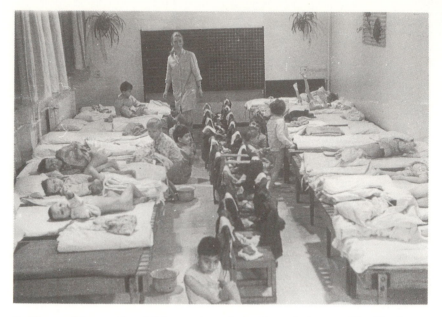

3 After waking up the children get ready to sit on their pots. The Conductor gives each child directive help as necessary in this 'task'.

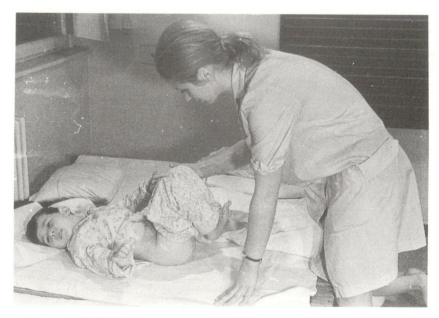

4 The child holds his pyjama trousers with his left hand.

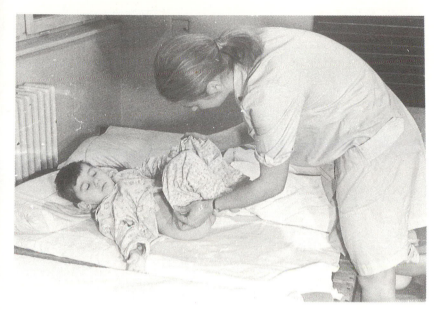

5 The Conductor ensures that he does not let go of them; she is directing the little
   boy's performance.

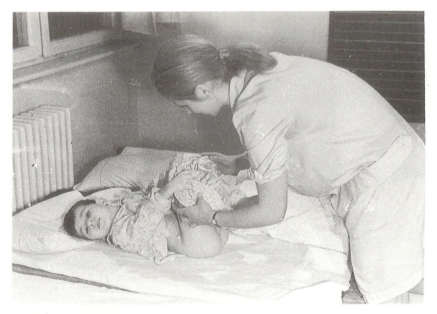

6 Grasping his trousers with both hands at the same time is a difficult task for an
   athetoid child.

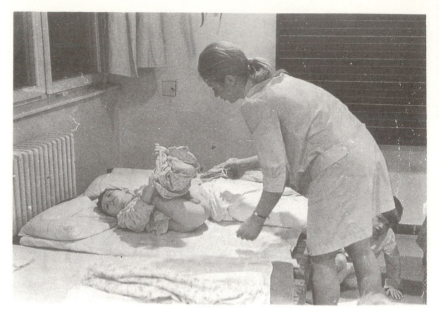

7 Simultaneous movement of head and hands is still uncoordinated and so the child is not yet able to look directly at what he is doing.

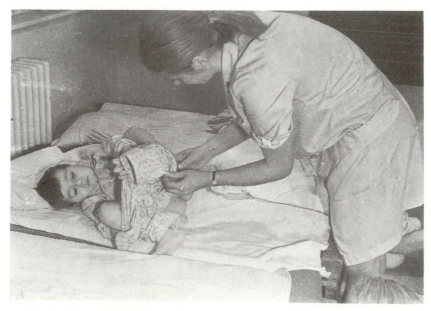

8 The Conductor has directed him so that he has turned on his side.

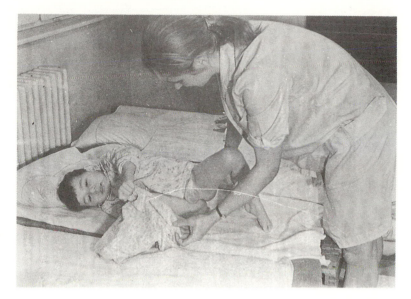

9 The task is easier to perform in this position but some parts of it are not entirely solved as yet. The Conductor helps at critical points so that the child can carry on by himself, ensuring that he makes maximum use of his abilities. In the course of the task-series, co-ordinated work using both hands during task-series in the daily schedule enables the child to accomplish this task, to undress more and more successfully.

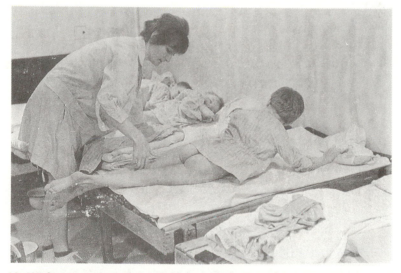

10 With quite a few of the children, sliding down from the slat-bed still needs direction to become sufficiently orthofunctional and here the Conductor directs the boy in positioning his legs.

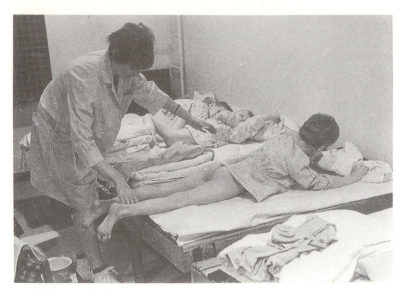

11 He 'intends' abducting his legs in preparing to slide down.

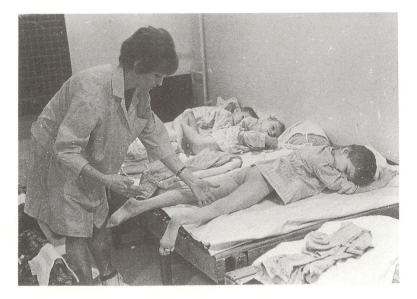

12 The intending has been successful; carrying out this performance has been patterned in previous task-series. Both Conductor and child monitor the exact application of elements of the skill which he has learned, the boy checking the result very carefully at each stage.

13 With appropriate preparation of his posture he is now capable of standing with his heels on the floor . . .

14 . . . then he can sit down securely on the pot in the right way.

15 Whilst chatting with the children the Conductor clears away the bed-linen. Meanwhile some of the children are beginning to dress of their own accord. Each one carries out the stages in dressing in whatever position best suits him. The child selects that position for himself.

16 Some of the children do the same task standing up . . .

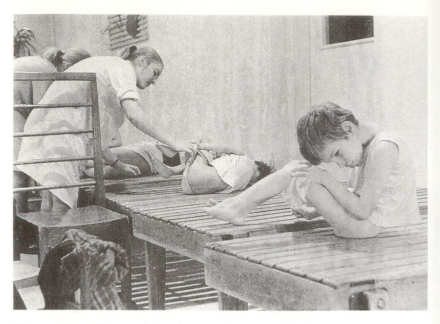

17 . . . others sitting or lying down, and some need help.

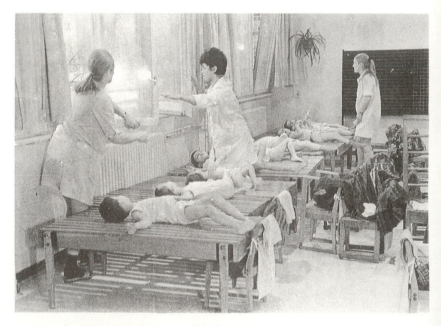

18 For the morning 'training' Conductors open the windows winter and summer alike.

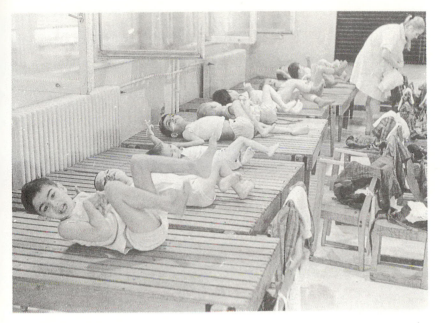

19   Training by the open windows . . .

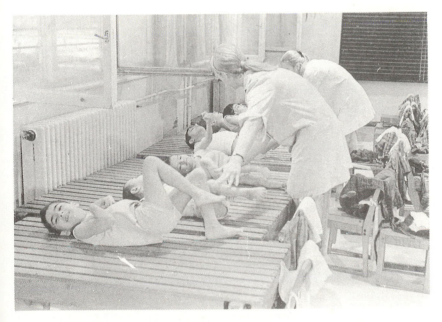

20   . . . some elements are directed by the Conductor . . .

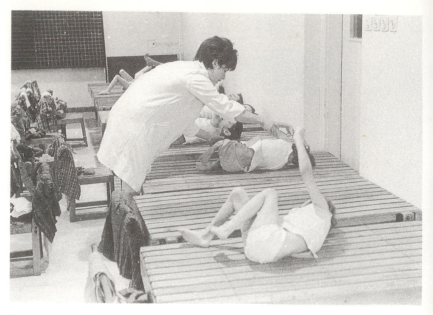

21 . . . who also gives help if necessary.

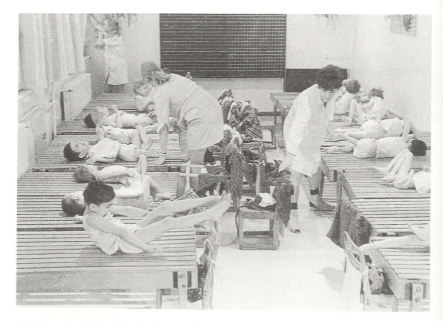

22 Training is finished, the windows are closed, and the children get ready to dress.

23 Pulling on socks.

24 One of the spontaneous manifestations of group spirit. The children draw each other's attention to an aspect of the task which might have been neglected.

25 The sock must be pulled up.

26 A detail of independent dressing.

27 Putting on shirts in different ways.

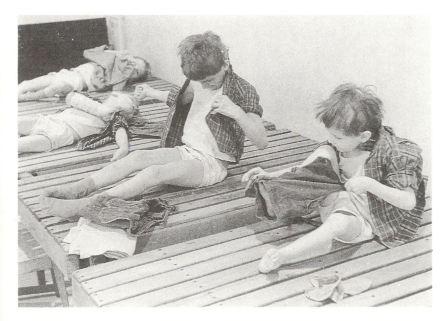

28 Stages in dressing. (The child wearing a plaster bandage had hurt his arm.)

29 Doing up buttons.

30 Preparation for washing.

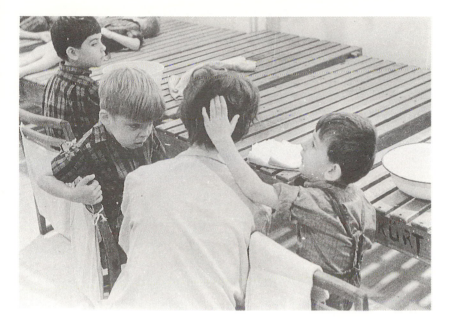

31 Morning chat.

32 Washing themselves, use of soap, nailbrush, and so on.

33 Opening the soap container. The child watches his own movements intently. Activities of practical personal use are always the most interesting (most strongly motivated) and also those which offer the greatest feeling of success.

34 To take out the soap, he has to sit still, hold the soap container steady, and get hold of the soap.

35 Washing one's hands is a complicated, co-ordinated task.

36 The nailbrush has fallen into the water and he has to take it out.

37 Both hands must be co-ordinated in using a nailbrush.

38 Some are already making their independent way into breakfast, or indeed, helping to push the chairs through.

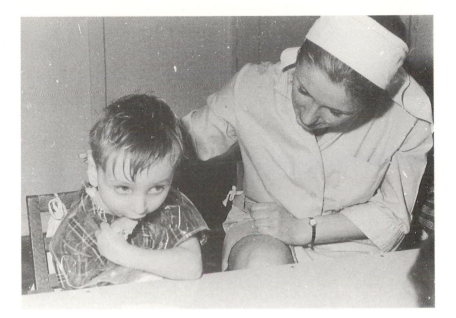

39 Eating independently.

40 After breakfast (and supper) mouths are washed out. The Conductors direct and so ensure that the task of toothbrushing is completed.

41 Every child . . .

42 . . . cleans his teeth . . .

43 . . . in his own way.

44 One child prepares to grasp the mug . . .

45 . . . to use it to wash out his mouth.

46 Using a method learned in the task-series, this little boy gets hold of his mug . . .

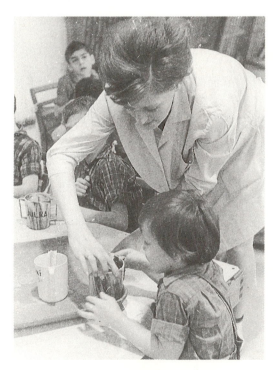

47 . . . and rinses his mouth.

48 The group cleaning their teeth and washing out their mouths.

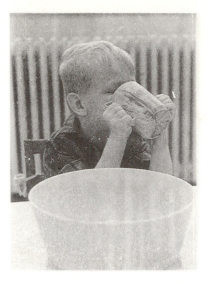

49 Holding the mug with both hands and raising it to his mouth.

50 The first task of a 'floor task-series' to be carried out on a slat-bed, climbing on to the bed. For this the child has to stand up from a sitting position. Some need directing.

51 Elements of the task 'standing up': stretching out his arms, the child has to grasp the slats. The Conductor shows how far he must reach. Demonstrating the goal to be achieved facilitates it. Stretching forward the arms as preparation for standing up.

52 An inappropriate posture must be corrected. Before this child was admitted, he had been lying down for eleven-and-a-half years. He has been in the Institute for only two months and already can sit on a chair but still needs direction for sitting properly.

53 An incorrect sitting position can be corrected with direction. The boy learns how he can correct his backward-leaning tensed posture by bending knees and hips.

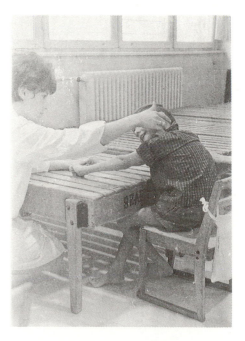

54 The good position achieved is maintained with a minimum of indirect help by ensuring that his left hand grasps the slat.

55 The goal is 'independent sitting' and so facilitation will have to decrease even further quite soon. By now facilitation by touch is no longer needed. The boy is able to maintain this position for shorter or longer periods by himself.

56 He is preparing to stand up. To do so, he has a little help by securing his wrist. To be able to stand up independently is essential for beginning the lying task-series. This is the boy's own designated goal. From the Conductor's point of view the educational goal is one method of teaching change of posture.

57 This way enables him to stand up.

58 In sitting, this child does not seem to be able to sit erect.

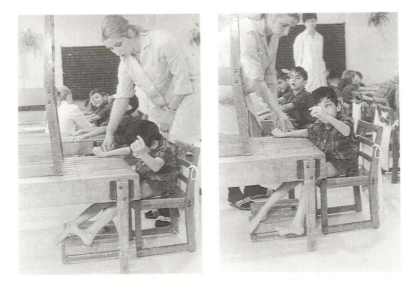

59 and 60 The general goal being to achieve independence, the Conductor only gives directive help. The child will learn to get up and stand by grasping the rungs of the chair in front of him. His goal is to reach the chair rung. Trying to achieve this he succeeds in sitting erect – something he had been unable to do by attempting it directly. Reaching the chair rung serves here as an indirect cortical facilitation by which he becomes acquainted with the concept of sitting erect through his own experience, once the result achieved has been brought into consciousness for him.

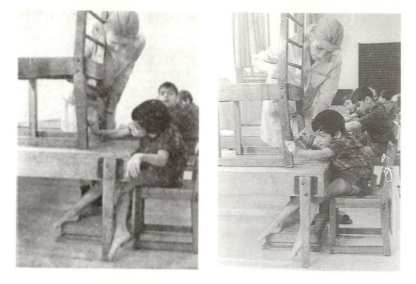

61 to 64   By breaking the task into parts and setting appropriate goals the
Conductor assists the process of learning by bringing experience
into consciousness. In this case she sees to it that the chair rung is
grasped successfully. For this child to reach and get hold of the
rung is very difficult. The Conductor creates the appropriate
educational situation for independent task performance and
ensures the total co-operation of the child, who was passive
initially, for without his co-operation any help would be unpro-
ductive. Success lends wings to his effort, so the Conductor only
intervenes in the activity by making suggestions about what to
do, with an unruffled voice and manner, according to her
knowledge of the system, always at the appropriate time, and
with a minimum of energy. Here she is securing the grasp the
child had managed with his right hand and so makes it possible
for him to grasp with his left hand. She has created the right
mood in the group for accomplishing the task and so promoted
group activity and individual intention.

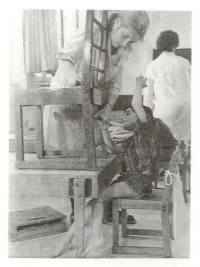
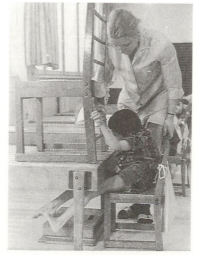

65 A new goal, to grasp a higher rung, the highest the child can reach. Standing up is built on previous tasks solved. The success previously achieved is the chief motivational factor. The child's main goal throughout the whole process was to be able to stand up while the Conductor's educational goal is different – to teach grasping and holding on. Through accomplishing the task both have achieved their goals.

66 The group is told to stand up when the boy in the foreground has reached this stage, then he, in unison with the other children standing up, tries for a moment to straighten out completely.

67 The children are standing up from being seated. Their next task in the series is to climb up on to their slat-beds and that means using their hands. The Conductor notices if a child is not putting his heels to the floor when standing up and lets him correct this fault. At the same time she teaches him how to grasp. He uses every method for changing positions, for example climbing up on to the slat-bed, not as a separate task but always where and whenever it would be useful.

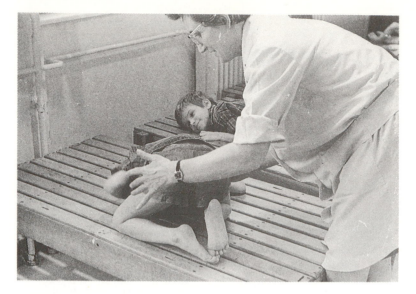

68 From lying prone to sitting back between the feet. This requires supporting oneself on one's hands. Elements in the task-series are very varied so the children have plenty of change but at the same time every task may have the same goal within it; for instance in this case learning to use their hands, or applying what they have learned in that respect. Individual tasks are repeated only in extremely rare instances. But the same goal may be achieved over and over again through different tasks.

69 Illustration 67 showed one variant of support on the hands for this boy and here the same pattern of action is used in sitting down. In both cases support is possible only with closed fists as yet. This is regarded as a successful result in the child's present condition when the emphasis is on supporting himself independently with arms stretched in an ortho-functional way compared with his previous state. (Progress here is not in the task but in the way in which it is carried out.)

70 The whole group has achieved the 'sitting back' position.

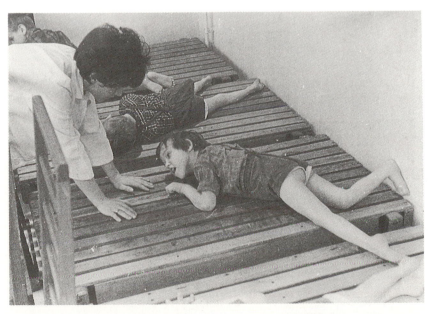

71 The task is to lie on the stomach and turn round to face the opposite direction. The goal again here is to support oneself on one's hands.

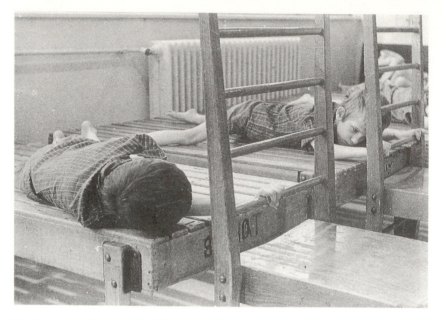

72 Arms must be stretched forward as far as the chair rung and children can do this successfully by turning on to one side.

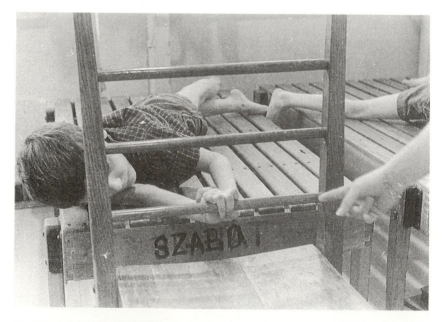

73 The athetoid boy has reached the rung with a precisely aimed movement. The goal of reaching out to the chair rung has facilitated extending his arms.

74 He has succeeded in keeping his hands on the rung although his grip is not yet perfect. There is no need for the Conductor to ensure his hold and he enjoys this independence. Straightening the elbow, dorsal flexion of the wrist, and grasping the rung are a facilitation for stopping involuntary movements.

75 Grasping the chair is a task common to the whole group. Individual solutions take shape within the framework of the group's collective effort.

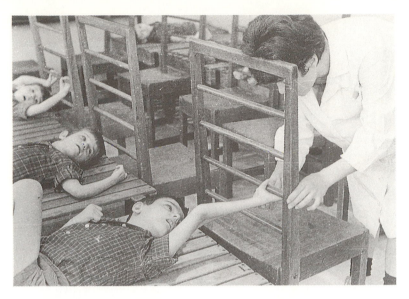

76 The task is to grasp the chair while lying on the back and stretching the arms back. The task of grasping varies under different conditions, and means in fact a different task every time.

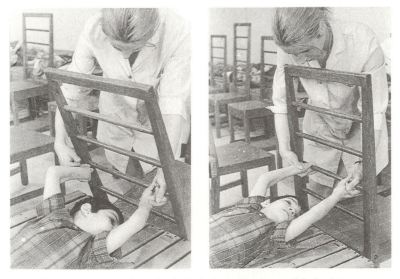

77 and 78 Tilting the chair back slightly makes it possible for him to grasp the rung independently. For a short time grasping may be directed at the wrist by the Conductor until the boy learns to recognize when his grasp is correct.

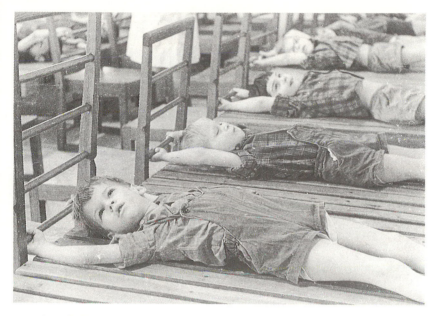

79 The whole group has succeeded in solving the task.

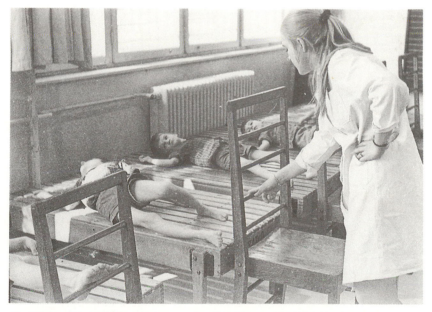

80 The goal is to lift one leg on to the chair rung. The children 'intend' this verbally. Some have achieved the goal, others are on their way towards it. At this time the task of the first ones is to keep their feet stretched out on to the chair rungs.

81   The nearest child has reached the rung with one foot . . .

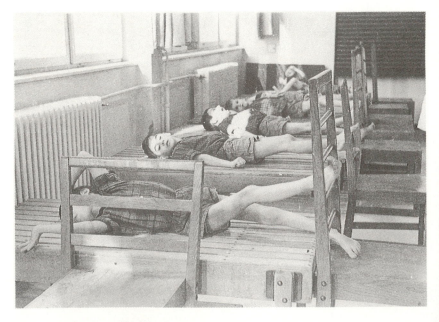

82   . . . and now with the other one as well.

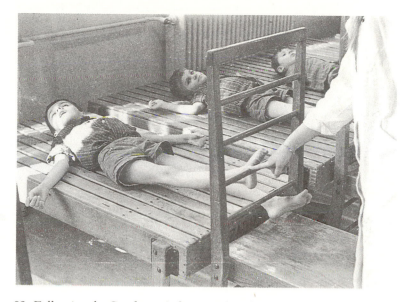

83 Following the Conductor's direction he adjusts his foot and at the same time corrects his body posture. In the course of the daily schedule he systematically achieves co-ordinated movements while restricting involuntary movements in the rest of his body.

84 We have selected only some elements here from a long task-series. Its goal is to master in a wide range of postures grasping, supporting oneself, and to learn how to consciously and adequately control positioning the legs. After achieving the goal, that is, after carrying out the last task, the children grasp a rung of the chair in front of them and prepare to stand up. Where necessary a stool is placed under their feet. A task-series done when lying always ends with standing up. From the very first day sitting down and standing up are included in every programme.

85   Their legs already do not need to be secured manually. A chair with rungs easy to hold on to can be used as facilitation. In some cases it may be a 'splay-footed' chair which will not tip up. Here the group is watching the success of the child standing up. The correct positioning of elbow and knee facilitates stretching his knee and putting his heel down. The athetoid child is grasping independently!

86   When he has grasped the chair rung, the Conductor secures his wrist dorsal flexion.

87 Applying the individually learned method of holding on, the entire group has succeeded in standing up.

88 Task-series form a unity with other parts of the daily schedule. At breaktime there is no need to teach sitting and stretching the arm forward separately but only to check up on the application of patterns learned already. The children's whole system of performance has undergone a change as a result of the previous lying task-series. Activity requiring a Conductor's facilitation at the beginning of the task-series is achieved independently now.

89 One child's particular way of grasping his mug!

90 The group holding mugs. In an athetoid group learning to support one-self on the elbows forms a facilitation for drinking. When drinking the children bend their heads forward to their mugs. Dorsal flexion of the wrists helps in grasping. The Conductor's manual assistance consists in directing the correct positioning of the wrist and tilt of the mug.

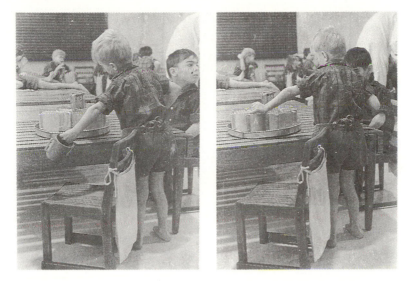

91 and 92 After break some of the children chat; others following their teacher's example help with tidying up. They put the empty mugs on the tray.

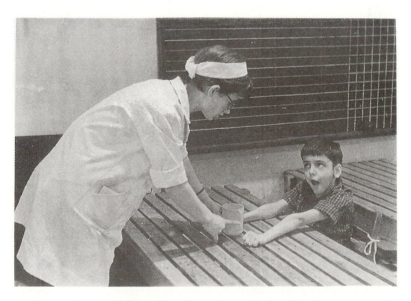

93 The task here is to learn how to grasp a mug. For this the arms must be extended as in the lying task-series in order to stop involuntary movements . . .

94 . . . and make grasping the mug handle easier.

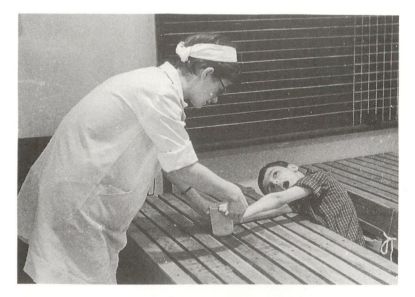

95 This child still needs facilitation to realize his goal. The Conductor secures the hand with which he has already grasped one mug handle and directs his other hand towards grasping the other one. It can be seen clearly that the child grasps the mug handle in the same way as he did the chair rung in the lying task-series. The Conductor offers the same assistance as she did then by ensuring the dorsal flexion of the wrists.

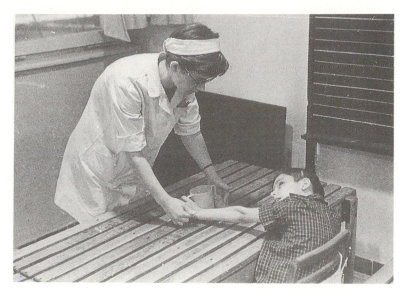

96 In this child's case too the facilitation is similar to that given him when
he was holding on to the chair rung.

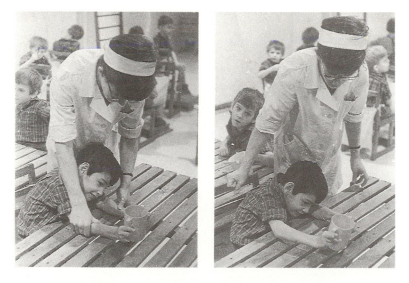

97 and 98 Facilitation is productive only if it is transitional. The child
grasps the mug by himself. Earlier task-series made it possible
for him to learn to stretch out his arms and so to find a way to
grasp the mug. During the next break the children make use of
things they have learned. The Conductor must take great care
that the new patterns should be applied in such a way that they
become consolidated.

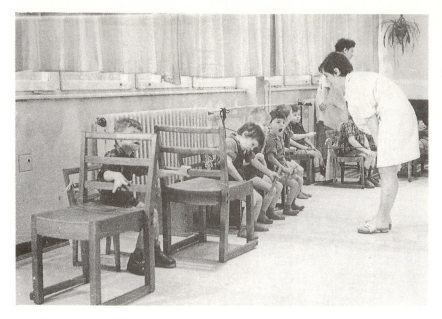

99 The next part of the daily schedule is individual and group standing-and-walking tasks.

100 Group members use individually differing methods.

101 A child walking independently between two ropes.

102 The children verbally intend walking. Those walking independently grasp sticks in their hands and this eases walking considerably. The Conductor stands in front of one child – this is facilitation, too, because he still needs reassuring by the Conductor's presence that he will not fall.

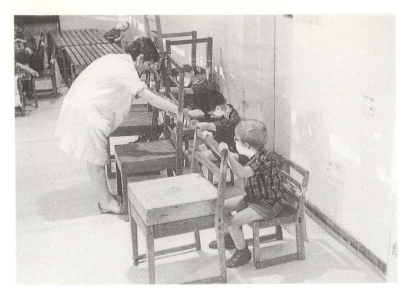

103 Across the room those children are preparing for standing up who still need to use a chair.

104 The first stage in standing up, pushing the chair forward and putting heels on the floor.

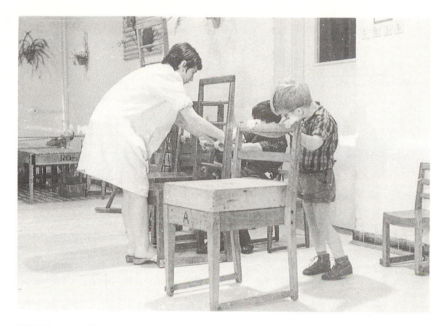

105 This is followed by standing up.

106 After standing up, the boy is told by the Conductor to check up on his feet and in doing so . . .

107 . . . puts down his heels.

108 A part of the (sitting) 'hand task-series', stretching the arms forwards. One boy's facilitation is to grasp a stick, while another's is to put his hands together. There are stools beneath their feet and they try to adjust their soles to keep them down.

109 Stretching out the arms in preparation . . .

110 . . . for the game shown here. If the work is to be really productive, a precondition for the Conductor is to gain and hold the children's attention and
active co-operation. Hence the Conductor plans all the details of the work,
for instance as to what goal is to be set, which games or other activities
encompass it and what facilitations will be given.

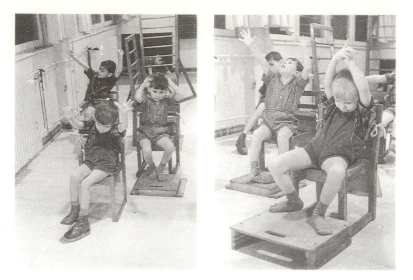

111 and 112 The task is to stretch the arms up and the children do this using their own methods.

113 The Conductor demonstrates the correct way to do it.

114 The child does it that way by himself.

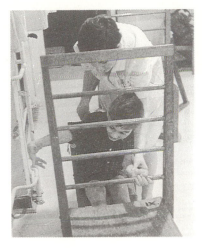

115 The task is to grasp the chair rung from beneath with both hands. The boy has already managed it with one hand. The Conductor gets him to correct his grip and now pays attention to the other hand which is beginning to move. Here facilitation is assistance not only in achieving a goal but also in learning how to get there.

116 An independent solution is always looked for. Here the boy puts his thumb on the rung and will turn his other fingers under it. He is not practising a movement but solving his task, not only to move but as an athetoid how to keep still as well.

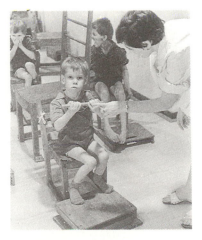

118 Here the goal is to grasp the stick from underneath.

117 A moment of triumphant achievement in his development! In this case it is accepted as an orthofunction. Success is always relative to the situation obtaining. A great achievement for one child may be quite the wrong solution for another.

119 Putting to use the form of grasp each child has learned, for instance here to grip and hold a flute in learning to play it.

120 Playing the flute . . .

121 . . . is also one way of developing speech.

122 A lot of attention is given to spontaneous activities within the daily schedule, for example 'work' . . .

123 . . . tidying up . . .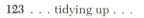

124 . . . rearranging the room.

125 Lunch. The children are sitting at the table in the way they have learned to sit during the task series.

126 How to eat lunch is another task. Here they change hands to drink their soup. Holding a spoon in one hand and using the other spoon for drinking they have stopped involuntary movements in the way they had learned. This forges a new link between intention and activity.

127 The little boy extends his left arm on the table and prevents his involuntary movements that way. He supports and controls his right (opposite) hand by leaning on his right elbow as he has learned to do, enabling him to raise that hand to his mouth to eat.

128 All the children can accomplish this task (eating doughnuts) by using the individual method shaped in their learning . . .

129 . . . to . . .

130 . . . cope.

131 Preparing for writing by learning to choose a stick and . . .

132 . . . lift it out . . .

133 from the box. All this is one way of bringing together seeing, touching, and grasping which, just like the appropriate way of sitting, results from the whole preparatory daily education.

134 Placing sticks . . .

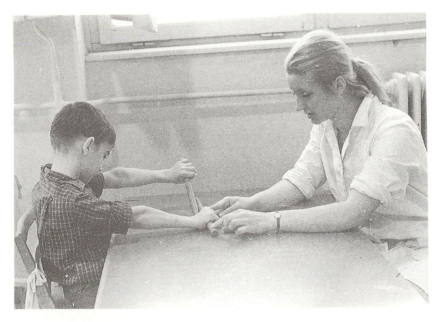

135 . . . upright is something else to learn . . .

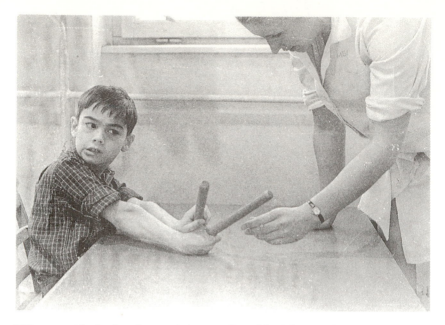

136 . . . with the hands remaining on the table. The Conductor sees that he intends this task.

137 He has worked out how to do it!

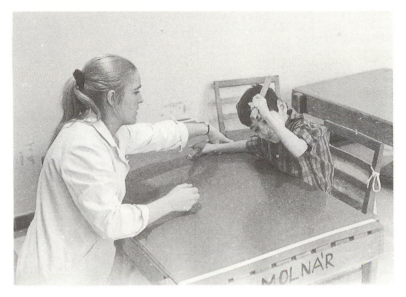

138 Here putting the sticks on the table is proving difficult. The Conductor ensures that what he has achieved so far is not lost and that the arm on the table does not slip off. The boy intends placing his other hand on the table with all the co-operation he can offer.

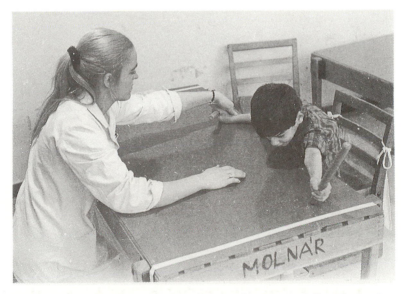

139 The Conductor has waited until it was done successfully. The boy has stretched out his arm slowly on the table while counting from one to five. If he had intended rapidly his arm would have sprung back into its bent position.

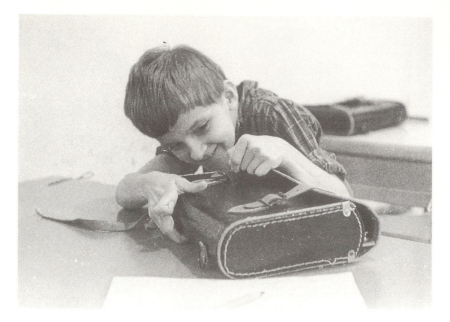

140 Preparing for school means learning to deal with its equipment – opening his satchel.

141 Taking out his pencil box.

142 Getting things ready for writing.

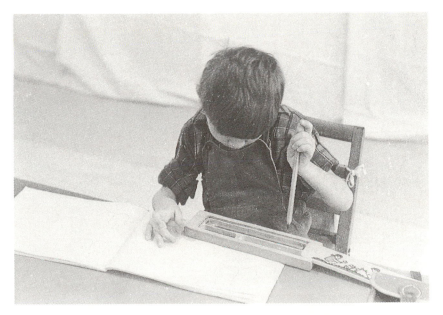

143 Now it's the pencil. All these are important tasks which the child manages by himself.

144 Getting ready to answer in class. Both children and Conductor see to it that while one arm is being raised the other stays on the table and the children stop their involuntary movements in this way.

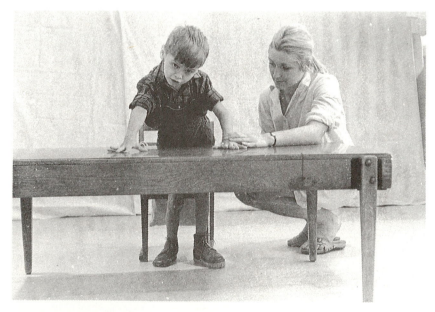

145 Questions in Hungarian schools have to be answered standing up and so the Institute does the same, as here, even if initially it is a slow process which needs several facilitations.

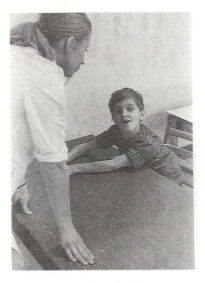

146 The pupil in the lowest class still unable to speak . . .

147 . . . learns to form sounds.

148 In order to write with his right hand his left hand is secured,

149 only if necessary.

150 The child shapes the position most convenient for him at the time even if this is not perfect yet. The Conductor watches and directs his every movement if necessary . . .

151 . . . until he is able to write independently.

152 Turning over pages needs very fine finger movement.

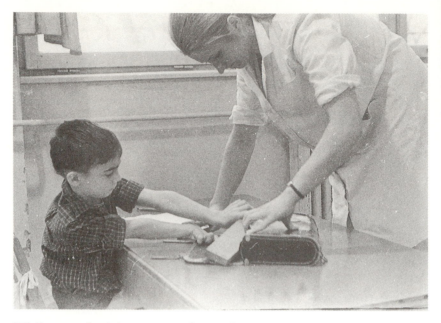

153 Putting school things away. The Conductor helps by creating the right situation only if necessary . . .

154 . . . otherwise the little boy does it quite by himself.

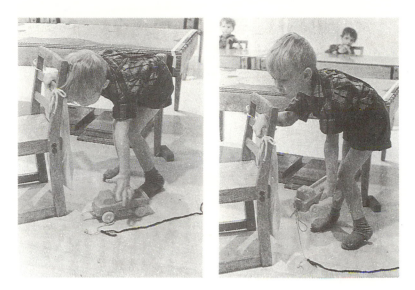

155 and 156 Nursery school activities – the child bends down for the toy.

157 The Conductor does not interfere in their play but teaches the children to learn how to play, bringing in the movement patterns they have learned.

158 They blow the paper boat along.

159 How to walk was taught in the walking task and must be used in every kind of occupation including play.

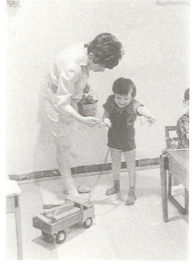

160 The child is getting about in the way he has learned.

161 A moment when the little boys are immersed in their play.

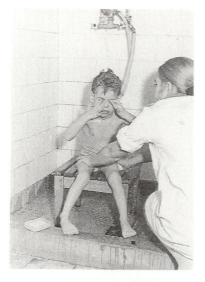

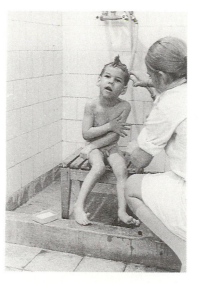

162 Taking a shower. The Conductor secures the boy's legs as long as it is needed so that he is able to use his arms with assurance.

163 He learns how to wash his arms . . .

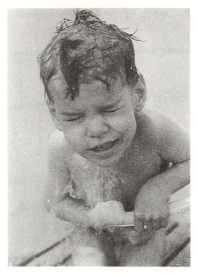

164 . . . and to handle . . .   **165** . . . the shower.

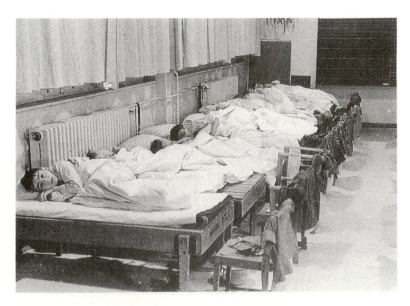

166 It is evening and the children have gone to bed.

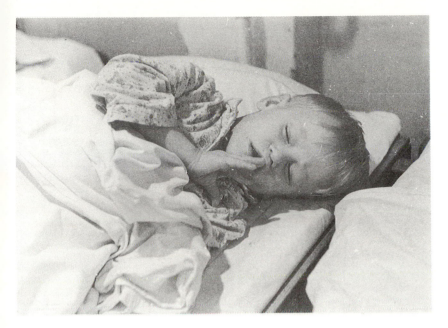

167 A day well spent is over.

Details of task-series, facilitations

Sitting as a task and as part of an activity

Completing the lying task-series leads on to shaping an ability to grasp and hold on, these in turn to learning how to sit up and all these actions can be used in dressing.

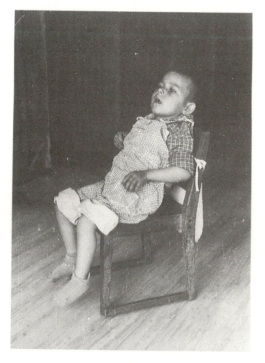

168 A child with double hemiplegia photographed on admission. He does not use his hands to support himself and is visibly afraid that if he even moved his hand he would fall down. His hip is in extension.

169 In his present condition, to begin to sit up he has to raise his head. He tries to find something to hang on to with his hands. (Behind him another child is sitting up by turning on his side.)

170 He holds on to the slats on both sides and bends his head forward. (The child next to him sits up by leaning sideways on his elbow.)

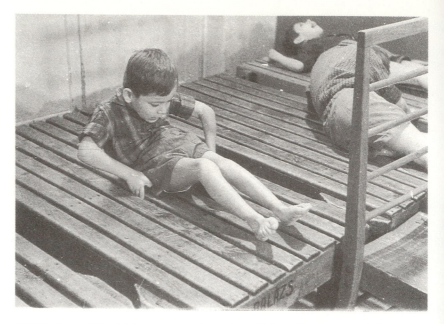

171 He is watching his knees pressed together. He has almost succeeded in sitting up.

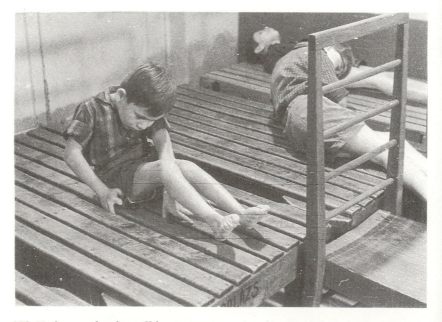

172 He knows that he will be sitting properly when he abducts his legs. So as a facilitation his left hand parts his legs by holding the slat between them.

173 He has adjusted his legs. He is sitting securely grasping the slats of his bed now with both hands.

174 Another detail taken at random from the daily schedule. He has to place the sole of his foot on a stick and for this he has to pull up his sole on to the seat of his chair, stretch out his arms, and incline his trunk forward.

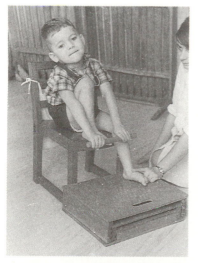

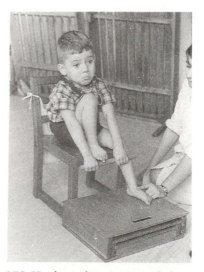

175 He has succeeded in putting his heel on to the chair, stretched out his arms and is leaning forward. The Conductor prevents his left knee from stretching out. He is not grasping entirely correctly because his left hand hyperpronates.

176 He has almost succeeded in getting his whole foot on to the chair. He has adjusted his left hand on the stick and placed that under his toes.

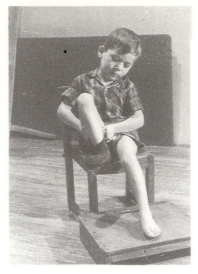

177 Pulling on socks – this pattern recalls the earlier ones.

178 He only stretches his left knee out a little way, has placed his heel on the chair, and managed to reach his foot with both hands very well, all this while sitting securely.

179 By paying attention to correct leg posture he does not need now to support his leg on the chair.

Standing up and walking as a task and as part of an action

180 The group is trying out standing without support. They already have no chair in front of them to provide security. They still need to concentrate on what they are doing and they do this for one another as well. While still seated they put their heels down, bodyweight forward, and verbally intend as they start to stand up.

181 Solutions to standing up, pace and method are individual to each child. They intend verbally and check up on the result achieved.

182 The goal of the action is a facilitation – a great motivational force. The body sets off to join his companions sitting at the table, standing up and walking independently, as he has learned to do. The Conductor ensures the appropriate conditions for him. (The chair is neither too far from nor too close to the table, for example.)

183 On his way to the table.

184 Independent walking with indirect help. About two paces in front of the child the small chair serves as a goal to be reached. He goes to it, stands, then pushes the chair forward.

185 This boy is able to walk round from chair to chair varying his direction. The distance he walks can be gradually increased by pushing the chairs (goals) further apart and the boy does this for himself.

186 The child shown in 180 and 181 on the extreme left is using two walking sticks to get about and checking his posture by lifting each in turn. To walk with two sticks is a transitional facilitation. The sticks are long so that they give as little support as possible and so serve to increase independence. He is not pressing his knees together now as he did in 180 and is standing securely.

187 To make him consciously independent he raises the sticks alternately as he walks.

188 One of the ways of learning to walk independently – walking between ropes in a group.

189 Any support and assistance is useful only if it can be dispensed with in its turn. This is prepared for by lifting up one arm while the other holds on to the rope which is stretched rather loosely and really only of help in maintaining balance.

190 Walking with ropes as an individual task. The little boy stands safely holding on to the two ropes, heels down and arms and legs extended. His wedge-shaped shoe soles help to keep his heels down. They are thicker at the front and thinner at the back of his foot.

191 He raises his arms alternately and shows how firm he is by stretching his other arm forward.

192 He lifts up and stretches out both arms. To increase his feeling of assurance two ropes (which hang quite loosely in any case) can be crossed in front of him. This photograph shows how it is done.

193 The child consciously holds the rope with two fingers only, so proving to himself that he is not using it as a support. If he does not check up on his knees they still tend to adduct.

194 He straightens and parts his knees, checking that his position is correct.

195 Standing up and getting about between chairs is the same facilitation as the ropes. The chairs are a more stable support, but more easily moved away. He is consciously lifting up his arms alternately.

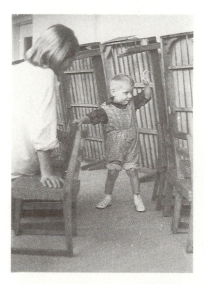

196 Walking between the rows of chairs, the child walks quite securely alone provided he is able to extend his supporting arm.

197 Between the rows of chairs he lets go with both hands while clapping and so stands independently.

198 One form of getting about with increased difficulty for a group of children with involuntary movements is to go on all fours. The children who still find this too difficult learn to straighten their knees with a stool or chair as facilitation. The goal is to put their heels down, extend their knees, and support themselves on their hands. All this is actually a preparation for standing up from the floor.

199 Gripping the stick facilitates standing and walking.

200 An athetoid boy is facilitating squatting by grasping small sticks. Practice in squatting and standing up also helps in getting up from the floor.

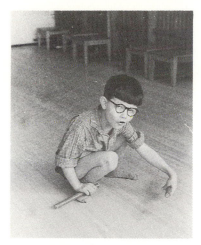

201 Squatting down.

202 Getting up.

203 Standing with extended arms and legs. He has learned to do this as a method of stopping involuntary movement.

204 Once he has learned to hold his legs straight he has to know how to bend them voluntarily too. Touching his knee with a heel as he walks means that he has to put all his weight on the leg he is standing on and to transfer his weight from one leg to the other in turn as he steps forward. Raising his knee, stopping involuntary movement while bringing the heel to touch his other knee requires a precisely aimed movement.

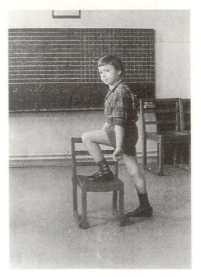

205 The same boy walking down stairs without any support. He is applying the knee-bending in another situation.

206 This little girl is standing securely even when she climbs up on to a chair and this again is a variation to make the task more difficult.

207 She stands well on the chair but at these times some involuntary movements recur, although generally they have become barely noticeable, by now.

208 Application of the results attained through the hand task-series in a ball game. Athetoid children stand securely stretching out their arms.

209 The little athetoid girl who stood up on the chair has learned to skip with a rope.

A diplegic group – Preliminary tasks preparing to stand up, with their practical application

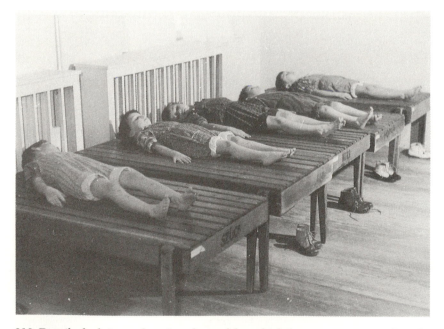

210 Detail of a lying task-series, the goal for which is preparing to stand on the soles of the feet. The initially uncorrected posture for diplegics when lying on their backs, with the feet in plantar flexion.

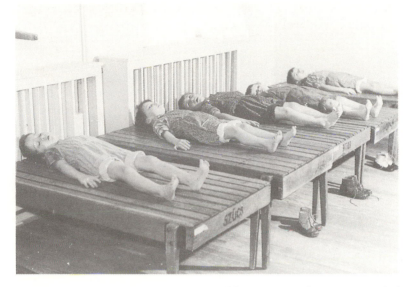

211 Shaping the conscious correction of foot posture. Continuous verbal intending facilitates dorsal foot flexion. The club-foot initial position seen in the previous photograph is less evident.

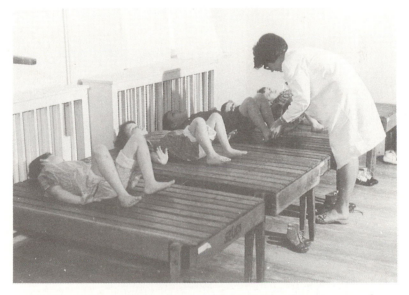

212 In this task-series dorsal flexion of the foot is used in very many forms and situations. Here bending up both hands and feet and parting the knees at the same time form a complex task. Dorsal foot flexion is facilitated by dorsal flexion of the hands and bending the hips.

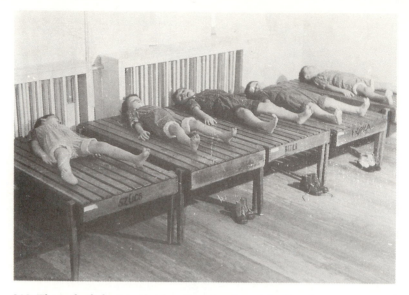

213 The task of placing a heel on the other knee is broken down into partial tasks. The first of these is to stretch out the legs previously flexed while keeping the knees apart (abduction of the hip). Even when keeping their knees apart the children do not forget to keep their feet bent up.

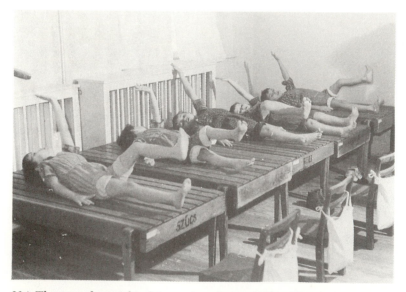

214 The second partial task is to raise an extended leg. Raising an extended arm facilitates this. Although meanwhile the knee bends in slightly, the children intend both extending their knees and the dorsal foot flexion and the latter is associated with every new partial task.

215 The third partial task is to place the heel on the knee.

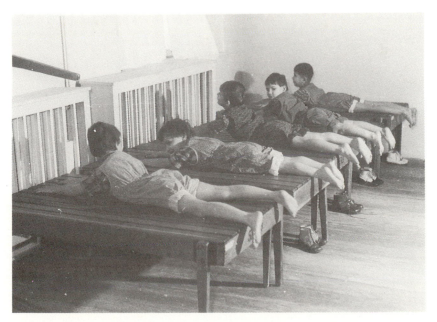

216 Even after turning over on to the stomach the previous requirements are maintained: dorsal flexion of the feet, knees apart.

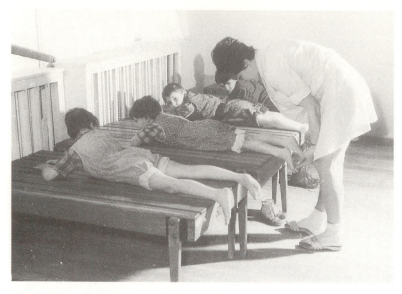

217 The Conductor directs if any facilitation is necessary. In this case it cannot be anything more than to ensure that the child understands what is required.

218 At the end of the task-series the children slide down from their slat-beds and stand on the floor in front of them with adjusted feet and parted knees. As a result of the preparation shown earlier they are keeping their heels down successfully.

219 Even when squatting down their heels stay down.

220 What they have learned can be applied later to sitting on the pot.

221 Abduction of the knees and dorsal foot flexion can be seen too when they are putting on their socks and boots.

222 A random detail from a hand task-series showing a seated group of diplegic and double hemiplegic children. The task is to bend up the feet and hands and check on the position of their feet.

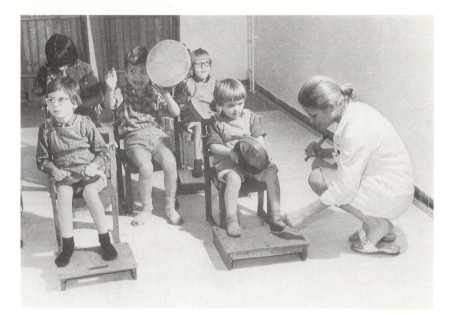

223 They also see to it that their knees are parted. Here they are sitting down applying tasks learned while lying down. At another time of the day the same group uses these patterns in an 'orchestral' situation. Here too they follow effectively the same requirements, learning to combine correct foot position with more complex activities.

224 The Conductor teaches them how to hold a musical instrument.

Preparation for writing in an athetoid group

225 Detail from a (sitting) hand task-series, the goal of which is to solve tasks of both spatial and precisely timed discrimination. The precondition for this is to prevent involuntary movements by fixing and then quick release of the fixing. The children raise one arm first while counting from one to five, then sing a song for lowering it and while doing so wave that hand up and down. Meanwhile they should keep the other hand fixed on their knees and heels down. Every beat of the rhythm is used, that is one element in the activity leads into another as beat follows beat. Some are still preventing involuntary movement through a pronounced arm extension and strong volar flexion, stretching their fingers. Others have learned to bend their hands down quite loosely. In the corner at the back of the left-hand side a child with torsional dystonia still needs to use the rung of a chair as facilitation. To the right in the row in front of him a choreo-athetoid child has found a peculiar solution to the problem of stopping involuntary movements in his feet.

226 The small stick must be held at one end on the knee and stood upright for one beat. The children stop involuntary movement in their feet and other hand. Some of them can already hold the stick with the tips of their thumbs and forefingers.

227 In the daily schedule linked with the task-series shown, occupations bring in what has been learned in a variety of ways, here for instance learning how to lace up boots. This helps to strengthen patterns learned previously.

228 Even at nursery school-age refined movements learned in the hand task-series are applied in practical situations. This child (seen in photograph 225 as well) is tensing his fingers to stop involuntary movements.

229 The boy is sticking coloured discs along a pencilled line on a sheet of drawing paper which he holds down with his other hand, sorting them out by colour. He can already hold the paper down and straighten his elbows. The dystonic child succeeds in holding his head correctly.

230 He is able to hold down the paper with his left hand without clenching his fist by stretching elbow and fingers. So his solution to the problem is increasingly orthofunctional (more adaptive). The child holds the adhesive with two fingers. Precision is indicated by the positioning of the elbow.

231 The coloured discs are assembled on each side, but the task is growing harder because it is more difficult to stop involuntary movements with a bent arm. Nevertheless the discs are placed relatively precisely. He holds the disc between two fingers but his left palm is turning upwards and his head has turned away from the proper direction.

232 Following a design he has to make a flower of discs and sticks on paper.

233 Adhesive must be squeezed out exactly with the pattern and the small stick fitted in accurately. He has managed to hold the paper down turning his hand inwards and has to work with his right elbow bent. He puts the adhesive on the line as required. By leaning a little to the left he has succeeded in turning his head the right way. He works precisely and extends his forefinger separately.

234 The final stage of making a flower showing again a form of both discrimination in action and hand–eye co-ordination.

235 Stopping involuntary movement of the left hand by grasping a stick and extending the elbow. Drawing vertical lines with the right hand between widely spaced horizontals.

236 He is already holding the paper down with his left hand. Elbow and wrist are bending in and involuntary movements beginning.

237 While working he has found the best position for both hands for completing his task and is now free from involuntary movement.

238 In an arithmetic lesson the child shown in photograph 229 is using an exercise book ruled with large squares to write and is applying what he has learned earlier.

239 Writing exercises done by this boy over two years.

240 Children with double hemiplegia are applying what they have learned in an occupational situation which requires spatial discrimination and accurate use of the hands.

241 Here two children with double hemiplegia are helping to sort out letters on to an alphabet board on tidying-up day. This means that not only do they have to hold the letters with the tips of their fingers and thumbs but also they have to distinguish between letter shapes when they both have severe perceptual disabilities.

The difference between assistance and the facilitation which leads to a result

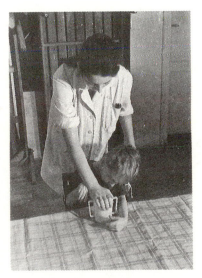

242 A 5-year-old contract athetoid torsional dystonic child on admission. He cannot even sit in a chair with no arms but sits in an armchair tensing his head back with his legs crossed. His arms always move in opposite directions. He cannot and does not even try to grip or hold objects.

243 Here he is learning to drink with a two-handled mug and his task is to hold it. However, to show what could happen, the Conductor holds the mug down this time, covering over the top of the drink, so not only is she preventing him from realizing what the mug is for but wrong too from the point of view of hygiene. Equally the handles of the mug are not within his reach.

244 He has managed to grip the mug by both handles. His task is to lift the mug to his mouth, bending his arms and head forward at the same time. This is a very difficult task for this little boy. He would need to be directed properly to hold it in the correct position.

245 The little boy finds the task hopelessly difficult. Encouraging words to urge him on do not help. Even what he had achieved has broken down now. Tensing in his left arm has pulled the mug away from the correct direction.

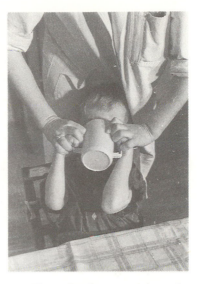

246 In the end, the Conductor exerts all her strength, gets hold of the child's hands and puts them on to the mug handles, bending his arms forcibly. With this the little boy's head tenses back and his trunk turns away.

247 The Conductor grips the child's hands and somehow forces the mug to his mouth. So the result has become totally passive and there is no chance of the adaptive reafferentative learning process developing through the boy's own successful activity.

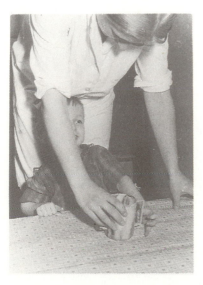

248 The same little boy with a two-handled mug busy with the same task, but in the series of photographs which follow the facilitations are correct and the goal will be achieved. Here the Conductor is bending over the boy and supports his head gently. He begins to relate to her and understand her directions. The Conductor holds the mug round the outside and turns it so that the child can grasp its handles.

249 After he has managed to grip one handle the Conductor secures the mug to ensure its remaining in the appropriate position.

250 To maintain the grasp which has been achieved independently the Conductor gently secures his left hand. Now he can hold on to the handle and so the little boy feels free to work with his right hand. He realizes already that he will be able to succeed and achieve his goal.

251 Once both handles are held the Conductor turns her attention to the correct wrist position.

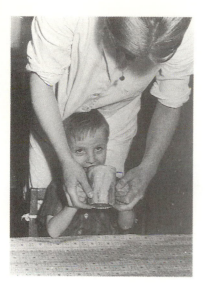

252 The most difficult task has been achieved – the little boy has lifted the mug to his mouth and the Conductor is not constraining his hands but letting them grip the mug independently, while merely ensuring the correct wrist position. She has waited until the child is in position for leaning on his elbows and has brought his hands up to his mouth by degrees. So that what he has learned will not be lost, she has supported his arms only towards the end of each of these stages.

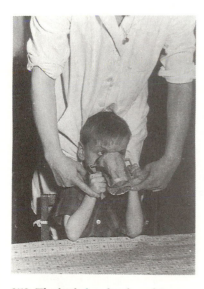

253 The little boy has bent his arms at the elbows actively without any strain and so they remain in the bent position. It is enough to secure each wrist with one finger.

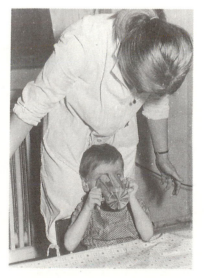

254 The next day when repeating the task-series leading to drinking, his hands can be left completely free. The ability to drink independently has taken shape.

Aspects of eleven case studies illustrating changes in symptoms

I

G.H. was born on 11 September 1965 and weighed 1,600 g. His twin died after birth.

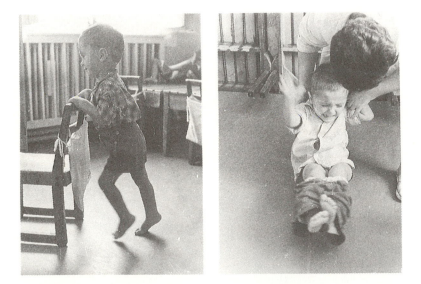

255 and 256 September 1968: on admission he could walk only by holding on to a chair, putting his weight on his toes. His right wrist is in flexion and he does not straighten his elbows. He uses nappies and has not sat on a pot before. He has to be supported when doing so. In this insecure position, his hips, knees and feet are in extension, his legs are adducted and rotated slightly inwards.

257 September 1968: he walks independently between two ropes and keeps his heels down while doing so.

258 October 1968: he walks independently but for the time being without boots.

259 December 1969: he walks wearing boots and at each step claps his hands above his head.

260 He crouches down.

261 He walks up stairs.

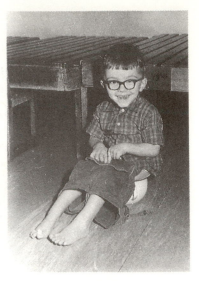

262 He sits on the pot.

263 During a nursery school activity he uses both hands. The volar flexion of the right wrist has disappeared now.

264 Continuing with the nursery school activity.

II

E.C. was born on 9 September 1962, premature at 7 months, weighing 1,700 g.

265 In September 1966 on admission he has increased flexional tonus in all four limbs, greater on the right side. Both legs are adducted at the hips and rotated inwards, most marked on the right side. The right hip is flexed. Feet are in the equinovarus position worse on the right side. The child cannot stretch his arms down by his sides.

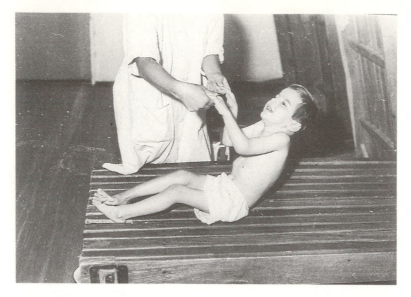

266 He does not sit up independently. When put into a sitting position he holds his head in line with his trunk. He cannot grasp and cannot stretch his arms out. His right arm is more bent than his left and both are adducted. His knees bend and the equinovarus position of his feet becomes more marked.

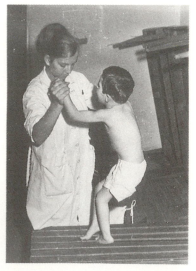

267 His high degree of insecurity in any position increases his spasticity and this can be seen when on the pot. The insecurity is increased by his inability to use his hands to hold on.

268 When he is put into a standing position his hips and knees go into flexion. If we attempt to keep him there, he puts no weight on his feet and the outer edges of his feet touch the slat-bed.

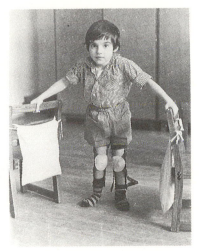

269 January 1967: in four months he has learned how to sit, consciously correcting the position of his knees and feet. He supports himself on his arms.

270 March 1968: he stands securely supporting himself with straight elbows and puts his weight on to his stockinged feet although in a valgus position especially on the right side. During some periods of the day he wears the practice leg-supports shown here to keep his knees straight.

271 May 1968: he is still trying unsuccessfully to put his heels down.

272 January 1969: he stands safely for a short time supported on outstretched arms. He rests his weight on his feet although mainly on the right side in a valgus position. He straightens his knees. In both of these pictures it is easy to see how hard he is concentrating on his position.

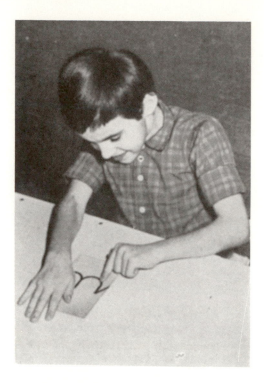

273 and 274 December 1969: the first class (most junior) has a reading and writing exercise. (This is the same child as in Illustration 241.)

III

H.T. was born on 26 November 1962, forceps delivery, weighing 3,100 g.

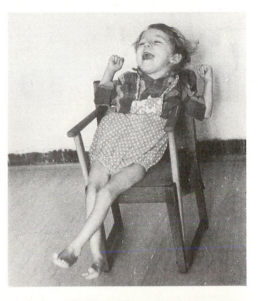

275 June 1967: on admission he is incapable of sitting in an ordinary chair. He sits here supported in an armchair with characteristic increased extension tone. His legs are crossed, the trunk is extended as stiff as a board, and he leans to one side. His arms are bent, hands at head height, unable to grasp because the fingers are tightly clenched.

276 December 1967: over the past six months he has learned to sit, to hold on, and to let go. His right hand is still often clenched into a fist and he tends to prefer to use his left hand.

277 When he reaches out for an object excessive athetoid movements appear in his other hand.

278 October 1968: behind a chair with an extended base, verbally intending, he stands up and holds on. He gets ready to stand up . . .

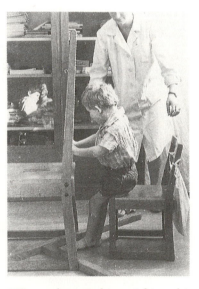

279 . . . he puts his weight on his feet . . .

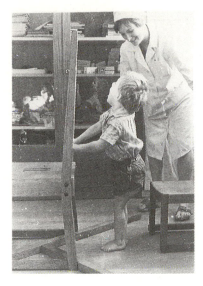

280 . . . and holds on very well.

281 June 1969: grasping the rungs of chairs placed on either side of him he takes a few steps, his legs uncrossed.

282 December 1969: the first attempt to hold a pencil. When he tries to write involuntary movement appears. He stops it by lying on his right arm and clenching his fist, but when he does this his arm turns in. He grasps the pencil in his fist and cannot hold the paper down.

283 He sits up straight with his arms stretched out.

284 He puts the stick upright and his left hand comes into a half-supinated position.

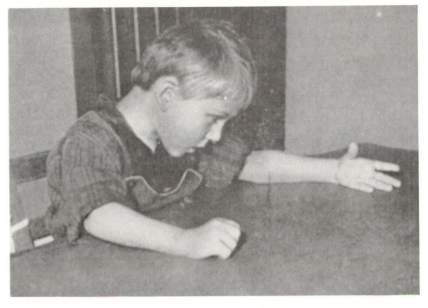

285 He supinates his left hand without any facilitation.

286 He holds the pencil upright with his left hand and holds down the paper with his right, but it is still clenched.

287 He sits up with his palms down.

288 He is still grabbing the pencil but he holds it upright on the paper and holds the paper down with his other hand.

IV

J.B. was born on 7 January 1960, after a seven-month pregnancy, weighing 1,950 g and with icterus neonatorum. Her blood was changed.

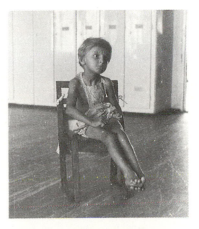

289 July 1966: on admission, in a sitting position she keeps her knees stretched and pressed together, feet slightly crossed, and in equinovarus and valgus positions. Her arms are bent and fists clenched. She is actually stopping her involuntary movements in this position.

290 She cannot stand. If her feet touch the ground the equinovarus position becomes more marked. This way she succeeds in keeping her feet on the ground and prevents them from flexing. Her feet cannot weight-bear and her hands cannot grip. The child supports herself on her head and trunk.

291 The arm position has changed from that in the previous photograph. Unlike double hemiplegics, the legs do not flex when the child is held to stand and there is no volar flexion of the wrists.

292 October 1967: photograph taken in course of task-series. (She is the first on the right.) The intended bending of the right arm causes the right leg to bend too. The task is 'I hold my nose'. At the time of intending (inadequately for the purpose) she cannot abduct her arm and it remains pressed against her trunk. For this reason she can reach her nose only by bringing her head to her hand. Involuntary movements occur, the fingers moving athetoidly.

293 (Now third from the right.) She has achieved the task, reached her nose, and found the right position to stop the movements.

294 May 1968: she has managed to control her involuntary movements by shaping tensions (appropriate contractions). She stretches arms and knees, and uses her heels in walking without any involuntary movements supported between two chairs.

295 December 1969: when she raises her arm, her heels still lift but she puts her correct weight on her feet. Involuntary movements in that arm are controlled by tensing and spreading the fingers. In spite of involuntary movements she does not let go of the chair as a support and maintains her balance.

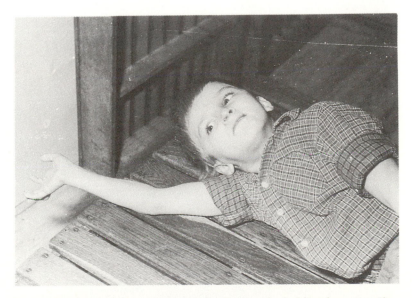

296 She has learned the appropriate facilitation for holding her nose. She stretches her arm out backwards . . .

297 . . . and pulling it down from above holds her nose.

298 Learning to write, stopping involuntary movements, holding the paper with one hand and the pencil with the other.

V

Cs. P. born 22 March 1966 at seven months pregnancy, precipitate labour, weight 2,250 g; asphyxia.

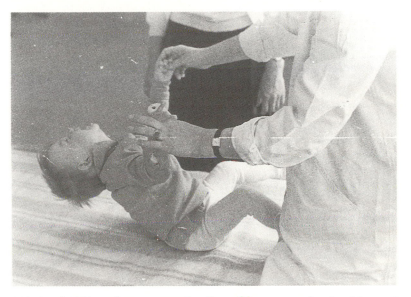

299 April 1968: at first examination is unable to sit up, has head lag and arms flexed, particularly the right. Grasping reflex is still seen.

300 When held under her arms she crosses her legs slightly, does not weight-bear, with the feet in marked equinus.

301 August 1969: no sign of the equinus seen on admission. Legs flex under her weight. Her trunk sags into the chair, arms are bent, and she cannot stand without support.

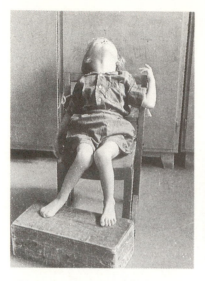

302 September 1969: when sitting, head flops back, arms are asymmetrical, legs adducted with a tendency to rotate inwardly on the right.

303 She tries to look at the object shown her but head is not turned appropriately, bent to the right and turning to the left. Arms are bent.

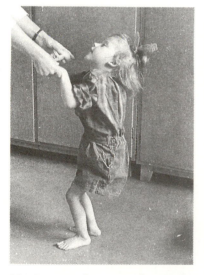

304 Supported to stand up, she leans back, head position incorrect as shown and she cannot grasp, arms are flexed.

305 December 1969: torsion of the head and asymmetry of posture are more marked than earlier. But she keeps her balance independently and straightens her knees rather better than she did before.

306 She sits upright. She has learned to keep her head up while holding on to the chair rung.

307 As before but in a group.

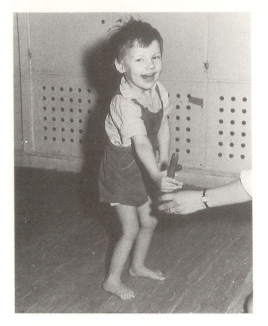

308 She walks with direction grasping a small stick. She straightens her legs almost completely, arms straight down and head up.

VI

T.O. was born on 11 February 1958, forceps delivery, weighing 2,500 g. After her birth she had severe 'convulsive spasms'.

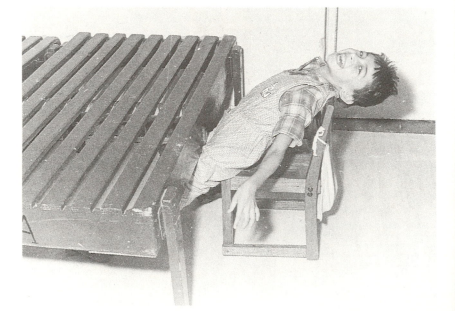

309 October 1968: at the time of admission she is opisthotonic, stiff as a board; her hips cannot even be bent passively.

310 Supine she crosses her legs and they are almost impossible to pull
apart.

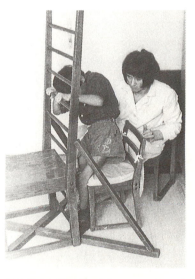

311 June 1969: she sits down from a
standing-and-holding
position.

312 Initially the hip extension is
still maximal but she is able to
control it.

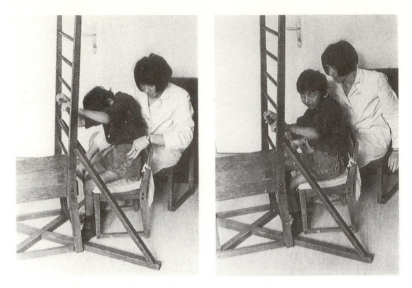

313 and 314 The Conductor directs her sitting down.

VII

K.H. was born on 17 January 1965, six-and-a-half month pregnancy, weight 1,500 g.

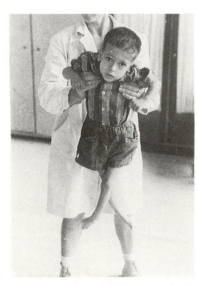

315 September 1968: on admission, when held up he crosses his legs maximally. Hips and knees show maximal extension. His feet are in maximal equinovarus position.

316 In trying to get him to stand up he cannot put any weight on his legs, bent-in knees, bends his arms, and does not hold on.

317 September 1968: sitting down (second from the left), legs cross maximally. He shows hip extension, right foot rotates backwards, elbows bent, hands maintained behind his head.

318 His method for sitting on the pot (on the right-hand side of the rim).

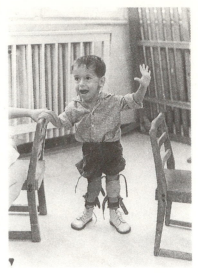

319 October 1968: he has learned to part his legs while sitting down, using his hands.

320 June 1969: wearing boots with small splints, he stands safely supported by one hand. The flexional tone has gone. Legs do not cross and he maintains his balance very well. To secure his grip on the chair facilitation is a gentle pressure on the wrist to hold it down.

VIII

M.H. was born on 21 January 1965 with spina bifida and myelomeningocele.

321 June 1967: on admission he is seen supported under the arms, the knees bent, feet in equinovarus position, and he cannot put any weight on them.

322 September 1967: his knee is stretched. With trunk bent forward he learns to put weight on his legs. Ankles are supported by boots . . .

323 . . . or the Conductor directs him and he raises one hand to increase the weight on his feet.

324 January 1968: starting from the floor he raises his hand-hold higher.

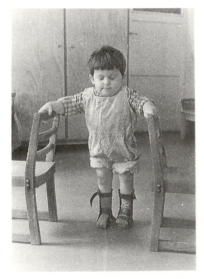

325 July 1968: supporting himself with two small chairs he stands up straight.

326 October 1968: with boots raised on the outside he stands supported without any leg rotation inwards.

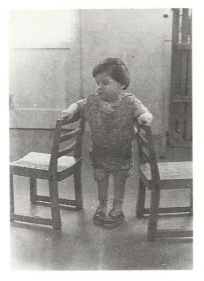

327 If he stands up straight his legs still turn in.

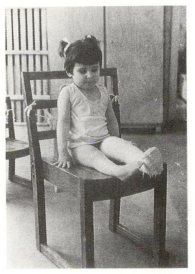

328 February 1969: after an orthopaedic operation to correct the varus foot.

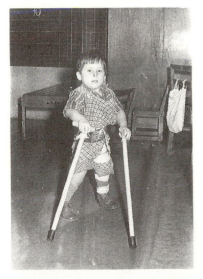

329 Beginning of December 1969: in normal boots he walks for the time being with two walking sticks and a walking aid with a pelvic basket and four circular splints.

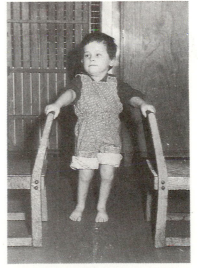

330 End of December 1969: without any help he can put his full weight on his legs.

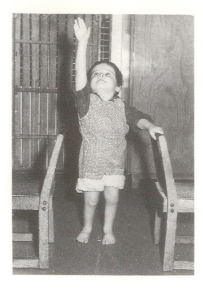

331 He stands letting go of the support with one hand.

IX

I.H. born 25 September 1963 with spina bifida.

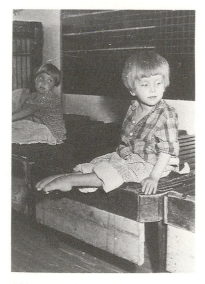

332 September 1966: on admission his feet are in maximal equine position.

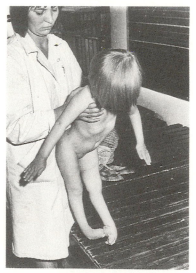

333 Held up beneath the arms he cannot weight-bear.

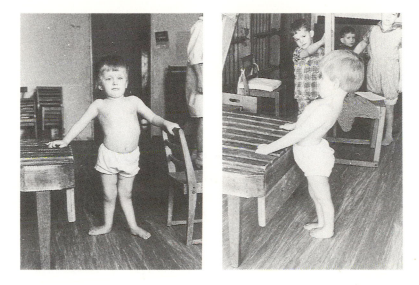

334 and 335 March 1967: he bears weight on both feet, shows lordosis.

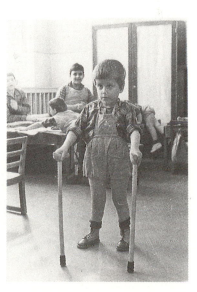

336 September 1967: standing, lordosis diminished.

337 July 1968: he walks in boots with two walking sticks.

X

I.P. was born on 8 November 1954, a spastic paraplegic.

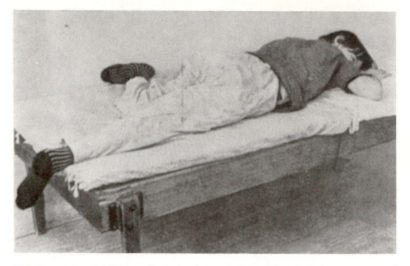

338 December 1968: on admission lying on her stomach, knees are pressed together and cannot be separated. Decubiti at the knees, left knee is bent in.

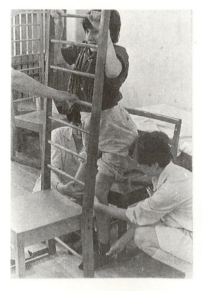

339 December 1968: she has succeeded in standing up for a moment with the help of three Conductors. She holds a chair rung but her knees are still bent and she can scarcely manage to keep her feet on the ground.

340 April 1969: she is standing supported by two chairs, no weight on her legs. She learns to put the knees back consciously, successfully so on the left but the right leg springs up and requires facilitation.

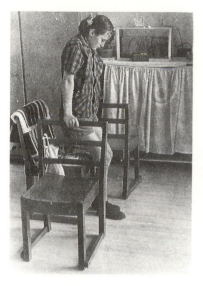

341 October 1969: she stands independently supported by two
chairs. She cannot take her
weight on her feet but they
remain down.

342 November 1969: she stands
independently supported by
two sticks. She straightens her
legs and puts weight on them.
The decubiti are healed. Provisionally she is using splints.

343 December 1969: she sits across
from the slat-bed to a chair.

344 December 1969: putting
weight well on her right leg,
she stands with minimal support for her left leg.

345 December 1969: she lets go of the chair with both hands and puts her weight equally on both legs.

XI

I.V. was born in November 1964.

346 September 1969: on admission he keeps his legs continuously flexed upwards, has never been able to walk, moves around sitting down, and cannot stand even with support. He does not speak and does not use his eyes adequately.

347 Early December, 1969: beginning to walk unsteadily as yet.

348 His walking is more secure.

349 End of December, 1969: learning to walk on the stairs.

350 He walks steadily.